Growing Up in the Greatest Nerd Generation

Scott Robinson

ISBN⬚⬚9798718368017

Cover art by Jim Wampler
Baby Boomer Fanboy logo by Jim Wampler
Artwork by Jim Wampler and Josie Robinson
Selected photos courtesy of Jim Wampler
Cosplay photos courtesy of Josie Robinson

Legacy photos by Annette Robinson
Author photograph by Elizabeth Castle

For my buddies Tim Buckley and Jim Kidwell –

who are, like me and Womp,

still nerding after all these years

Also by Scott Robinson ...

AI in Sci-Fi: Fictional Artificial Minds
    and the Real World Awaiting Them
The Children of Babel: Essays on the Inherent Nature of
    Artificial Intelligence and Consciousness
A Conversation with Hofstadter's Brain
HAL 9000: An Unauthorized Biography
Red Brains, Blue Brains:
    Neuroscience and Donald Trump
Red Brains, Blue Brains: Authoritarian We Will Go!
A Chill in the Air: Profiles in American Authoritarianism
Lucy's Courtship: An Integrated Perspective
    on the Feminine Role in Human Sexual Evolution
Really Great Things That I Didn't Say
The Smell of the Lord (and Other Charming Heresies):
    Growing Up Fundamentalist in the American Midwest
The Heart of the Scots:
    Love, Sex and Romance in Scottish History
A Dark and Stormy Night in Scotland! Folk Tales, Legends, and
    Disturbing Bedtime Stories for the True Believer
Uncle Scott's Treasury of Useless Knowledge
Uncle Scott's Treasury of Random Information
Chasing the Enterprise:
    Achieving *Star Trek*'s Vision of the Human Future
Rock Candy: The Beatles
Rock Candy: Elton John
Rock Candy: Boston
The Quotable Beatles
To the Toppermost of the Poppermost:
    The #1 Hits of the Beatles, Before and After
The Progressive Beatles
On the Yellow Brick Road:
    Analyzing the Music of Elton John, 1968-1977
More Than a Feeling:
    Analyzing the Music of Boston, 1976-1988
YesTales: An Unauthorized Biography
    of Rock's Most Cosmic Band
This Is What I'm Saying:
    Burdens of a Midwestern Suburban Polymath

My Work Here is Done!
>More Very Random Essays on Weighty Matters

I Think I'm Right in Saying That?
>The Intellectual Chaos Continues!

All My Thoughts, Unfiltered:
>Further Esoteric Explorations for Untethered Minds

I Think I've Said Quite Enough Already!
>Still More High-Quality Pablum for the Intellectually Ill-Nourished

Why Is He Telling Us This?
>The Best of Uncle Scott, 2012-2020

Don't Encourage Him!!! A Raucous Compendium of
>Irrelevance, Improprieties, and Serious Lapses
>in Judgment

Shadows of Shadows

Table of Contents

Introduction   *1*
Origins: Libraries   *3*
Nerd Theory   *5*

FANBOYHOOD
    Stowaway to the Mushroom Planet   *8*
    Major Matt Mason   *10*
    TV Sci-Fi of the Sixties   *13*
    Danger, Will Robinson!   *14*
    Ultraman & 8 Man   *17*
    My First *Trek*   *20*
    FANBOY DEBATE: Does the Transporter Kill You?   *22*
    "Na-na-na-na, Na-na-na-na..."   *29*
    Andy Buckram's Tin Men   *34*
    Volume S   *36*
    Enter the Seventies   *37*
    The Juveniles   *38*
    Scooby Doo & Jonny Quest: Young Nerd Values   *40*
    UFO   *43*
    Second *Trek*   *46*
    "Get your stinking paws off me, you damn dirty ape!!!"   *48*
    That Tribble Guy   *51*
    I Like Ike!   *56*

The New Wave   *60*
Land of the Lost   *63*
The Legion   *64*
Trek Toons   *66*
Trek Books   *68*
The Six Million Dollars, Man!   71
More Comic Books   *73*
Trek Lives!   *75*
Fanzines   *78*
K/S: The Birth of Slash Fiction   *80*
Conquest of Space, Failure to Launch   *82*
"Let My People Go!"   *84*
The Closet Scientist   *89*
Parallel Universes   *91*
Published!   *94*
Holy Texts   *97*
Run, Logan, Run!   *101*
Womp   *103*
The Science Fiction Book Club   *108*
Boucher's Treasure   *111*
Cousin Jimmy   *113*
September 24, 1976   *114*
My First Cognitive Clusters   *116*
Fake Beatles in Space   *119*
Nerd Theory: Monty Python   *123*
Interstellar Rock   *125*
TV Sci-Fi of the Seventies   *129*
Roddenberry Theater   *132*
Sci-Fi Cinema of the Seventies   *137*
Nerd Theory: Nerd Rock   *140*
Space: $19.99   *142*
FANBOY DEBATE: Are We Alone in the Universe? *148*
Aslan on Mars   *157*
Nerdy Grrls   *161*
HAL and Me   *163*

Wizards!   *166*
The Summer of *Star Wars*   *169*
Move Over, Spielberg!   *173*
FANBOY POP QUIZ: Name That Movie!   *181*
Nerd Theory: *The Rocky Horror Picture Show*   *183*
The Showkiller   *184*
Girlfriend in Canada   *190*
Babbatar Gaggita   *192*
FANBOY DEBATE: *Enterprise* vs. *Galactica*:
      Who Would Win?   *195*
Comics as a Sci-Fi Fix   *199*
Chasing Frodo   *200*
The Sands of the Front Desk   *202*
She Went Back for the Cat   *204*
Dungeons and Dragons   *206*
30 Months That Changed the World   *208*
My Parents' Basement   *217*
Gems   *219*
Afterword: The Fanboy at 60   *222*

FANBOY LEGACY
Zygotes   *226*
Cosplay   *230*
AI on the Trail   *232*
Golden Apples – Ray Bradbury and Me   235

FANBOY REDUX
Star Trek – Discovery   *240*
FANBOY DEBATE: Can a Human Brain be
      Downloaded into an Android?   *243*
Gene, George, and JJ – The Stars Awaken   *250*
Prometheus Rebound   *256*
The Art of Creative Destruction   *260*
Ever Going, Boldly   *264*

Ape Shall Not Kill Ape!   *270*

FANBOY REVIEWS
    Classic Kamandi   *276*
    Pay No Attention to the Man Behind the Curtain!   *278*
    He is Legend   *284*

Bibliography / Recommended Reading   *292*

Introduction

Born amid the contrails of Project Mercury – between Shepherd and Grissom, specifically – I entered the world toward the end of what we refer to in hindsight as the Baby Boom.

It can be fairly described as a moment in time when the US – and most of the rest of the planet, by extension – was reaching, in earnest, for the future. Our first steps into space harmonized with the arrival of vast blue machines filling up refrigerated rooms in large businesses – the first commercial computers – and the diseases that had killed tens of millions in the previous generation were being rapidly eradicated. Telephones and televisions now lived in every home; cars had the sleek contours of spacecraft.

What a moment to join the party! The future was actually arriving.

And the future had its heralds: I had just missed science fiction's Golden Age, when giants like Heinlein, Clarke and Asimov roamed the Earth. They would persist for decades more, and be joined by nimble mammals like Harlan Ellison and Thomas Disch and Kate Wilhelm and Joanna Russ and "James Tiptree, Jr." and Larry Niven and Samuel R. Delaney.

Star Trek was already a gleam in Roddenberry's eye, and Serling's *Twilight Zone* had just opened. Television was about to bloom in splendid hue, and with it the first round of sci-fi for mass consumption, courtesy of a guy named Irwin Allen.

The stage was perfectly set for growing up nerd in America.

Here follows that tale, but let the Gentle Reader be on notice: this is no mere starry-eyed memoir of Baby Boomer youth in the post-war Midwest; this is an explicit argument that the Baby Boomers are *the* starry-eyed generation! We were the first true nerds, and we set both the tone and the expectations for the amazing, culture-morphing generations that have followed.

Sprinkled among the stories of nerd days gone by are a few commentaries on the clichés that define us, as well as some explications of the debates that most entertain us. I hope these turn out to be entertaining!

My friends of that era will be right alongside me as we take this journey together, pursuant of my intent to acknowledge and honor that deep core commitment of fandom that the Gentle Reader certainly knows well: *fandom* - also known as *community*.

This document is a labor of love, offered in fond memory of my original fandom community.

As I write these words on a yellow pad in an airplane five miles up, the book itself is done, and Womp has sent me a digital file of the cover art. There's a certain sense of full circle in my heart and mind as I forward Womp's delectable art to my kids, via a ubiquitous device in my pocket that transcends the most ambitious dreams of all of sci-fi's prophets.

It's been a long but beautiful six decades; time, I think, for some appreciative reflections on days past...

STR
May 2021

Origins: Libraries

It is a September Saturday morning in 2018, and my youngest daughter has resumed her weekend dance class – and I, once again, have the happy duty of being her transportation. Our routine, over the two years she's been in this class, has been for me to pick her up and drive her to class, chatting and singing and joking as we go, then stealing away to the nearby Jeffersonville Public Library with laptop and a few reference books in my backpack for an hour of journalistic solitude.

Today, I noticed for the first time that there are administrative rooms here, free for public use, a bit quieter than the open main floor. I inquired, and was cheerfully escorted to one of these rooms, where now I sit, with my work waiting patiently in my backpack.

But I'm swelling with gratitude right now for this happy feature of our modern world, the Library - and feel I should say a few words.

My life is a progression of such buildings, and I can reconstruct who I was and how I became who I am from that progression.

Let's begin in the Garden Springs Elementary School library, where I met *Alfred Hitchcock's Three Investigators*, and the concept of the short story collection. It was here I picked up the notion that thinking could be the true action in an adventure story.

Then there was the East Point Public Library in Georgia, where I read *Andy Buckram's Tin Men*, the first science fiction I encountered, a book that assured me that young minds were capable of invention – and which I took to my grandparents' farm, where my grandfather and I began constructing a robot from tin cans.

Then came the East Union Elementary library, where I befriended Encyclopedia Brown – learning that girls were as smart as (and often tougher than) boys – and discovered *real* science fiction, in the form of *Revolt on Alpha C* by Robert Silverberg and *The Runaway Robot by* Lester del Rey. From these readings sprang my first thoughts of what human society might someday become, and how technology will increasingly reflect our humanity.

The best was yet to come. Junior high school beckoned, and I attended Darlington, an old *Hoosiers*-style pile of faded brick three stories tall (with dingy basement), high ceilings, thick oak banisters and a gym built in the

Twenties – with a musty-sweet library on the third floor, where Study Hall took place: my personal heaven.

My friends and I would zip through our homework, raise our hands, and be granted grazing rights in the stacks - where I found Asimov's *I, Robot* and Heinlein's *Space Cadet* and Bradbury's *A Medicine for Melancholy* and *Something Wicked This Way Comes* – manna from heaven, all of it! - and decided to become a writer.

It was a heartbreak, but only a brief one, when I graduated to North Montgomery High, an ultra-modern building that could not have been more different – with a library that hosted Clarke's *The Nine Billion Names of God* and Bradbury's *Martian Chronicles* and a Hugo Winners collection that featured Tom Godwin's gut-wrenching "The Cold Equations" (to which I wrote a reply story, decades later).

All of that culminated at the nearby Crawfordsville Public Library, where I found *The Illustrated Man* and Asimov's *Buy Jupiter* and the novel version of *2001: A Space Odyssey* – a paperback I failed to return, and upon which there must now be a $5,000 fine, these 42 years later.

In my freelance months, when I have no office to go to, I dislike working at home. Being surrounded by my own books is a comfort, to be sure, but it's terribly lonely. I have grown accustomed to sauntering up the road to the New Albany Public Library, where I can write in peace but still be around the smiles and warmth and courtesies of other human beings – as I am this moment.

Needless to say, all of my children have subsequently had deep indoctrinations into the joys of libraries.

Libraries made me who I am.

Zeus willing, I will die in one.

Nerd Theory

Going forward, let's have some qualifiers in place.

To begin with, I'll use the word *nerd* frequently, alongside the word *fanboy*. The two words are not interchangeable, and I want to make clear to the Gentle Reader that I understand this.

All nerds are not fanboys. I myself am certainly both, but as a former engineer, I can testify that there are millions of nerds in the world who are not fanboys (or fangirls).

Let's distinguish the two.

By formal definition, a *nerd* is a person who is obsessive regarding technology or academia, to the point of inspiring social distancing in others. In my engineering days, I knew many guys who would rather read a tech magazine than sleep with a beautiful woman. Nerds abound in this world, and our numbers are growing.

A *fanboy*, by formal definition, is likewise obsessive – but about pop culture domains. Such a person (who can just as easily be female) tends to have the same social shortcomings as a nerd. They are nerd-like in every particular: they are obsessive and socially stunted.

But... while all fanboys are nerds, by definition, not all nerds are fanboys. It is possible to be a nerd and not give a rat's ass about *Star Trek* or *2001* or *Westworld*.

Why is he telling us this?

I'm telling you this because I'm going to be making similar clarifycations, moving forward, and I want to make sure these distinctions are understood.

Fanboyhood

Stowaway to the Mushroom Planet

It began here - with a little book I discovered in the library mentioned above, at Garden Springs Elementary in Lexington, Kentucky - a book called *Stowaway to the Mushroom Planet*. This would have been early 1969, when I was in the third grade.

Written by Eleanor Cameron, *Stowaway* is the first in a series of space adventures for elementary school minds, including *The Wonderful Flight to the Mushroom Planet, Mr. Bass's Planetoid, A Mystery for Mr. Bass,* and *Time and Mr. Bass*.

The story concerned Chuck and David, two Earth boys who travel to the planet Basidium[1] in a homemade spaceship, and Theo Bass, a man who

---

[1] It's simpler than it sounds: Basidium, the Mushroom Planet, is an invisible

appears human but is in fact from that world. He sees an opportunity to return there when he learns of Chuck and David's spaceship.

Bass makes his flight to the mushroom planet, but the assistant of a famous Earth astronomer has hidden in the ship, and causes all manner of trouble, once they arrive.

This was my first-ever exposure to science fiction in print form. I was already watching *Lost in Space* and had glimpsed *Star Trek* (read on) and picked up a bit of other great SF content here and there, but this was the first science fiction *book* I ever held – the first of many thousands.

I had only just learned to read, of course. I remember following my mother around the kitchen a year or two before, stumbling through *Dr. Seuss's Green Eggs and Ham*, reading aloud; my grandfather would, the following Christmas, start me on The Hardy Boys, and I had picked up Alfred Hitchcock and the Three Investigators' *Mystery of the Green Ghost* in the school library.

But this was something different. Something new. This was where I belonged.

So powerful was the lure of *Stowaway* that I resolved to build my own spacecraft, two years later in the summer of 1971. I took an old 50-gallon milk can and decided it would make a good fuel tank, and drew up plans for the rest of the ship.[2]

"Mom," I asked from the back seat, "how much gasoline does it take to achieve orbit?"

"You are not to play with gasoline!!!" came the immediate response.[3]

---

planetoid orbiting the Earth at a mere 50,000 miles distance.

[2] This was not wasted effort; my design efforts led me to team with 5th grade classmates on a science project to show the cutaway construction of actual spacecraft, using a cardboard towel roll for the main Saturn V booster and long balloons to represent the fuel tanks. We won something for that, as I recall...

[3] Mom and Dad never found out that I was making gunpowder in the garage in those days. They did, however, ban me from matches for a year for other pyrotechnic offenses. Nor did they ever learn that I and my neighborhood friends were sneaking into the auto parts junkyard at the bottom of the hill, where lurked a bulldog that would have mauled us in a heartbeat, to steal old radios and headlights for our experiments.

Major Matt Mason

It was 1968, I think. I'd have been seven years old. Kennedy's quest for the moon was well underway, and as young as I was, it somehow came to my awareness and grabbed my imagination.

Perhaps it came to me by way of other kids in my neighborhood. Neal, two years older than me, always seemed to be aware of the latest awesome toy or the cool new TV show; Mike, who lived in the house behind ours (we shared a chain link fence in our backyards), was a year younger but likewise kept up on all the latest fads. It could be that one of them suddenly presented the little rubber action figure in the cool spacesuit with the rubber joints and removable helmet and backpack with a real recoiling cable.

Major Matt Mason.

It might have been my parents, who seemed to sense my interest in space and bought me toys in that domain (including, believe it or not, a silver spacesuit and Mercury capsule for my GI Joe). Major Matt Mason was all the rage – TV commercials teasing his lunar exploits could be seen on Saturday mornings – and it could be that my folks saw me mesmerized by one of them.

In any case, I eventually had a Major Matt Mason of my own.

About the Major himself: he was Mattel's attempt to cash in on the raging popularity of NASA, which was launching Gemini missions right and left at the time of his debut (1966); by the time he came to my awareness, the program had transitioned to Apollo, and to an anxious nation, the Moon actually seemed to be within reach.

Going out of its way to make this toy authentic, Mattel designed the Major's space suit along very realistic lines, taking its cues from real-world astronaut photos in *Life* magazine, *Jane's*, and other military sources. It also bore a more-than-casual resemblance to the suits used in *2001: A Space Odyssey*, which already existed in 1966 (though that movie didn't go public until 1968).

The Major's backstory placed him on the Moon in the near future, where his jetpack aided him in crater-hopping, when he wasn't scooting around on his powered sled or Astrotrack crawler. His lunar base (purchased separately) was three stories high, and was roomy enough for his colleagues Sgt. Storm and civilian astronauts Doug Davis and Jeff Long.

Mason's spacesuit was white; Storm's was red, Davis's yellow and Long's blue, so you never mixed them up. In a for-the-time progressive move, Long had the additional distinction of being African-American.

There was also a Captain Lazer, an alien giant who seemed menacing but was actually a Mason ally. I never owned Lazer (or the civilians, for that matter), but I treasured the Major and the Sergeant, who came to me on some subsequent birthday.

If you listen to the commercial, you'll pick up a certain Trekkish tone:

Meet Major Matt Mason, Mattel's Man in Space,
And the bravest astronaut yet!
He lives on the Moon (we may all be there soon),
And he gets around with a jet
Until Sergeant Storm, in his red uniform,
Major Matt worked all alone;
Now together they face the dangers of space
And seek to learn the unknown...

...but my Major Matt Mason days preceded my Trek indoctrination.

I'd have to characterize Major Matt Mason as the very first nerd indulgence of my boyhood. My other toys were far more conventional: GI Joe, Johnny West, and so on. *Lost in Space* and *Batman* had impinged on my consciousness (read on), and my one exposure to *Star Trek* had damn near left me scarred (see page 20); but these did not yet represent any real investment on my part.

Major Matt Mason, on the other hand, was cherished – as *LiS* and *Batman* and *Trek* would soon be. He represents my one small step on a giant, lifelong nerd journey.

TV Sci-Fi of the Sixties

It's important to understand, as I describe my exposure to TV sci-fi of the Sixties, that I was not from a TV-watching family. We only owned a single old black-and-white set, and my parents were utterly uninterested. I have vague memories of a guy named Chet Huntley and another named David Brinkley who would soberly talk about a place called Saigon, far away somewhere else, but my parents never watched TV recreationally. And my sister and I only watched on Saturday mornings.

Still, occasionally at home and at friends' houses, I would see some of the offerings that were out there. And the mid-to-late Sixties were a *wonderful* time for sci-fi on television!

Most breathtaking was *Land of the Giants*, a series by a guy named Irwin Allen – the god of Sixties TV sci-fi. It was the story of small group of people in a suborbital craft called the *Spindrift* that gets pulled through a space warp to a planet of giant humanoids, where they struggle to survive.

Irwin Allen had been around. There was *Voyage to the Bottom of the Sea*, which had run four years, starring Richard Basehart and David Hedison as the captain and first officer of the futuristic submarine *Seaview*, having all sorts of Cold War-inspired adventures.

There was *The Time Tunnel*, which for two years bounced James Darren and Robert Colbert hither and yon through history – to the *Titanic* on the night of its sinking; to Pearl Harbor on Dec. 7, 1941.

And there was one great show that wasn't Allen's - *The Invaders*, starring Roy Thinnes,[4] a show about a guy who realizes an alien invasion has covertly begun and will do anything to stop it. The aliens appeared humanoid, but really weren't; my prominent memory here is that when one of them would die, the body would glow red, as if hit by a *Star Trek* phaser beam, and disintegrate. I remember arguing with friends over whether they were dying or being transported somewhere.

But the two biggest hits of Sixties TV sci-fi were – of course! - *Star Trek* and *Lost in Space*.

---

[4] Thinnes would resurface on *The X-files* three decades later, and was a finalist for the role of Captain Jean-Luc Picard.

Danger, Will Robinson!

Yeah, that Irwin Allen guy did get around. He *was* the television sci-fi of the Sixties. His most famous creation, however, endures to this day.

That creation was, simply put, an open-throttle thrill machine for kids. The full-color teaser would show the heroes about to tumble into some wild adventure, the screen would freeze, and the music would shift to a pounding V chord, as a countdown flashed –

7...6...5...4...3...2..1...

...and once again, we'd be *Lost in Space!*

That teaser/countdown, followed by the awesome intro music by the peerless John "Star Wars" Williams, jacked up to 11 immediately. Our excitement was palpable - *"I have no idea what's happening, but it's gotta be really cool!"*

Cool, at least, to young children; to everyone else, the adventures of my namesakes, the Space Family Robinson, were pretty silly. Space circuses... walking, talking vegetables... geezus! But when you're nine years old, it just works.

Even viewers who thought *Lost in Space* was goofy are familiar with the concept: several decades in the future, a brainy family heads into space in the *Jupiter 2*, bound for the colony world of Alpha Centauri, with a handsome pilot, a sentient robot, and a nefarious stowaway along for the ride – and go far off course, landing (and stranded) on a planet where anything could happen.

Loosely based on the 19th century classic *Swiss Family Robinson, LiS* began, not as a TV series, but as a Gold Key comic book. Irwin Allen stole the concept, retooling it for television, then took it to CBS, where it was favored over *Star Trek.*

The adventures of Professor John Robinson, his wife Maureen, daughters Judy and Penny, son Will, Major Don West and the sniveling Dr. Smith were more or less based on fairy tales and armchair mythology, with simplistic plots and over-the-top characters. The whole thing was woefully undercooked, and the science was openly laughable. Still, it was friendly, funny, adventurous in a campy way, and undeniably warm-hearted. It was an easy show for a kid to love.

It lasted three seasons, as did the rival *Star Trek*, running 1965-1968 to *Trek*'s '66-'69. And, like *Trek*, it assigned a certain tone to each season: the first year was undeniably the best for both shows, with the sharpest stories and most engaging character moments; the second season wasn't as sharp but still had plenty to love; and the third season – well, by then a certain rot had set in. But these variations in tone went right past the nine-year-old mind; *any LiS* was great *LiS!*

The *Jupiter 2*, the family's home (as well as its interstellar transport), quickly came to feel like home to us, too. We memorized its layout and drew pictures of it in flight during idle moments at school. We imagined taking Don West's place as pilot beside Professor Robinson.

Planetside, we imagined taking the Chariot out for a spin, or roaming the landscape with the Robot in tow, scanning for danger, or a lurking Dr. Smith. Daydreaming of standing in Will Robinson's shoes, it was easy to conjure a colorful alien or two at any excuse.

And what a parade they were! Half of Hollywood clamored to guest on *LiS*, just as they did on the neighboring *Batman* over on ABC – Ted Cassidy from *The Addams Family*; Werner Klemperer from *Hogan's Heroes*; Disney's Kurt Russell; Arte Johnson from *Laugh-In*; and Wally Cox, the *Underdog. Trek* sent over Michael Ansara, Sherry Jackson, and Michael J. Pollard, and Michael Rennie of *The Day the Earth Stood Still* even appeared.

It was the simplest thing to take Will's place, rerunning an episode in the imagination – heading south in the Chariot to escape an approaching ice storm in "There Were Giants in the Earth"; floating across the water in "The Hungry Sea"; hearing voices in a cave along with Penny in "My Friend, Mr. Nobody"; fighting the alien gladiator in "The Deadly Games of Gamma 6"; dealing with an alien-possessed Smith in "The Cave of the Wizards". It's more than a kid can stand!

We didn't know at the time that the show recycled monster outfits and props from Allen's Voyage to the Bottom of the Sea; nor did we realize that the show's not-so-gradual shift from focusing on the Robinsons as a family to the triumvirate of Will, Smith, and the Robot were the product of the manipulations of Jonathan Harris (who played Smith) to make himself indispensable to the show and secure his paycheck.

We didn't know that Guy Williams (Professor Robinson) despised the show's campy tone and badly wanted out, or that the network killed it because by the third season it had simply become too expensive to produce.

All we knew was that *Lost in Space* was *fun* – a perfect escape for the restless suburban kid, complete with a red-headed role model wo was (like us) smarter than all the adults around him.

The reruns persisted into the Seventies, and even though *Star Trek* ascended far above *Lost in Space* in my priorities, I would still fondly indulge an hour here or there. I never let go of the show, and own it on DVD today.

Though the 1998 film version fell flat, the 2018 Netflix reboot manages to rise far above the original, as so many of the 21ˢᵗ century reboots have done. Still, as much as I love the new version, I'll never tire of Smith calling the Robot a Bubble-Headed Booby, Will bailing Smith out of whatever fix he'd gotten into, or the Robot intoning, *"Danger, Will Robinson!"*

Ultraman & 8 Man

These two do not play as big in my memory (or my affections) as the others, but they were undeniably part of my formative mix.

Part of this is to do with their formats, which were brand new at the time to both me and the genre. *Ultraman*, a Japanese life-action import where the actors dress in fully-obscuring body armor and shoot laser beams from their eyes, wrought sci-fi adventure basically as a dramatic acting-out of Gerry Anderson puppet shows like *Fireball XL5*. *8 Man* was early anime, an Asian visual style that became truly Americanized with the arrival of *Speed Racer* (1967-1968).

For the uninitiated, Ultraman is not one man but many – and is not a man, but an alien. And, though man-shaped, is actually a space-faring race of cyborgy guys who are, for all practical purposes, the Japanese incarnation of the Green Lantern Corps: they go to other worlds to police them and defend them against monsters and so on.

Ultramen can only stay in Earth's atmosphere for a little while because it's so polluted. After that, they have to bug out or merge with an actual human. And they're very hard to kill. They are generally red and silver with yellow domes for eyes.[5]

This all sounds a little goofy, and of course it is, but don't sneer: the Ultraman franchise earned $7.4 billion between its inception in 1966 and 1987, making him the Asian Superman.

---

[5] Peyton Reed, who directed the *Ant-Man* films for Marvel, said that Ant-Man's uniform was based on Ultraman.

Many, many series followed the first over the decades, several of them produced in the US (one by Hanna-Barbera). There are almost 3 million copies of Ultraman manga out there, and several motion pictures.

8 Man is something else altogether. An animated adventure, it presents the exploits of a detective killed in the line of duty and reanimated in an android body that can run really fast – kind of *Knight Rider* meets *The Six Million Dollar Man* (but 8 Man can also assume the appearance of other people).

Debuting in 1963, *8 Man* didn't do near the business that *Ultraman* did, but nonetheless generated a live-action movie in 1992, a follow-up series, and a comic strip.

Why is he telling us this?

I'm telling you this because for the year my family lived in East Point, Georgia – 1970 – *Ultraman and 8 Man* were the only sci-fi available to me, apart from the library book *Andy Buckram's Tin Men*.[6] I needed my fix, and these two shows were it. They made a huge difference, because they bridged that space between the Irwin Allen of the Sixties and the *Trek* and *Apes* and *Space:1999* to come.

The thing is – *they scared the living piss out of me.*

[6] See page 34.

Maybe it's just that the Japanese have a different sensibility about imagery, but there were many occasions when something I saw on *8 Man* or *Ultraman* sent me running from the family room to my room. This, however, did not deter me; I dutifully returned, week after week, to keep watching.

My First *Trek*

My ultimate fate was decided on the night of October 27, 1967. How do I remember that so precisely? It's right there in Wikipedia, actually; it was the night that the *Star Trek* episode "Catspaw" first aired on NBC.

I was six years old, and my baby brother Dan was being born that very night. My memory is fuzzy; I believe my sister and I were home with a sitter, a neighbor lady who also went to our church. In any case, I turned on *Star Trek*, which I'd never seen (I was already a *Lost in Space* kid).

If you know the episode, you can guess what happened next. Jackson beams back up to the ship and falls over dead like a chopped-down tree – and a voice emanates from his dead body, warning Kirk away from the planet below. Kirk, Spock and McCoy beam down anyway, of course, and encounter the terrifying apparition of the Three Witches from *Macbeth*:

Go back, they moan, *Go baaaaaaack!*
Remember the currrrse!

Wind shall rise,
And fog descend,
So leave here, all, or meet your end![7]

Scared the living piss out of me. I bolted from the bedroom where our black-and-white TV lived, wailing, and jumped into the arms of whoever was babysitting us, shaking.

I wanted no part of that show. *Lost in Space* for me, thank you!

I didn't go near the TV show itself, but I should acknowledge its presence in my social world. My friend Neal, who was two years older and lived just down the street, was watching *Trek* and tried to get me past my fear of Shakespearean witches. There was so much cool stuff on *Trek*, and I was missing it!

---

[7] I lit out of that room before I heard it, but the next three lines are not only the funniest in all of Trek, but demonstrate why Kirk and Spock were, and remain, the epitome of cool. It's not enough that they are utterly unperturbed by the terrifying scene in front of them: Kirk calmly turned to Spock and says, "Analysis, Mr. Spock?" to which Spock replies, casually, "Very bad poetry, Captain." The look of annoyance on Kirk's face is classic; "Something a little more useful, Mr. Spock?"

The transporter beam, for instance. He described how it worked, how an *Enterprise* crewmember could step into the transporter chamber and instantly be taken to the surface of a planet.

"But..." I had to ask, "...how do they breathe?"

I just wasn't ready...

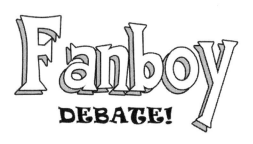

Does the Transporter Kill You?

Surprisingly, our first revisitation of a popular fanboy debate focuses on a question that really wasn't asked much back in the first nerd generation, to wit: when Scotty beams Kirk down to the surface of a planet, is it really Kirk that arrives, or a copy? And if it's a copy, then isn't the original Kirk destroyed? And doesn't that mean that the first time a person goes through the Transporter, they've basically been killed?

No, this particular fanboy debate is a modern one, rather than a classic: but it's apropos to bring it up now, as we've just seen the eight-year-old me engage in the somewhat similar (but much less informed) question of how one breathes while beaming.

Let's imagine two fans watching an episode of classic *Trek* and seeing Kirk beam down...

FANBOY   **FANGIRL**

...and another Kirk bites the dust.

                                                                 What?

What does that make, counting from "The Man Trap"? Fifty or more?

                                                I have no idea what that even means.

Kirk just died again. Surely you noticed? Except, of course, that wasn't the original Kirk; that was Kirk 57 or something.

                        You want to pick another fight? In the middle of an episode?

No better time.

What are you saying?

I'm saying that every time somebody steps into that thing, they die, and what comes out the other end is someone brand new.

Oh, for gods' sake...

Prove me wrong.

At least pause the episode first!

Paused! Prove me wrong.

You and I have both had this debate with other people. You're slipping into the Information Fallacy again.

The what?

Oh, don't pretend you don't know what I'm talking about! The Information Fallacy!

Remind me.

There are two understandings out there in fandom about how the transporter really works.

Only two?

The two main ones! The first one is that the transporter disassembles the particles of your body, sends them to another location in an annular confinement beam, and reassembles them exactly as they were.

Got it.

That's the popular description of the process. But there's this other idea that the transporter simply scans every particle of the body, assembles the information, sends the information to the target location, and assembles a new version there.

And the scanning process destroys the original. Yes.

That's what I meant by the "Information Fallacy" version.

Why is it a fallacy?

Because that's not how Scotty and Geordi and all the other engineers in Starfleet say it works, for one thing.

Okay.

First, let's review the process: the person to be transported is scanned, as we were saying, with "molecular imaging scanners", creating a pattern image of the person; next, they are subatomically deconstructed, and the "matter stream" of resulting particles goes into a buffer...

Okay so far...

Then that "annular confinement beam" is fixed on the destination, the matter stream is pushed into the beam, and the particles collapse back into their original configuration according to the information collected in the imaging scan. Call it the Matter Stream transport.

That was almost perfect. I am in awe.

"Almost"?

You forgot to mention the Heisenberg Compensators.

Not germane to my argument.

Well, we're going to stop calling it the "Information Fallacy" argument and start calling it the "Information Only" argument.

If you say so.

We have plenty of evidence that the transporter sends information, not matter itself, to the target location.

Enlighten me.

"The Enemy Within". If the transporter can only re-materialize the matter of which the original person was composed, then where did the extra matter for the extra Kirk come from? Answer me that!

Same goes for the duplicate Riker in "Second Chances."

Okay.

Also, the Information Only version is far less energy-intensive than the matter-stream thing; moving information from one place to another has a very low energy cost; moving the mass-equivalent of a human body thousands of kilometers in a matter of seconds has a huge energy cost. Why move the entire body when you only really need to move the information?

Well, now we have all kinds of problems.

Such as...?

In *any* transport, not just "The Enemy Within", where does the matter to re-assemble the person come from?

I'll admit that's never made clear, but we can assume it's the same basic technology as the replicator.

No, we really can't; replicators only work within a chamber where the replicated object materializes. We can safely assume there is a store of starter matter that they exploit.

I guess...

But the transporter re-assembles people and objects in the open air. There isn't any source of matter for them to work with for the re-assembled object or person, if not the original matter of the transported person or object.

We don't know that!

Of course we know that. If the transporter worked the way you want it to, there would need to be a receiving station for every transport; no open-air "landing" would be possible.

So it's your position that the Information Only transporter kills you, but the Matter Stream version doesn't.

I didn't say that.

I'm lost. What exactly are you saying?

They *both* kill you.

Okay. How does the Matter Stream transporter kill you?

It disassembles your molecules into their subatomic constituents completely. *That's disintegration, by definition.* It's exactly the same thing, from a physics standpoint, as being hit with a phaser set on Kill, except that your particles don't dissipate into the air.

Exactly, your particles *don't* dissipate into the air! They're all preserved in the matter stream and perfectly reassembled.

Yes, but in the meantime, you die.

Okay – even stipulating that you are "dead" when beaming, aren't you brought back to life?

Are you?

It's your musical, you sing and dance it.

Let's say you have a laptop...

Okay.

We scan the laptop and get a perfect image of every last physical detail of it, down to the subatomic level.

Okay.

Now – we take it completely apart, and melt down every single component into liquid.

Okay...

Then we recreate every single component necessary for building a laptop to the exact specifications of the original and assemble all the parts, according to the instructions provided by the original scan.

What's your point?

Would anyone in the world say it's the same laptop? No; they'd say it's a new laptop, built from the raw materials of the old one.

That's nitpicking. That's pure semantics!

Is it?

Yes! No matter how you say it, you get taken apart and put back together, and as long as you're back together, exactly as you were, that's all that matters! And you're built out of your original molecules, which is even more than my version requires!

That part doesn't help my argument.

What? What does that mean?

I'm telling you your Information Only transporter kills because the result is a copy – and so, in essence, is yours.

It isn't a copy if the molecules are my original molecules!

Sure it is. The fact that the original molecules are used is philosophically arbitrary: the preservation of the original molecules, we've already established, isn't about the integrity of the original object of transport; it's a necessity if the transporter is to reassemble it in open air, with no receiving station or starter matter source.

Now you're just making shit up.

I'm not! Let's do one final analogy.

If you insist.

Let's imagine a Play-Doh version of you.

Seriously?

Let's do an image scan of Play-Doh you, then smoosh up the Play-Doh into a lopsided ball. Can we agree the Play-Doh is no longer you?

I suppose.

Now, let's make a new Play-Doh you from our image scan. It's the same Play-Doh. But is it the original you?

There's absolutely no difference between the two!

We're already established that isn't our criteria. Suppose you had a kid, and they brought you the first Play-Doh sculpture, then smooshed it up and made a second one – what would you say to your kid? You'd say, "You made a new one! How nice!"

This is getting ridiculous.

The whole premise is ridiculous. Transporters are ridiculous. But now, every time you see someone transport, you'll think Play-Doh.

This was your plan all along, wasn't it?

Un-pause the episode, Play-Doh Boy...

"Na na na na, Na na na na..."

The nerd gestalt isn't all science fiction, of course. Comic books and the superheroes who inhabit them, though ubiquitous and owned by all today in this era of the billion-dollar Marvel Cinematic Universe, were *our* turf, back in the day. Ours and nobody else's!

For me, that began at Rexall Drugs, on the corner of Lane Allen Road and Harrodsburg Road in Lexington, about a mile from our Honeysuckle Road home. An old-school comic book rack – the kind that spins, with four sides and space for 36 different titles – stood near the drugstore's door, and in those days, comics cost 15 cents: a whopping 3/5ths of my weekly allowance.

I plunged into the world of Captain America and his buddy Rick Jones; got on board with Batman and Superman and the Justice League. And I became no small fan of Archie comics. Spider-Man, not long after.

But it was Green Lantern on the DC side and the Silver Surfer on the Marvel side that really grabbed me. These guys weren't just superheroes; they were *space-dwelling* superheroes! They became my superheroes of choice.[8]

The Silver Surfer was, of course, the herald of the world-gobbling Galactus, a humanoid alien with metallic skin from the world of Zenn-La, who flew faster than light on a surfboard-shaped spacecraft. Green Lantern was, of course, terrestrial test pilot Hal Jordan, chosen by the dying alien Abin Sur of the Green Lantern Corps, an interstellar police force, to replace him and bear his green Ring of Power, which allowed him to travel the stars.

I memorized these magical words:

> *In brightest day, in blackest night,*
> *No evil shall escape my sight*
> *Let those who worship Evil's might*
> *Beware my power – Green Lantern's light!*

---

[8] To this day, I'm still pissed that Green Lantern wasn't in the 2017 *Justice League* movie, and – worse! - that the studio barred Ryan Reynolds from appearing as GL in that final scene with Bruce Wayne, rather than the Martian Manhunter, in the Snyder Cut...

Yeah, baby!

But – alas! - I just didn't have the budget, as an eight-year-old getting 25 cents a week, to truly begin collecting comics. Fortunately, the TV had me covered.

You can laugh all you want, but William Dozier's *Batman* on ABC is classic stuff! Yes, I love Keaton and Bale and Affleck as much as anyone – and more than most, I'd guess – but it will always be Adam West and Burt Ward in stately Wayne Manor, sliding down the Batpoles into the Batcave beneath... Robin's checklist – *Atomic batteries to power! Turbines to speed!*... the Batmobile blasting out of the hillside, over the fake roadblock... and the two of them leaping down the stairs into Commissioner Gordon's office. *That's* Batman!

...or it was, for a wide-eyed seven-year-old in the Sixties.

In this modern era of serious, scary Batmen and absolutely disturbing Jokers, it's difficult to convey just how compelling the campy TV version of the Caped Crusader was to young eyes. The Villain of the Week – whether the cackling Cesar Romero as the Joker, the waddling Burgess Meredith as the Penguin, the wily Frank Gorshin as The Riddler – sent chills down my spine! The roar of the Batmobile, the clickety-chatter of the Bat-Computer, the beepy Bat-Phone, the drawl of Chief O'Hara, the soothing voice of the dignified Alfred – all of these were my immersive reality. The *KAPOW!* and *THWACK!* and *ZLOTT!* word bubbles, every time Batman or Robin threw a punch? It was my gospel.

It never occurred to me that Jerry Lewis popping his head out of the window as Batman and Robin climbed the side of a building was intended as camp; I took it all in stride, and completely missed the jokes.

It was all ridiculous, of course, in hindsight; but the show's tonight-tomorrow 30-minute cliffhanger format mesmerized me. I totally bought into all of those death traps between Part One and Part Two, where the seconds were ticking away and the Dynamic Duo were hovering on the ragged edge of death. I actually worried that *this* time they might not get out alive!!![9]

And Batgirl, in season three? Don't get me started!

The series went into syndication after its run ended in 1968, of course, and so it began airing in the afternoons, after school, in the Seventies. I was right there, soaking it up all over again.

Today, I own the series (of course), and have read West's memoir, *Back to the Batcave*, several times, enjoying it more with each reading. From time to time, I break out the DVDs and watch an episode or two, and have tried repeatedly (in vain) to get my own children to give it a chance.

Alas, I fly solo on this one, but I just can't get enough, even 50 years on. I see it through adult eyes now, of course, and I pick up on all the stuff a seven-year-old can't. Batman's Catwoman lust; Shelley Winters (playing Ma Parker) eyeing Burt Ward; and one can't get too much of Yvonne Craig in her skin-tight Batsuit.

---

[9] Halloween, 1968: my mother, using a pattern she bought at the department store, made me a Batman outfit for trick-or-treat and made my sister Amy a Robin costume. For years, I retained the utility belt pouches she'd made for it. I'd give anything to have saved the entire outfit.

But the all-time winner, appreciated in the modern era but totally missed at the time, was Batman's admonition to Robin as the latter picked up a metallic cat statue in one episode: *"Drop that golden pussy, Robin! It could be radioactive!"*

Andy Buckram's Tin Men

That first magical decade ended for me in East Point, a quiet suburban extension of Atlanta, where my father had taken up a post in a church as pastor. That summer, my mother regularly took my sister and I to the nearby public library, keeping our emerging reading skills fresh. And I picked up a book that changed my world, a book that was technically science fiction, though really more a child's fantasy – *Andy Buckram's Tin Men*, by Carol Brink.

Stowaway to the Mushroom Planet had alerted me to the existence of fantastic fiction the year before in Lexington; now Andy Buckram was bringing it home, with the story of a boy (my age!) who cobbles together a family of small robots out of tin cans. When lightning strikes them, they come to life, and all sorts of adventure ensues.

This story set my imagination on fire. When I was sent to my grandparents' farm in northern Kentucky for the week of my ninth birthday, I immediately begged for tin cans, and began to assemble my own robot.

My grandfather was greatly amused by this exercise and encouraged it, pulling together supplies to aid me in my invention. He came up with the nickname "Robby" on his own, with no help from *Forbidden Planet*, and pronounced 'robot' with a soft 'o' - 'robbit', rhyming with 'hobbit'. The robot survived, such as it was, for years, eventually rusting to nothing in the out-building behind my grandparents' house.

Why is he telling us this?

I'm telling you this because it's charming, of course, but also because it shaped the man I would become. I spent the Nineties as a systems engineer, designing and prototyping – you guessed it! – robots, for the US Department of Defense, Department of Energy, and NASA.

And today, I'm an artificial intelligence designer. Thank you, Carol Brink. Thank you, Grandpa. Thank you, mom!

Volume S

It was largely *Star Trek* that focused my mind on science and reason, starting around 1972 – but it was the World Book Encyclopedia that first got it moving.

Dad had bought the 1970 edition for the family while we'd been living in East Point, and Mom stressed that it could be an invaluable homework tool, if I gave it a chance – which I did. The previous year, they had kept me up *way* past my bedtime to watch Neil Armstrong take his one small step, and that moment had captivated me. So when we arrived in Crawfordsville in December of 1970, I pulled Volume S out of the World Book, sat down in the living room with it, and read the article "Space" for the first of dozens of times. Within a few months, I had the entire history of the space program memorized, from Explorer 1 through Apollo 11.

Next came the Lunar Lander model. And the Saturn V model. And the plastic-sheet 45 rpm record from an issue of *National Geographic* that gave a five-minute summary of Apollo program highlights. And the *National Geographic* Moon Poster, made famous in Lou Grant's office on *The Mary Tyler Moore Show*, went up on my bedroom wall.

And so it went. My interest in science would expand to include a great many areas, from chemistry to anthropology to psychology to computer science and systems engineering – but space was my first love.

It wasn't just a *Star Trek* thing, nor was it all about the thrill of thinking about the future; I began to get into the nuts and bolts of science itself, and found it to be a wonderland.

I undertook this excursion with no small trepidation, understanding all too well that science ran afoul with the faith of my fathers – and this, of course, would only get worse with time. But that wouldn't - couldn't! - stop me; the wonder I felt when I opened Volume S and re-read the thrilling details of the space program would be repeated thousands of times, with volumes like *Gödel, Escher, Bach: An Eternal Golden Braid*; *The Selfish Gene*; *A Brief History of Time*; *The Origin of the Species*; *The Sixth Extinction*; *In the Shadow of Man*; *The Dragons of Eden*; *The Cosmic Code*; *Pale Blue Dot*, and countless others.

Enter the Seventies

I was nine years old as the Sixties ended, the Beatles broke up, and the moon became truly ours. And that last event set the stage for a bold new decade, filled with possibility.

Yes, Vietnam wore on, and yes, it was hard living in a world without the Beatles. But the next Apollo mission went to the moon, and the next, and the next. It felt very much like the dawning of a new age.

I was still a boy, but adolescence was fast approaching, and with it a new understanding of this magical world I had begun to inhabit. The razzle-dazzle of starships and aliens and other worlds had zapped me right between the eyes, for sure; but I was still a long way from any of the meaning to be found in this new universe.

It didn't take me long, however; early in the new decade, I'd taken up *Star Trek*, discovered the New Wave, and reading books that were far, far beyond my years. And it's especially important at this point to note the context; recall that I was growing up in the Midwest, in the home of a Fundamentalist Evangelical minister[10] – bug-eyed monsters and ray guns were one thing, but non-Western philosophies and disturbing social dystopia and other mainstays of the new sci-fi literature would have been *verboten*, had my parents realized what I was reading.

The timing was, of course, perfect. Just as I was reaching an age where I could understand these new ways of seeing the universe, the nerd landscape decided to open up all the way, with the socially poignant *Apes* films, the unsettling dystopia of *Zardoz*, the ascendance of sci-fi's feminist auteurs. Technology itself seemed to have sniffed the air and noticed the nerds, and begun heading in the direction of our dreams and visions – digital watches and calculators, do-it-yourself computers, even velcro tennis shoes. The world had begun moving in our direction.

This little fanboy was on his way...

---

[10] The story of the author's Fundamentalist Evangelical upbringing is told in *The Smell of the Lord and Other Charming Heresies*.

The Juveniles

My first nerd books – *Andy Buckram's Tin Men* and *Stowaway to the Mushroom Planet* – seriously whet my appetite for sci-fi tales of wonder before I even turned 10.

Once I crossed that threshold, I was able to discover some more developed works, written by real sci-fi pros especially for kids like me. I would later learn that the industry referred to these works, wherein the established novelists of the adult sci-fi world would target younger readers, as "juveniles".

Check out the list below, Fanboy; are any of these familiar?

In a classroom at East Union Elementary School in Crawfordsville, Indiana, my buddy Greg found and shared the following paperbacks:

The Runaway Robot (Lester del Rey): 16-year-old Paul lives on Ganymede with his family, and his dad tells him they're going back to Earth – very exciting, until Paul learns that the family's robot Rex will be remaining behind. Paul can't accept that, so he and Rex concoct a plan to thwart the forces that would separate them forever.

Tunnel Through Time (Lester del Rey): Paul Miller, teenage son of scientist Sam Miller, is amazed by the time ring his father has invented – a portal to the past. When his friend Pete's paleontologist father is lost in the Mesozoic Era, Bob and Pete plunge into the past to find and rescue him. (This book, I later learned, was not actually written by LdR, but by Paul W. Fairman, under LdR's byline.)

Lester del Rey was, of course, one of the grand masters of science fiction, churning out hits like *The Sky is Falling*, *Nerves*, and *The Scheme of Things*. He was also one of the field's leading editors.

Then there was Robert Heinlein, whose kinky work – which included *Stranger in a Strange Land* and the Lazarus Long novels - couldn't possibly have been more inappropriate for children. But his juveniles were among the very best. I discovered these a couple of years later, in the library of Darlington Junior High School:

Space Cadet (Robert Heinlein): Matt Dodson is an Iowa teenager bound for adventure, attending the military academy that will train him for service in the Space Patrol, entrusted by Earth's government with the only cache of nuclear weapons left in existence. The book is packed with themes that tease adult sensibilities, but the adventure component wins out.[11]

Red Planet (Robert Heinlein): Like *Space Cadet*, this novel about two boys in a boarding school on Mars contained themes for more mature minds, as their colony finds itself in conflict with the native Martians. The description of these Martians foreshadows the elders of *Stranger*.

Then there's Robert Silverberg, with a different spin on the whole teenage-boy-in-training-for-the-space-patrol theme...

Revolt on Alpha C (Robert Silverberg): Cadet Larry Stark comes from a long line of Space Patrol commanders, but he is unprepared for his final training voyage – a cruise to Alpha Centauri IV, where the inhabitants are about to fight for their independence. The story is a poignant exercise in moral ambiguity.

All of these books hit me in my pre-teen years, and all of them thrilled me. I was already treading into the much more questionable waters of the New Wave (see page 60), where a boy my age had no business, but these youthful adventures kept me firmly anchored.

Later in my teens, when I was really beyond the juveniles, I learned that my beloved Isaac Asimov (see page 56) had done a series of juveniles about a space ranger named Lucky Starr, written in the early Fifties and reissued in the late Seventies, just in time to catch my attention. It goes without saying that I bought and read every one.

---

[11] The book served to inspire the *Tom Corbett, Space Cadet* franchise.

Scooby Doo and *Jonny Quest*:
Young Nerd Values

We can say with some assurance that the designation *nerd* carries with it a system of distinct values: there are certain convictions and commitments that you'll find inculcated in anyone brandishing the name, whenever and wherever you might find them.

These include, but are not limited to, a belief in science and reason; a thirst for novelty; progressive tendencies; and a perception of the world as a planet and humans as one race.

The first two of these values were cultivated in our young Boomer minds from 1969 onward through the cartoon adventures of a motley quartet of crime-busters with noses for the spooky and mysterious: Fred, Daphne, Velma and Shaggy – and their cowardly canine companion, Scooby-Doo.

Created by Joe Ruby and Ken Spears for Hanna-Barbera product-ions, *Scooby-Doo, Where Are You!* was an instant Saturday morning hit, pitting Scooby and company against all manner of apparent ghosts, vampires, werewolves and other supernatural threats wherever they found themselves. Cruising around in their Mystery Machine, a period-perfect mini-van, they solved crimes hither and yon, creepy monsters and apparitions notwithstanding.

There was Fred, the Fearless Handsome One; Daphne, the Coy Attractive One; Velma, the Brainy Inquisitive One; and Shaggy, the Gangly Nervous One.[12] And, of course, Scooby - who was so slovenly, impulsive and easily spooked that he made Shaggy look composed and intrepid by comparison.[13]

---

[12] The Scooby gang stood out among Saturday morning cartoons as perhaps the most personality-driven ensemble around, being of such distinct individual appearances and temperaments. Only the Archie gang compares. Interestingly, this made Fred and Daphne and Velma and Shaggy a sub-genre of modern porn, as shameless as that may sound; but even the noblest nerds, we suppose, have their shameless moments...

[13] Based on their perpetual snacking, scruffy façade, sartorial indifference and passive paranoia, there has been a pervasive assumption over the years that Shaggy and Scooby were avid stoners. This, of course, is pure conjecture, unsupported by any canonical evidence in the episodes themselves.

From this wonderful gang, a generation of budding nerds drew a set of values worthy of Carl Sagan – for, of course, the answer to each mystery was that the evil being done by the monster of the week was in fact the work of a human villain in a suit; and that villain, of course, would invariably utter the words, *"...and I'd have gotten away with it, too, if it hadn't been for those nosy kids and their mangy dog!!!"*

Monsters Aren't Real was, of course, the on-going theme of the show – or, more to the point, the Real Monsters Are Always Human. That's a lesson worth learning early on, and the show didn't stop there; the kids always got to the bottom of things through – wait for it! - empirical investigation, using observation and the gathering of evidence, basing their conclusions on sober deduction. And that, too, is a lesson worth learning early on.

Of lesser fame and tenure was *Jonny Quest*, the embodiment of those other two values. Also a Hanna-Barbera property, *JQ* was the work of comic book artist Doug Wildey – and, unlike *Scooby Doo*, was a prime-time enterprise, rather than a Saturday morning cartoon.

Premiering on Friday night prime time in 1964, the adventures of the young Jonny Quest – 11-year-old son of a globe-trotting professor and his small entourage – foreshadowed Indiana Jones, serving up international adventure and even intrigue. This was a lot for a cartoon aimed at the blooming Boomer boy, but the happy truth of it is that we were totally up for it.

Motherless, young Jonny traveled the world with his scientist dad, Benton Quest, who worked for the US government. Then there was the square-jawed Race Bannon, Benton's pilot and Jonny's bodyguard;[14] the mystical Hadji, a street-wise Indian orphan and Jonny's best friend; and Bandit, Jonny's distinctive white-with-black-spots bulldog, who had a nose for trouble.

This wonderful entourage bounced around the globe on all manner of government missions, solving mysteries and investigating scientific mischief, facing down villainous bad guys and pulling off the occasional rescue.

Though *Jonny Quest* only ran for one season, it went into regular syndication, where Boomer boys could enjoy it for years and years. Prior to that, it managed to air on all three of the major US networks of the day. There would be a 1986 reboot for *The Funtastic World of Hanna-Barbera*, and *The Real Adventures of Jonny Quest* in the Nineties.

---

[14] In hindsight, Race's rendering was more than a little homoerotic.

While *JQ* shared *Scooby-Doo*'s devotion to science and reason, it also served up a message of tolerance and global awareness through the presence of Hadji – accepted as a member of the Quest family – and the many people of all lifestyles and nationalities they would encounter in their travels. That doesn't seem like a big deal now, but from my white-bread, mid-Sixties suburban perch, it was a *huge* deal then.

Blond of mane and modest of build, I fancied that Jonny was a cartoon version of myself; and in my private inner arrogance, I imagined his brainy inquisitiveness to be modeled on my own – I, of course, would have done just as well against spider-robots and slave traders and Mexican pirates as Jonny did (if not better!).

It goes without saying, I suppose, that I have that magical TV series on DVD; alas, however, I've been unable to inspire any of my own children to watch it.

The values, even so, live on: *Scooby* and *Jonny* made my fanboy generation what it is: dedicated to reason, curious and inquisitive, tolerant and open. I'll take it, and I hope I pay it forward...

UFO

This wonderful unknown gem from British superpuppeteer Gerry Anderson of *Thunderbirds* fame appeared in syndication on my rural Indiana television in the summer of 1973, not long after *Trek* had hooked me. At the time, I didn't fully understand syndication and I'd never seen a TV show made in Britain – but it was right in my wheelhouse.

UFO is a single-season sci-fi action-adventure series made in 1970 by Gerry Anderson's production company and distributed by ITV. It takes place in 1980, when Earth is regularly visited by aliens who kidnap humans for their organs.

Defending Earth from these insidious incursions is SHADO (Supreme Headquarters, Alien Defense Organization - both an organization and a central command), located underneath a film studio in England, commanded by Col. Edward Straker, who masquerades as a studio executive.

SHADO has clever hi-tech resources at its command. The first line of defense is SID, the Space Intruder Detector, orbiting the Earth with a stuffy British demeanor. SID identifies incoming alien craft and notifies both SHADO on Earth and the strike force at Moonbase, which hosts three missile-bearing attack craft.

If an alien gets past the moon, SkyDiver takes action. It's a submarine that hides from orbital detection in Earth's oceans, sending out an aerial attack fighter to pick off the alien before it can land.

Finally, if the alien makes it to the surface, there are tank-like missile platforms that can be deployed to pick them off before they can kidnap any organ donors and escape.

Alone for the ride with Straker are Alec Freeman, his second-in-command; Col. Virginia Lake, his advisor; Col. Paul Foster, a civilian pilot recruited by Straker; Lt. Gay Ellis, commanding Moonbase, and a dozen or so others.[15]

The aliens are humanoid, but we learn that they are liquid-breathers. Their ships are small, scoutship-sized, and look like spinning tops the shape of Hershey's chocolate kisses.

Now you've got the gist: each episode involves another attempt by one or more of these little alien ships to get through SHADO's defenses, land, and make off with some humans for their organs.

---

[15] The SHADO team is played by Ed Bishop, George Sewell, Wanda Ventham, Michael Billington and Gabrielle Drake, respectively.

Why? We learn that they need our organs because they are dying and require them for transplant.

Let's count the plot holes, for they are endless:

SHADO's film studio cover. This one is just bonkers. The rationale is that the secrecy keeps the public at large from knowing that aliens are constantly trying to kidnap them for their livers and kidneys, lest panic set in. But aren't there about ten thousand military cover stories that would be just as misleading but much less constrictive?

One Moonbase, three fighters. Seriously? Against an endless stream of alien invaders? They know where Moonbase is; can't they just slip past on the opposite side of the moon, before the attack fighters can reach them? For that matter, can't they just wait for the moon to be on the sun side of the Earth, leaving the night side wide open?

One SID. Seriously? If there's only one SID satellite, it can only scan half the sky at once. Again, easy to slip past.

One SkyDiver. Seriously? What if SkyDiver is in the wrong ocean to intercept the aliens? The wrong hemisphere?

Where are these little alien ships coming from? Reason dictates that they are being launched from a mothership somewhere in the solar system. (If not, we are asked to accept that they are interstellar ships. Really? They're the size of gas station fuel tanks.) Wouldn't it be more efficient to just bring that mothership to Earth and overwhelm SHADO's forces in a single mass attack?

The aliens are harvesting humans one or two at a time. Seriously? They're trying to save their species by stealing our organs for transplant, and they're going to accommodate their entire race by collecting humans individually? Don't they want to either take over the planet and put us in supermarket-like concentration camps, or invade *en masse* and capture several thousand of us, or at the very least several hundred, to take home and use as breeding stock?

Do I quibble? Yeah, I get that a lot.

This is all so avoidable. Just bolster SHADO's resources by shooting the same Moonbase and attack fighters and SID and SkyDiver over and over from different angles, and change the dialog to imply dozen of bases, hundreds of fighters and satellites and subs.

As for the lunacy of the aliens' strategy, well, they're on their own.

Swiss cheese plotting aside, *UFO* is breathlessly exciting. The effects are astonishingly effective for a British TV show in 1970, and the stories are remarkably sophisticated and compelling if you can sufficiently suspend your disbelief in the premise itself.

For instance, there's an episode where an alien invader wants to defect, bringing with him knowledge that can be strategically invaluable to SHADO's success – but Straker must choose between saving the defector and saving his own son's life.

There's an episode where Foster is stranded on the moon's surface – with an alien in exactly the same predicament, requiring that they trust each other and cooperate.

Or the episode where a SHADO fighter pilot thought dead suddenly turns up alive. Or the episode where the SHADO team discovers an underwater alien base. Or the creepy episode where an alien ship makes it through and freezes time in a single nanosecond, leaving on Straker and Lake able to fight back.

It was more than 12-year-old Me could stand. But try as I might, I couldn't get any of my school friends interested enough to give it a try. And by the time we migrated from Crawfordsville to Frankfort, where I had plenty of nerd companions, *UFO* wasn't being shown anywhere anymore.

Though *UFO* didn't take off (so to speak), Gerry Anderson did begin work on a sequel series, *UFO 1999*, focusing on a greatly-expanded Moonbase.

That series became, of course, *Space: 1999...*

Second *Trek*

November 1972. I'm twice as old as I was when I first saw those three minutes of "Catspaw" on the night my little brother was born. I'm a pre-teen, living in north-central Indiana – old enough, at 11-going-on-12, to stay up late on the weekends. I'm in the basement, watching that same old black-and-white TV, and Part I of the first-season *Trek* episode "The Menagerie" comes on.

There they are again – Kirk, Spock and McCoy. And Captain Christopher Pike. And the Talosians. And Vina.

I fell in love. I'm been a die-hard Trekker from that day to this.

That particular story was a great one to really come on board with – a story of love and mercy and sacrifice. I was back the next Saturday night. And the next. And the next.

Then came the James Blish paperbacks. And *Spock Must Die!* And *The Making of Star Trek*. And David Gerrold's *The Trouble with Tribbles* and *The World of Star Trek*. And the animated series. And its Alan Dean Foster books. And then came others like me, at school. Endless study hall drawings of space battles between the *Enterprise* and a Klingon D-7 cruiser. The *Starfleet Technical Manual*.

And I watched every episode over and over and over, as did my friends.

My parents didn't know *Trek* from *Lost in Space*, and who could blame them? To the casual eye, they were just shows about spaceships and ray guns and scary aliens – mindless and harmless.

Except there was nothing mindless or harmless about *Trek*. If my parents had had the slightest clue what I was watching, it would certainly have been banned in our home.

These were stories about bigotry and racism ("The Corbomite Maneuver", "Let That Be Your Last Battlefield"); stories about the Vietnam War and US military espionage ("A Private Little War", "The *Enterprise* Incident"); tales of genocide and class struggle and overpopulation ("Patterns of Force", "The Cloud Minders", "The Mark of Gideon").

Starfleet was a place where opportunity was unfettered; the Federation was ethnically diverse. None of the prejudices and misogynies or other dysfunctions all around me were in evidence; instead, the first officer in the very first episode I watched front-to-back was a woman; the show's cast was multiracial (a television first); and peace, cooperation and compassion were the defaults in episode after episode.

I paid a heavy social toll for this new loyalty; in junior high school, I had bushy blond hair that fell over my neck and ears and into my eyes, and class bully Roger Smith liked to lift my hair to see if my ears were pointed. But by the time I arrived in the 10th grade at Franklin County High, there were allies aplenty, a phalanx of friends with whom that *Trek* bond persists to this day.

I don't need to tell you that my guys won. At this writing, there have been nine *Trek* TV series (with more to come), 13 *Trek* movies, more than a thousand books, and I've soaked up every last minute and page.

At 13 I made my own Spock costume from scratch, complete with tricorder and communicator; the *Enterprise* and *Galileo* hung from my bedroom ceiling.

In the late Seventies, my family had attended a church a mere quarter-mile from our home. At that time, Louisville WAVE-3 TV broadcast *Trek* reruns every Sunday morning at 11am (those who were then and there will certainly recall). I would sneak out of church, run home to watch the episode, and be back at the church before my parents were done shaking hands with people. They were never the wiser.

In 1989, I wrote a *Trek* novel. I've since written three non-fiction books about *Trek*.

All of this occurred within the context of my Fundamentalist Evangelical upbringing. Why do I mention this?

In September of 1976, my *Trek* pals and I journeyed from Frankfort, Kentucky to Louisville, where Gene Roddenberry was speaking. I got to shake the man's hand and get his autograph. And it was clear in the talk he gave that a certain strand of thinking, which glowed bright that night, weaved its way through everything he'd created. *Trek* was a reflection of Roddenberry's own personal philosophy and vision of the human future.

It's a future where war and hunger and inequity and injustice have been vanquished; where women and people of color enjoy their full birthright; where poverty and jealousy and racism have no quarter, where plenty and opportunity abound for all.

No, had my family and adult monitors had any clue what that show was really about, it would never have been allowed in our home.

Star Trek, in its original incarnation and every one since, is a template for humanism.

Gene Roddenberry was a humanist. Most of the show's writers were humanists.

And at age 11, there in the basement, I was about to become one.

"Get your stinking paws off me, you damn dirty ape!!!"

It's 1974. I'm a 13-year-old junior high student in north-central Indiana. *Starlog* and its fan service peers have not yet emerged on the newsstands, so the only path kids like me have to What's Out There is TV Guide and whatever pops onto the marquee at our local cinema.

In Crawfordsville, Indiana, that marquee is the Strand Theater, downtown – an ancient temple of cinema erected in 1919. And a year after the release of the fifth *Planet of the Apes* film – *Battle for the Planet of the Apes!* - our beloved Strand did a Saturday marathon showing of all five of them.

It is possible I saw the original on television before that marathon. I remember being very familiar with the franchise, although I could be remembering the *Mad Magazine* interpretation, rather than the actual 1968 movie. In any case, that marathon was a key moment in my nerd evolution.

Planet of the Apes – Taylor and his peers crash-land on an Earth-like world where talking gorillas, chimpanzees and orangutans dominate, and humans are dumb, stupid beasts. Taylor engages them and prevails, escaping them in the Forbidden Zone, only to find the Statue of Liberty protruding through the North Atlantic beach.

Beneath the Planet of the Apes – Astronaut Brent, sent to learn the fate of Taylor's mission, walks in his footsteps into a confrontation between the ape civilization Taylor stumbled into and a tribe of telepathic mutants living below the ruins of New York City, which Taylor – rescued by Brent – manages to set off, destroying the Earth.

Escape from the Planet of the Apes – But wait! Earth is destroyed in the 40th century, but Taylor's chimpanzee advocates, Cornelius and Zira, manage to escape back through time in his recovered space-craft![16]

---

[16] The return of Taylor's ship through time and space is the Suspended Disbelief of all time. We are asked to believe that 1) three chimpanzees managed to pull the craft from the middle of a deep lake, using... what? Ropes? Pulleys and gears? and then 2) restore it to working condition, after it had been submerged in a lake for months, using NO TECHNOLOGY WHATSOEVER, and then 3) refuel it for a return-trajectory trip, using... kindling and firewood? And then 4) understand its

There they are greeted as celebrities, catching the public's imagination, until a somber scientist makes clear that their superior intellectual chimpanzee genes, introduced into the present day, will result in the overthrow of humanity by apes – a self-fulfilling prophecy. They are chased and executed, but their infant child Caesar survives, hidden away...

Conquest of the Planet of the Apes – Raised by the kindly circus owner Armando,[17] Caesar observes the oppression of his kind, forced to human servitude in an authoritarian near-future. He leads an uprising of apes, bringing his masters to heel, and points both humankind and apekind toward their eventual shared fate.

Battle for the Planet of the Apes – The world has gone to hell, and cities are in shambles. Caesar rules the apes, and humans exist in isolated pockets. Rebellion within the ape community results in Caesar's death, and the remnants of both species are left to negotiate a future course.

All of this made perfect sense to my 13-year-old mind. The marathon had been, I learned decades later, a promo for the upcoming CBS TV series, which co-starred *Trek*'s Mark Lenard (Sarek, Spock's father), as well as Roddy McDowell, who had played both Cornelius and Caesar in the films. I watched every episode (and the DVDs are sitting on my shelf today).

There was also a Saturday morning cartoon, *Return to the Planet of the Apes*, and I watched every episode of that one, too (and it, too, is in my collection).

This was right in my wheelhouse. I'd transitioned from my pre-teen *Lost in Space* and *Batman* and Japanese cartoons and become immersed in *Trek*, and along comes the Ape movies. Very different from *Trek* and its kin, but also very in the dystopian tradition of the genre, with easily-digested bits of pop philosophy and plenty of heart-stopping action and suspense.

But the *Apes* movies represented something new: they were science fiction, yes, but *they were also mainstream! Everybody* loved them, not just nerd kids like me! My very non-nerd peers also saw those movies and talked about them at lunch.

controls well enough to pilot it... *hello!!! Taylor and Brent and ALL OF NASA couldn't have pulled that off!!!*

[17] Ricardo Montalban, of *Wrath of Khan* fame.

Put another way, the *Apes* series represented a shift in the general public culture gestalt – and this foreshadowed the revolution that would eventually sweep away the prevailing landscape, and escort the nerds to their rightful place in the cultural hierarchy...

That Tribble Guy

It would be hard to overstate the impact of *Star Trek*'s David Gerrold on my writing career.

If you're reading this book at all, you're certainly familiar with the author of "The Trouble with Tribbles", one of the most popular episodes of the franchise – and you likely know that he is also the author of a slew of great sci-fi novels of the Seventies and Eighties, one of the unsung creators of *Trek: NextGen*, and you might be aware that he co-created the Saturday morning sci-fi gem *Land of the Lost*.

If you're a *Starlog* veteran, you'll remember that he had a column in the magazine for the longest time, which became a play-by-play of the development of *TNG* (in which he played a critical role) until his unjust sacking.

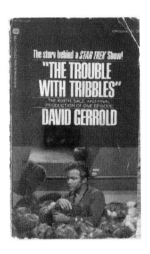

I was in my early teens when I bought David's *The Trouble with Tribbles*, a non-fiction book about how TV episodes get written – and how *Star Trek* episodes get written, in particular. Then there was *The World of Star Trek*, wherein he took all us Midwestern loner nerd kids on a tour of the fandom we were too isolated to experience first-hand. I read them and read them again and read them again, along with Stephen Whitfield's *The Making of Star Trek*.

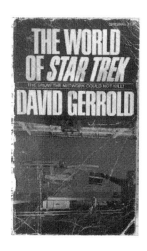

These books opened up worlds to me, beyond the imagined worlds found in the fiction of Bradbury and Asimov and Heinlein (and Gerrold himself, who had cranked out *When HARLIE Was One* and *The Man Who Folded Himself* and the novelization of *Battle for the Planet of the Apes*). These books brought the science fiction universe out of the imagined and into reality. These books *connected me to other kids like me!* Understanding how *Star Trek* happened, and how big the universe of fans really was, wow – that made me feel special. It made me feel empowered. Part of something.

No longer alone.

I still have the copies I dog-eared almost 50 years ago.

The accessible, you-and-me style of *The Trouble with Tribbles* and *The World of Star Trek* spoke to me. I felt like David was sitting on the couch in our family room with me, watching a *Trek* rerun. Already aware that I was destined to be a writer, I was taking subconscious note of this style. I wanted to come across in the friendly-yet-informative way that he did.

Then it all got cranked up several notches when David Gerrold started writing for *Starlog*.

An aside: *Starlog* was a fan magazine launched in 1976, dedicated to nerds like me. It was all about *Trek* and *Space: 1999* and *The Six Million Dollar Man* and, in its second year, *Star Wars* and *Close Encounters* and on and on and on.[18]

David's column had that same easy, informative tone that I'd come to love in his books. When I got my monthly issue of *Starlog*, his column would be the first thing I'd read.

It wasn't all thrills. There came a point at which he went on an ugly rant against William F. Nolan, creator of *Logan's Run*, that was condescending and off-putting – and ironic, since the movie inspired a TV series (see "Run, Logan, Run!", page 101), with Dorothy Fontana as story editor and David himself as a contributing writer.[19]

I stuck with his column, month after month, year after year. I soaked up his style. I checked out everything he mentioned or recommended.

Eventually, when Paramount committed to a *Trek* sequel series, *Star Trek: The Next Generation*, and Gene Roddenberry brought on both David and Dorothy Fontana as key personnel, his *Starlog* column became a behind-the-scenes tease of the evolving series. If I had been rabid about his column before, at this point I was manic – I couldn't *wait* to get the next tidbits about the upcoming show!

David's connection to *NextGen* went south, and with it his column.[20]

---

[18] What's noteworthy here is that I snagged the first issue, and on the back cover was Lindsey Wagner, *The Bionic Woman*, walking next to a man whose back faced the camera. There was a contest: identify the actor and the episode, and you get a free subscription to *Starlog*. Twenty-five responses were drawn. Seven got it right: It was Andy Griffith, in the episode "Angel of Mercy". I got my free subscription.

[19] Though he stripped his name from the episode due to rewrites, tagging it with his pseudonym "Noah Ward", the *LR* episode "Man Out of Time" is by far one of the best of the short-lived series.

[20] Many if not most readers know the tale. But for those unfamiliar, Gene Roddenberry – upon being handed the task of recreating *Star Trek* as *The Next Generation* – brought David and Dorothy Fontana and Bob Justman and Eddie Milkis from the original series, back into the fold. For many months, this really

By that time, I'd already resolved that I wanted to be the kind of writer David was. Especially in the area of "essay", at which he excelled (and wherein I suspect he borrowed technique from his pal Harlan Ellison, who might be the science fiction community's finest essayist, next to Asimov).

But the story didn't end there.

As *NextGen* faded in David's story, his own ideas re-emerged. The Star Wolf, in particular.

The Star Wolf, a series about interstellar conflict and adventure on a par with *Trek*, is about a leader-to-be, jacked up in the throes of war, anxious to take his big steps but unprepared. He winds up under the wing of a master warrior who becomes his unsettling mentor, and the story is about how he finds himself.

We can imagine such a story taking place in *Trek*. Who mentored Jim Kirk? Was it Captain Garrovick of the *USS Farragut*? If so, what was that like? How did Garrovick shape Kirk into the commander he would become?

David answered those questions in the story of first officer Jon Korie and his own mentor, the Star Wolf, a legendary commander whose lessons for Jon go down hard. What an amazing story it implies – that the journey of Jim Kirk, from disillusioned Iowa farm boy to quintessential star voyager, must have been something special.

I'm not connected to David's "War Against the Chorr" stuff – Earth invasion stories, which never grabbed me in principle – but I'm good with all the rest. And I took notes. Wow, did I take notes!

David likes to say that Harlan Ellison, whom he deeply loved, is truly a *writer*, while he himself is a *storyteller*. I get the distinction he's teasing out; he puts forth words about how Harlan gets into the "oatmeal of your soul" (and I take that as Harlan getting into your conscience), while David wants to inspire – and that works for me. Because David's stuff definitely inspires, while Harlan's stuff is sometimes deeply depressing.

I started writing like David in the Eighties, and went out of my way to become an essayist – writing first-person opinion stuff, reaching for that

---

worked well, and David even contributed to the creation of the series (the notion of a first officer who did the away missions, rather than the captain himself, was his; and there is reason to believe that he had a lot to do with the creation of Data). But Gene was in poor health, and was abusing meds and alcohol; he brought in a lawyer, Leonard Maizlish, to protect him, and that lawyer manipulated both Gene and the show to secure his own position and power. Gene's relationships with David and Dorothy Fontana were damaged by Maizlish's machinations, and in the end, both left the show for cash settlements. History has corrected much of it, but the full story isn't yet known, to this day.

easy, informative connection. I drifted into tech writing, and managed to maintain that personal tone I'd crafted by emulating David.

And now, here we are – more than four decades on. Today, I'm friended to David on Facebook, and those of us who follow him closely have shared his experience with his adopted son Sean,[21] and now his early days as a grandparent to Sean's own son – and enjoyed the best writing of his career... not his fiction, not his non-fiction, but his biographical offerings – his explication of the joys of family, from his poignant and unique perspective.

David – you'll never read these words, but *wow*, what a writer you made me! Your ability to be the nerd and the industry all at once, and draw us in – you escorted a generation into fandom! The way you put your thoughts out there to others, inviting theirs – and your fiction, picturesque and inventive – just *wow*. All of that, I've sought to build into my own style, for years and years.

A postscript: I write both a column and bits of fiction for a wonderful gamer periodical, *Scientific Barbarian*. The editor, none other than Jim Wampler (whom you've come to know well in these pages), is a suburb talent in his own right, a cartoonist and painter extraordinaire (and a fan of yours!), and recently pushed back on a column of mine, saying the following: "It reads like a Ted Talk transcript of a Robinson lecture! Make it more like a David Gerrold column in *Starlog*!"

I've never, ever gotten a better editor's note...

---

[21] The story of David's adoption of Sean in the Nineties became the basis of "The Martian Child", which won a Hugo, a Nebula, and a Locus Award.

I Like Ike!

It would be hard to overstate the impact of legendary author Isaac Asimov on my writing career – but, more deeply, on my humanity.

While David Gerrold's writing helped me find my own style and voice, the voluminous works of Asimov almost single-handedly shaped my aspirations. He wasn't one writer, he was 10 – a science fiction writer, a mystery writer, a humorist, an essayist, the Great Explainer – a commentator, an academic. A historian. A biographer. And, before it was a thing, a blogger.

I became aware of Isaac Asimov at an early age, picking up on his magnificent short stories in various collections - "The Billiard Ball", "The Last Question", "The Martian Way", and of course the incomparable "Nightfall". And so many more. It took me no time to seek out his longer works – *The Stars, Like Dust*; *The End of Eternity*; *The Caves of Steel*; *The Gods Themselves*.

This was great stuff, and I couldn't get enough! These books were as easy to read as the Heinlein juveniles (see "The Juveniles", page 38), but were packed with sophisticated ideas and themes. I sought them out in the school library, in the public library, at the drugstore paperback rack.

And that's before we get to the really good stuff: *I, Robot* and The Foundation Trilogy.

I, Robot grabbed me by the nose and never let go. Asimov's seminal short story arc about a series of positronic robots emerging in the near future, and the impact they had on those around them – from nanny-bot Robbie to the passes-for-human android politician Stephen Byerly – grabbed not only my imagination but my intellect, and I made it my mission in life to be part of the emerging field of robotics (a term Asimov coined).

And the Foundation Trilogy – I don't have words to describe how completely it impacted my thinking. The astonishing thousand-year sweep of the Fall of the Galactic Empire, against which the saga evolves, was beyond anything I'd ever encountered. The lure of psychohistory – a fictional science by which the path of history can be anticipated and made inevitable – still lingers in my own social science career.

He won the Best Series Ever Hugo for the Foundation Trilogy. He won subsequent Hugos for *The Gods Themselves* and "The Bicentennial Man", a robot story. Along with Robert Heinlein and Arthur C. Clarke, he was one of the "Big Three", the voices who shaped the genre in science fiction's Golden Age.

And beyond the science fiction, the mysteries! *Murder at the ABA*, his insider whodunit featuring a hero based on his pal Harlan Ellison, with himself as a supporting character; the Black Widowers, his gentlemanly sextet of professional men who entertain puzzling problems over a monthly dinner, always to be outdone by their incomparable waiter, Henry... like the science fiction, the mysteries were top-drawer, as engaging as could be. I couldn't get enough.

And it became what I wanted for myself – to write stories as grand as sweeping and thought-provoking as these, stories that explored ideas that challenge our ideas about ourselves.

And all of this is before we get to the *real* Asimov.

Though he cranked out bales and bales of science fiction in his youth, Asimov wrote more non-fiction than fiction by a ratio of about 10 to 1.

My grandfather John Emrich encouraged me into that non-fiction. Every time we visited his Columbus, Ohio home, a new Asimov science essay collection would be laying around for me to discover. Ace Books was publishing these collections at the time, one after another, and each contained discussions that ranged across the scientific spectrum – from astronomy to physics to chemistry to science history to mathematics to biology. *Adding a Dimension... Of Time, Space, and Other Things... View from a Height... Of Matters Great and Small.* Year by year, he cranked them out; year by year, my grandfather bought them, and year by year, I learned all I could from them.

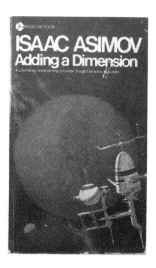

This, too, was something I decided I wanted for myself – to be a scientist, and to be a voice that could effectively promote it to the masses.

And there was the social Asimov – the shining light at the center of the science fiction community, the brotherly peer of the established giants of the field, the beloved uncle figure of fledgling writers and fans alike.

You met this Asimov in the pages of *The Hugo Winners*, an anthology series he edited, where he'd share very humorous and self-deprecating anecdotes about his friendships and adventures with writers and editors of all stripe; of his friendly, decades-long feud with Harlan Ellison; of his family, especially Robyn, the daughter he doted on; and his own struggles to win a Hugo (which, of course, happened several times in the long run).

That engaging first-person style (much like David Gerrold's) was utterly winning, and gave rise in the late Seventies to two thick volumes of autobiography – *In Memory Yet Green* and *In Joy Still Felt*, both of which I bought through the Science Fiction Book Club and re-read many times, hoping for more clues about how to follow in his footsteps with each pass.

There I learned of his striving, from age 19, to break into the field as a writer; of his early dealings with editors like John W. Campbell;[22] of his emerging friendships with other writers of his era, including Frederick Pohl and Lester del Rey.

---

[22] The editor of *Astounding Science Fiction* – later *Analog* – Campbell single-handedly defined the modern science fiction genre, lifting it above its pulpy origins to a place for literate, intelligent, inventive work. He discovered not only Asimov but also Heinlein and Clarke. Indeed, Ray Bradbury is the only giant of the genre who was not a Campbell discovery.

I also learned of his career struggles, as he tried to balance his work as a biochemistry professor at Boston University with his hugely successful status as a prolific author. I realized that I would face similar struggles, if I followed in his footsteps.

I learned of his friendship with *Star Trek* creator Gene Roddenberry, and how that friendship stimulated Roddenberry's interest in humanism – which, of course, became *Star Trek*'s foundation.

So important was Asimov's work to me that I collected as much of it as I could. He wrote 500 books before his death in 1992, and I have an entire bookcase dedicated to him.

The book you're holding now is my 33rd... so I think I have some way to go! But I'll never stop trying...

The New Wave

As the Seventies opened up and I proceeded into adolescence, my burgeoning interest in science fiction rapidly moved beyond *Star Trek* and comic books and began luring me to the drugstore paperback carousel. I'd already discovered Bradbury and Perry Rhodan and the Heinlein juveniles at school; I was primed for more.

There, in the corner of the drugstore, I happened upon a thick green paperback: *World's Best Science Fiction: Tales of Wonder and Adventure by Isaac Asimov, Harlan Ellison, Brian Aldiss, Samuel R. Delaney, Larry Niven...*, edited by Donald A. Wollheim and Terry Carr. It set me back 95 cents.

It covered the year 1967, which at the time was five years in the past. A better sampler of science fiction as it was in the transformative Sixties, I could not possibly have chosen.

A quick word about those transformative years. Though I could not have known this at the time (and wouldn't have understood it if I had), the Sixties represented a sea change in science fiction. The old guard of the Forties and Fifties – Arthur C. Clarke, Robert Heinlein, et al – had written grand, epic, science-driven stories that spoke to the connection between humankind and its technological product, the consequences of our invention and exploration. But in the Sixties, a new generation emerged, with writers like Delaney and Ellison and Zelazny and dozens of others taking over the genre with more experimental work, new forms and new themes (most of them social, rather than scientific) that challenged the sensibilities of the pre-Boomer sci-fi audience.

Asimov himself, one of the original masters of the genre, confessed that he found this transformation – known as the New Wave – more than a little baffling, far afield of his own understanding and approach (nonetheless, he managed to make it into the collection I then held in my hands). I, on the other hand, was too young and innocent to fully grasp the difference.

This collection, which you can still find on Amazon, is astonishing.

It kicks off with a laugh – Richard Wilson's playful "See Me Not", about a suburban everyman who finds himself the unwitting subject of an invisibility experiment by Big Pharma. That was more than enough to hook me, but *oh*, what followed...

"Hawksbill Station", about an all-male penal colony for deviants and dissidents, situated a billion years in the past; "The Number You Have Reached", my first exposure to the astonished Thomas Disch – a last-man-on-Earth tale with an unsettling tone and even more unsettling conclusion; Andrew Offutt's "Population Implosion", a philosophical terror-fest foreshadowing the winding-down of our species. "Full Sun", by Brian Aldiss; "Handicap", by Larry Niven; "Thus We Frustrate Charlemagne", by R.A. Lafferty.[23]

And then comes Asimov, the Golden Age relic, who had actually been long away from fiction, feeling the field had moved beyond him. In "The Billiard Ball", he resurges with a vengeance, spinning an uneasy tale of two old college enemies – a theoretician and a businessman (read: Neil deGrasse Tyson and Elon Musk) sparring in public over a new and deeply disruptive technology, coalescing into an unprecedented (for Asimov) excursion into the terrifying darkness that can take up residence in the human psyche.

And then there's Ellison.

"I Have No Mouth, and I Must Scream".

---

[23] As amazing as this collection is, it is notable for its utter lack of female talent; it would be another decade before women such as Ursula LeGuin, Joanna Russ and Kate Wilhelm began to receive their due.

Keep in mind, I'm *12 years old* here! Not yet even a teenager, and here I am absorbing Ellison's signature descent into the blackest bowels of human despondency.

The computers of the world have all been connected into one vast network (how's that for prescience?), and the resulting AI grows more and more powerful (and physically all-consuming, with infrastructure permeating the surface of the planet and below) - AM,[24] the Allied Mastercomputer turned Adaptive Manipulator turned Aggressive Menace, humankind's ultimate Judge-Jury-Executioner. The story's narrator is one of five remaining humans, kept alive by AM as playthings to torment, rendered immortal and invulnerable that they might suffer AM's eternal slings and arrows.

And I thought Ray Bradbury was creepy.

I had, of course, already been through Ray's stuff and the Heinlein and del Rey juveniles, but this was my introduction to the grown-up stuff.

I still have that paperback. It's sitting next to me. It opened the door to more Disch and Delaney and the works of the three women mentioned above – *The Left Hand of Darkness*, *The Female Man*, *Where Late the Sweet Birds Sang*, *The Word for World is Forest*. Then came Philip K. Dick and "James Tiptree, Jr." and Vonda McIntyre and so many others.

A part of me realized that what I was reading was beyond my years. A part of me realized that it was so completely at odds with the world in which my parents had raised me, in its wildly heretical concepts and themes, that I risked severe punishment they ever realized what I was reading.

But this astounding world of ideas and possibilities spoke to me; as I was contorting with kick and scream into young adulthood, it was awakening my dormant sense of tomorrow within the growing aches and pains of my adolescent today.

This was where I was born to be. I was discovering my home.

---

[24] As a global supercomputer complex enabled by an endless network of networks, AM brilliantly foreshadowed the Internet.

Land of the Lost

Star Trek writer/apostle David Gerrold is the uncredited creator of this Saturday morning children's program, under the imprint of Sid and Marty Krofft of *H. R. Pufnstuf* fame. Why does a children's program merit its own chapter?

Well, it's not because the show had a tremendous impact on my childhood; I watched it, I loved it, I fondly recall it – but its exalted place in this memoir is more a celebration of just how much the science fiction community was capable of accomplishing by the time I was coming of age.

Land of the Lost, a half-hour adventure about a father and his two children trapped in a bizarre land populated by the primitive Pakuni and the reptillian Sleestak. Their goal is to find their way home – but many things stand in their way, besides the hostile Sleestak: dinosaurs, time portals, and mysterious Pylons.

Resourceful and determined, the Marshall family brave the dangers of this strange world week after week, befriending the occasional native and puzzling out the mysterious technology they encounter as if living in a game of Myst.

All of this sounds a bit too sophisticated for Saturday morning – but remember, this was in the days when *Star Trek* itself appeared in the line-up. And *Land of the Lost oozed Trek* pedigree.

Gerrold himself, the show's story editor and writer of the series pilot, is obvious. But he also brought along his pal Dorothy Fontana to write for the show, along with Margaret Armen. Walter Koenig – "Meester Chekove" from the original series – wrote for the show (Fontana also got a script out of him for the animated *Trek*) as well.

And Gerrold went absolutely nuts, recruiting within the sci-fi community for writers. That strategy worked wonders for Roddenberry when pulling Trek's first season together – and sure enough, Norman ("The Doomsday Machine") Spinrad and Theodore ("Amok Time") Sturgeon turned in scripts.

Then came two real surprises. Larry Niven, who had been coaxed into an animated *Trek* script ("The Slaver Weapon"), wrote his own episode and collaborated with Gerrold on two. And Ben Bova, editor of *Analog*, did a script for the show – the only television credit of his career.

The show lasted three seasons, with 43 episodes total, and spawned a reboot in 1991 and a comedic film version starring Will Ferrell in 2009.

The Legion

Alas, it wasn't all sophisticated experimental fiction by the genre's most inventive minds. There were still those comic books. And they served up plenty of sci-fi to love.

In my particular case, it was in DC Comics. There was Green Lantern, of course, the interstellar superhero I'd discovered in grade school; but there was also the Legion of Super-Heroes, a group of teenagers in the 30th century who defended honest worlds against interstellar threats. They were friends with Superboy – the young Superman – who would travel into the future via his super-speed to participate in their adventures.

This had all been going on in DC's Adventure Comics in the Sixties, but that was before my time. The group was rebooted with a new look and feel in the early Seventies, becoming a feature in the *Superboy* comic itself, which was eventually retitled *Superboy and the Legion of Super-Heroes*.

This became my must-have comic. A monthly, it usually featured a pair of stories, and every quarter there'd be a special 100-page edition that would include a new full-length adventure, plus one or more reprints of a classic Legion story from the *Adventure* years.

What was this Legion?

It began with three teenagers – Rokk Krinn of the planet Braal, who could control magnetic fields a la Magneto over at Marvel; Imra Ardeen of Titan, a telepath; and Garth Ranzz of Winath, who could generate bolts of lightning.

The three were traveling on a shuttle to Earth when they foiled an attempt by bad guys to kidnap R.J. Brande, a billionaire industrialist, who offers to finance a headquarters for the team if they'd care to go into the superhero business. They take on the names Cosmic Boy, Saturn Girl and Lightning Lad, respectively, and become the Legion.

They are soon joined by a vast array of fellow teen heroes: Phantom Girl; Chameleon Boy; Colossal Boy; Brainiac 5; Invisible Kid; Star Boy; Shrinking Violet; Ultra Boy; Mon-El; Dream Girl; Element Lad; Timber Wolf; Shadow Lass, and others.

All told, more than 30 teen heroes joined the Legion over the years. Most had powers with distinct sci-fi elements. Notable among these was Wildfire, a young engineer who was caught in an anti-matter blast and became a being of pure energy.

While some of their missions took place on Earth, a fair number happened on other worlds or in space. I have an unbroken string of perhaps five years of the comic, and consider many of the stories to be classics.

It's noteworthy that in the mid-Seventies, with the rising popularity of *Trek*, the art of the Legion increasingly resembled it: the Legion space cruisers were blatant variations of the *Enterprise*; they began using something similar to transporter technology. I should have found this derivative and irritating, but (unsurprisingly) it totally worked for 13-year-old me.

Trek Toons

My memory is that I was in Columbus, Ohio, at the home of my maternal grandparents – where my Grandpa John lived, the one who bought the Asimov science essay collections and left them laying around for me – when I turned on Saturday morning cartoons and got the surprise of my life.

There it was – *the Enterprise!!!* And there they were – *Kirk, Spock, Bones, and the gang!!! On Saturday morning cartoons!!!*

I had truly discovered Trek and started obsessively watching in November of 1972. Now it's September 1973, and I'm watching something called "Beyond the Farthest Star". And even though it's a cartoon, the story – which I later learned was written by Samuel Peeples, who wrote "Where No Man Has Gone Before" - is as serious as any *Star Trek* story I've seen yet.

I am stunned. I am dazzled. When we return to Indiana, I tell my handful of *Trek* friends.

The following week: "Yesteryear", written by Dorothy Fontana, a story involving Spock, Sarek and Amanda, and the Guardian of Forever, a story that is so serious and authentic that it is considered canon, while the animated series in general is not.

So begin two splendid years of Saturday morning *Trek* adventures, with that wonderful standard maintained. The original actors are back, doing the voices;[25] memorable characters return, including Harry Mudd and Cyrano Jones;[26] alongside veteran writer Peeples we see Dorothy Fontana and David Gerrold and Stephen Kandel[27] and Margaret Armen[28] and Paul Schneider[29].

---

[25] ...with the exception of Walter Koenig. For budgetary reasons, the producers (including Roddenberry) sought to keep the talent pool as shallow as possible, excluding even Nichelle Nichols and George Takei. Leonard Nimoy rebelled, insisting that if Nichols and Takei were not invited, he was bowing out. Koenig's consolation prize was that he got to write the script for the episode "The Infinite Vulcan".

[26] Voiced by the original actors, Roger C. Carmel and Stanley Adams.

[27] "Mudd's Women", "I, Mudd".

[28] "The Gamesters of Triskelion", "The Paradise Syndrome", "The Cloud Minders".

Larry Niven of *Ringworld* fame weighed in with "The Slaver Weapon". Popular TV actor Ted Knight voiced a guest starring part in "The Survivor".

The *Enterprise* returned to the Shore Leave planet, encountered tribbles once again, and had its first holodeck installed.

It only lasted two seasons – 26 episodes altogether – but it was glorious. It was serious *Trek*, treated with the love and respect that *Trek* deserves, and ended all too soon.

It goes without saying that the DVDs are sitting in my living room.

---

[29] "Balance of Terror", "The Squire of Gothos".

Trek **Books**

Trek reruns, *Trek* toons, *Trek*... paperbacks?

It's spring 1974, more than a year after I've settled into the syndicated reruns and just after the first season of the animated *Trek*s. I'm in the local mall, browsing a paperback rack – and there I spot *Star Trek #10*.

It's the latest in a four-year string of paperback novelizations of the scripts from the television show, written by author James Blish. I plop down three quarters – most of my allowance! - for a copy, which sits on my nightstand for the next week.

It contains written versions of six more-or-less randomized episodes - "The Alternative Factor", "The Empath", "The Galileo Seven", "Is There in Truth No Beauty?", "A Private Little War", and "The Omega Glory".

Remember, this is an era before streaming services, before DVR, even before VHS. We can only see episodes of *Star Trek* when they roll around in the rotation in syndication. Imagine the cornucopia of having the episodes right there next to you, where you can re-live them on a moment's notice, just by picking up a book!

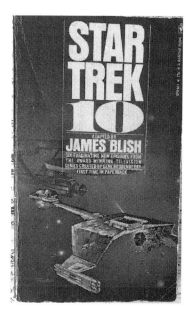

I made it my mission in life to collect the other nine. I learned that Blish had done an original novel – *Spock Must Die!* - and snatched it up.

Then came *Star Trek #11*... and *Star Trek #12*. And that was it, except for the Harry Mudd episodes. James Blish died, and his widow finished off the series in a volume called *Mudd's Angels*.

After Blish's death, it was open season. Bantam, publisher of the novelizations, began cranking out *Trek* novels right and left.

Ballantine joined the party, hiring Alan Dean Foster to write novelizations of the animated episodes.[30] Then followed several years' worth of novels, until Pocket Books took over the franchise with the first *Star Trek* movie.

Since then, *Trek* in print has been endless, in hardback, paperback, comic book, and graphic novel form. The books number well into the hundreds, covering every incarnation of *Trek* – *NextGen*, *DS9*, *Voyager*, *Enterprise*, *Discovery*, *Picard*, and even some customized spin-offs - and kudos to the fanboy/girl who owns them all.[31]

Myself, I'm no slouch, but neither am I anything to write home about. Here's my own wall:

---

[30] Foster managed to turn 22 episodes into 10 books, and expanded many of the stories with his own subplots. He also did the novelizations of the *Alien* movies, the Kelvin Timeline *Trek* films, and the original *Star Wars*, as well as its first sequel, *Splinter of the Mind's Eye*.

[31] A huge honorable mention goes here. When *Star Trek: The Motion Picture* came out, Pocket Books took over the *Trek* paperback franchise from Bantam Books. A flurry of new *Trek* novels emerged, including *The Entropy Effect* from Vonda McIntyre (known for *The Exile Waiting*, *Dreamsnake*, and the *Starfarers* quadrology), an entry that expanded the backstory of Sulu and gave him the first name Hikaru (and bestowed Nyota on Uhura). So successful was McIntyre's take on *Trek* that she was given the assignment of novelizing the *Star Trek II, III* and *IV* movie trilogy; in each instance, she improved on the film version. Her contribution culminated with another original novel, *Enterprise: The First Adventure*, which told the story of Kirk assuming command for the first time. This tale was filled with interesting twists, from the reason Spock became first officer rather than Gary Mitchell to the distrust Scotty felt for the inexperienced Kirk early in their relationship.

Federal operative Oscar Goldman steps in and arranges for Austin to be reconstructed, using the latest in cybernetic technology – bionics, a synthesis of man and machine. Austin is given three new robotic limbs, far stronger and faster than the originals, and an eye that can not only see perfectly but telescopically and microscopically.

In exchange for this bounty, Austin is obliged to enter into a new kind of government service, as a superspy. And there you have the series, which lasted five seasons, from 1973-78.

It was hugely popular, prompting school kids everywhere to shift into slow motion, with a vocalized *dit-dit-dit-dit-dit-dit-dit-dit!* sound effect, emulating bionic action in the show. We all imagined that we could throw a tree like a javelin, just like Steve Austin; that we could overturn a truck, just like Steve Austin; that we could run 60 miles an hour and see a mile away, just like Steve Austin.

But the sci-fi didn't end there. In his adventures, Austin encounters Bigfoot – who turns out not to be a rogue terrestrial anthropoid, but an extraterrestrial robot. He meets Shalon, a woman from another world. A friend is kidnapped and replaced with a humanoid robot that's indistinguishable from the man. And so on.

All this and international espionage, too!

The show spawned a spin-off, *The Bionic Woman*, starring Lindsey Wagner, about a love interest of Austin's who gets the same cybernetic treatment. Both shows were canceled in 1978, but not for lack of popularity (See "The Showkiller", page 184).

The following year, I started college at the University of Kentucky. There in the school bookstore, on a paperback rack, was a re-issue of *Cyborg*. I snatched it up and eagerly re-read it.

More Comic Books

I've already mentioned DC's Legion of Super-Heroes, super-powered teenagers in the 30th century where Earth is part of a huge multi-planet, space-faring consortium. Superboy time-travels to have play dates with them - sci-fi to the core! But then, sci-fi in comics, it turns out, is the rule rather than the exception.

The granddaddy of the all - Superman – is, of course, a humanoid alien from a red-star planet far, far away. Kal-El of Krypton may be a contemporary fellow by many measures, but his story is all sci-fi, from his childhood journey to Earth to his solar-powered, gravity-defying body.

And so it is with many if not most superheroes, across the various comic houses. At DC, there was the interstellar Green Lantern Corps that we've already noted – space cops from many different worlds with energy-based, thought-guided powers.

The Justice League put its headquarters into a satellite in geo-synchronous orbit over the Earth in the early Seventies, and got to and from by means of a transporter ripped off from *Trek*. One of its members, the Martian Manhunter, was not only a bona fide Martian, but a shape-shifter.

And Jack Kirby, liberated from Marvel in 1971, served up the New Gods – beings from the worlds of New Genesis and Apokolips, delivering essentially an interstellar mythology. Notable among its sci-fi innovations were the Boom Tubes, portals that could take you from one world to another in the blink of an eye. Then there were the Mother Boxes – metallic cubes that could alter the state of matter, even returning it to a prior state.[32]

Kirby also offered up OMAC, a character set in the near future, in an era when technology has run amuck and society is way out of balance. He began life as a small, nondescript man who is rebuilt from his cells up into a god-like superman by Brother Eye, an intelligent satellite with formidable powers. OMAC works for the Global Peace Agency, helping to hold the world together in a world too dangerous for large armies.

Over at Marvel, sci-fi themes and tropes abounded. There are the persistent Kree, a militaristic race from the planet Hala in the Large Magellenic Cloud, who constantly pop up in many Marvel titles (and in the Marvel Cinematic Universe movies, particularly *Captain Marvel*).

---

[32] Both Boom Tubes and Mother Boxes figure prominently in Warner Bros.' *Zack Snyder's Justice League* (2021).

There's Galactus, Devourer of Worlds, who sustains his own life force by draining it from entire populations; there's his herald, the Silver Surfer, the metal-skinned humanoid we met in the Batman chapter above.

And Spider-Man, who's as down-to-earth as any superhero, experienced a harrowing sci-fi-driven ordeal in his own Clone Saga, when his enemy the Jackal made a copy of his dead, departed Gwen Stacy, then made one of him, too.

Some themes and conventions are shared by both comic houses. Both, for instance, are big on cyborgs: DC's premiere cyborg superhero is called just that – Cyborg – and can not only fly and shoot energy blasts from his arms, but tap into the Internet and control anything and every-thing.[33] Marvel has quite a few cyborgs of its own, but most notable is Deathlok, whose story takes place in a dystopian, post-war near-future. Deathlok is interesting because his non-organic parts include a computer, which he addresses as 'Puter, with which he can carry on internal dialogs.

There are other major characters on both sides – star-traveling, interdimensional aliens like Darkseid[34] and Thanos – but you get the idea: superhero turf is decidedly a sci-fi domain.

And, as we'll see, this rich source of nerd narrative went on to rebuild pop culture.

---

[33] Ibid.

[34] Ibid.

Star Trek Lives!

David Gerrold is credited above with opening up the existence of *Trek* fandom to me (and countless others) with his book *The World of Star Trek*. This gave us all a serious taste of what was out there, *Trek* community-wise, and that was pretty exciting to think about – there were thousands, even *millions* of folks out there *just like us* who loved *Star Trek!*

My next window into *Trek* community came in 1974, the year after Gerrold's book came out, when the older brother of my friend Mike offered me a box of books and memorabilia – it seems he was about to move out of the house into a place with others, and he was shedding stuff he didn't want to carry around.

Inside that treasure box were a couple of Blish books I didn't already have – and the program books from the 1973 and 1974 international *Trek* conventions!

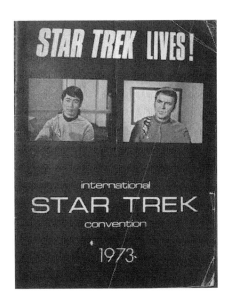

Well, if I'd wanted to feel connected to the great Trek community out there, those programs did it. I saw that those who attended got to hear Isaac Asimov speak; got to meet Dorothy Fontana and David Gerrold and Jimmy Doohan and Nichelle Nichols and George Takei and Walter Koenig. There were film screenings and art exhibits and exhibition halls filled with memorabilia and cosplay contests and discussion panels. I wasn't there; but I could *imagine* being there.[35]

And if we had been awakened, the newsstand made clear that the press itself was likewise alerted. *Star Trek*, a long-since canceled TV show, was popping up *everywhere* – not just on the paperback rack, but in magazines of all kinds. *Trek* fandom helped fuel the rise of nerd print media, culminating in *Starlog*, the big daddy of such journals, in the fall of 1976.

---

[35] Those early conventions, of course, led to hundreds more over the decades, and were the precursor of the now-ubiquitous ComicCon, a more general conference. My buddy Jim Kidwell, to whom this book is co-dedicated, still regularly attends them.

All of this nerd content steadily rose in volume throughout the mid-Seventies. In 1975, Jacqueline Lichtenberg, Sondra Marshak and convention organizer Joan Winston followed up Gerrold's earlier book with an update on the *Trek* fan universe, *Star Trek Lives!*, filled with wonderful reports and anecdotes about happenings in fandom. I snatched it up and read it repeatedly.

It's no wonder that it rapidly became clear to the culture at large that *Star Trek* wasn't going away any time soon. Add to this the fact that Gene Roddenberry, after several years of cranking out failed pilots[36] a nd giving lectures on tour,[37] was about to enter into discussions with Paramount about bringing the series back – *Star Trek* lived, and there were even better days ahead than there were behind...

---

[36] See "Roddenberry Theater", page 132.

[37] See "September 24, 1976", page 114.

Fanzines

In the age of the Internet, when the website is the standard platform for all things nerd and fanboy, it's hard to conceive of what preceded it.

But David Gerrold, mentioned above, gives us a clue in his *World of Star Trek*. Before we had websites, fanboys/girls shared their passion and obsession through... fanzines.

Fanzine is a truncation of *fan magazine* – a home-grown publication created at home on a typewriter and reproduced (in the pre-Xerox years) on a machine called a mimeograph.[38] They are amateur productions, to be sure, but they were also the torch-and-flame of fandom as *Trek* was first taking root in the public gestalt.

Gerrold recalls that there were hundreds of such publications, lovingly created at kitchen tables and mailed out to subscribers across the nation and beyond. Certainly labors of love, they included commentary, opinion, whatever tidbits of news about *Trek* that could be shared with fellow fans, and – of course – fan fiction.

"The fanzines appeared shortly after *Trek* appeared on the air," Gerrold writes in *The World of Star Trek*. "As the *Trek* fans discovered science fiction fandom, they began to adopt more and more of its conventions (pun intended). Articles about *Star Trek* in science fiction fanzines turned into *Star Trek* fanzines with occasional science fiction articles.

"As the *Star Trek* phenomenon developed and grew," he continued, "more and more of the Trekkies, many of whom had never heard of science fiction fandom before *Star Trek*, began to put out their own zines. They paid little attention to either tradition or structure – but then again, few fans do – substituting enthusiasm instead."

Gerrold goes on to list some of the fanzines of the Sixties/Seventies: *Star Date*, *Impulse*, *Babel*, *T-Negative*, *Guardian of Forever*, *Quadrant*, *Kivas & Trillium*, and *Grup*, to name a few.

I came across a few of these over the years, and you'd think that I, of all people, would have been the type to immediately sit down and start cranking them out. But I chose a different outlet for my fanboy enthusiasm, as I'll share shortly.

---

[38] There was a mimeograph in my pastor father's church office, used to print the Sunday morning church bulletin, among other things. When I started writing movie scripts – a story that follows – I printed them on just such a device.

But there was one other aspect of the fanzine that I found fascinating, and one that persists even today (while fanzines in the traditional format do not). That topic – *Slash fiction* – immediately follows.

K/S: The Birth of Slash Fiction

A cornerstone of fanzine content was, as mentioned above, fan fiction – stories of Kirk, Spock, and the gang written by adoring fans. These stories ran the gamut – some were serious efforts that were well worth a reader's attention, while others were nothing more than wish fulfillment. What they all shared was that passion and enthusiasm that defined the fanboy/girl in those days.[39]

There emerged a fascinating sub-genre with this home-grown *Trek* fan fiction: the Kirk/Spock story, or K/S for short.

Mind you, Spock alone made for great fan fic material, which (as the Gentle Reader might guess) often took an overtly sexual turn, in the fangirl's typewriter, with special attention often given to the savage brute lurking beneath his cool Vulcan façade. Commentary on this phenomenon is rendered by one such female writer is quoted in *Star Trek Lives!*:

> *"Many are the fanzine tales that wax enthusiastic about Mr. Spock's amorous qualities. With our hero in the grip of pon farr, the reader is besieged with stories of his tender and solicitous regard toward his current bed-partner, her sharing of his satisfaction seems to be of paramount importance. Now I also find Mr. Spock sexually exciting, extremely masculine, and undeniably intriguing. It is part of his mystique, a projection of his restrained sexuality that is so apparent to all of us…"*

You can imagine.

But what you might not imagine is that they didn't stop there, oh no. In the K/S stories, the object of Spock's lust is… James T. Kirk.

The K/S stories imagined the captain and his trusty first officer as more than just fellow officers, more than comrades, more than friends. In the K/S stories, they can't fight this feeling anymore, as it were, and they go all the way – becoming lovers.

Once this got rolling, there was no stopping it: hundreds of such stories emerged, and female fans the world over couldn't get enough of them.

---

[39] Bantam Books, publisher of the James Blish paperbacks, did two volumes of this fan fiction – *Star Trek: The New Voyages* and *Star Trek: The New Voyages 2*, in 1976 and 1977. They were edited by Sondra Marshak and Myrna Culbreath. Roddenberry wrote a foreword to the first volume.

And it gets even more interesting: these 'slash' stories, as they came to be called, birthed a genre beyond *Star Trek*. Slash fiction emerged in every franchise you can imagine: over in *Star Wars*, Vader was getting it on with the Emperor, Han was getting it on with Luke, and Luke was getting it on with Chewbacca. In *Lord of the Rings*, Frodo and Sam got friendly, Arwen was getting frisky with Eowyn, and it was open season on Legolas. In a more contemporary franchise, Harry Potter has done just about everybody at Hogwart's.

As slash spread, it spilled out of sci-fi/fantasy into more conventional domains, such as *The Brady Bunch. Archie. Bonanza.* I kid you not.

This is as fascinating a phenomenon as anything I've ever come across in pop culture, and if it's of interest to you, a moment's Google search will turn up countless sites where you can read this stuff till your eyeballs bubble. I'm more interested in the phenomenon than its contents, but I appreciate that it was Trek fandom that set it all in motion.

We'll wrap this topic up with an interesting nod to K/S that occurred in the novelization of *Star Trek: The Motion Picture*, where Alan Dean Foster (writing as Gene Roddenberry) includes a footnote in the story, quoting James T. Kirk himself:

> *"I was never aware of this lovers rumor, although I have been told that Spock encountered it several times. Apparently he had always dismissed it with his characteristic lifting of his right eyebrow which usually connoted some combination of surprise, disbelief, and/or annoyance. As for myself, although I have no moral or other objections to physical love in any of its many Earthly, alien, and mixed forms, I have always found my best gratification in that creature woman. Also, I would dislike being thought of as so foolish that I would select a love partner who came into sexual heat only once every seven years."*

Conquest of Space, **Failure to Launch**

Whatever shortcomings I might bemoan from my Fundamentalist upbringing, I have to say that the church my father pastored in my early teenage years had one very prominent plus: beautiful teenage girls. And when my dad created a youth center, ReachOut House, near the town high school in the early Seventies – where we would go a couple of nights a week and have Bible study with other church kids, and I got to play guitar for praise chorus time, I had plenty of opportunity to study them.

One of them, Bambi, was not only staggeringly fetching but whip-smart; I always hoped she'd sit close enough to me to notice how awesome a guitarist I was. Also, she smelled wonderful.

Bambi's younger sister Beth was my age and in my group, and every bit as smart. I remember getting into it with her in the fall of 1974, not at ReachOut House but at church, where we were both part of a youth activities committee. It was our job to plan some ReachOut House events, and the board had given us a little money to play with.

The church had a 16mm film projector (this was a decade before VHS tapes became a thing) and we decided to rent a movie for a Reach-Out House movie night. Beth and I were assigned the task of select-ing a movie.

You'd think I'd have had the brains to make the most of this opportunity to get to know a brilliant, beautiful young woman my own age much better, but I was in my early *Star Trek* days – all I could do was seize the chance to expand my reach for the stars. Browsing the provided catalog of 16mm prints available for us to rent, I locked onto *Conquest of Space*, a 1955 George Pal classic about a Mars mission gone awry.

Beth favored the far more accessible *Please Don't Eat the Daisies*, a 1960 Doris Day romp featuring David Niven that would undoubtedly have been a far more popular choice with the audience we had. Beth and I argued and argued over this across several phone calls, and I wouldn't budge. Her annoyance was palpable, and I don't think she ever forgave me for my intransigence.[40]

That my behavior was inexcusable goes without saying, though the event itself went very well. All the guys my age loved the movie and all the girls hated it, but we *all* loved the pizza and popcorn and snacks and the novelty of our own private movie screening, there at ReachOut House.

---

[40] As an apologetic homage to Beth, I bought both movies on DVD many years later.

Many invited friends who had never been there before, which was part of the point.

The more distressing take-home point is that my behavior was *inexplicable*: here I'd had an opportunity to work closely with a peer whose considerable beauty was exceeded by her brains, and I hadn't been self-aware enough to simply work with her and enjoy the collaboration. Sadly, my dull-wittedness in this area would persist for years. Decades, even.

"Let My People Go!"

Before Harrison Ford flew the *Falcon* or cracked Indy's whip; before Michael Biehn knocked up Sarah Conner or went steady with Ripley; before Mark Hamill voiced the Joker or kissed his on-screen sister, there was... *Charlton Heston???*

It's hard to convey to millennial fanboys or Zoomer fanboys that the sci-fi on-screen hero of the Boomer fanboy was Moses or Ben-Her (I'm always getting those two mixed up). To begin with, the odds of their having seen *The Ten Commandments* grow fainter with the passing years; and within Heston's sci-fi legacy, the only bell-ring for fanboys under 40 is *Planet of the Apes.*

But there was more. Oh yes.

As the Sixties were becoming the Seventies, science fiction and fantasy began making a return to the silver screen, after about a decade in limbo. There hadn't yet been a specific actor in sci-fi who had appeared often enough to become a familiar face, even in the more prolific Fifties. But after the back-to-back successes of *Fantastic Voyage, 2001,* and *Planet of the Apes*, more and more sci-fi projects began appearing on studio to-do lists – and Heston, having led *Apes* to an astonishing $35 million box office (more than *2001* and *Fantastic Voyage* combined), must have seemed like money in the bank.

After setting the *Apes* film series in motion in 1968, he agreed to cameo in the first of four sequels. He then became *The Omega Man* (1971), a military scientist in a world populated by cultish zombies, made so by a virus he hoped to cure. He was then tapped to play Frank Thorn in *Soylent Green* (1973), a severely dystopian overpopulation fable. This film was a stunner, with a twist ending almost as notorious as *Apes'* Statue of Liberty scene – and it fixed Heston in the minds of the Nerd Nation as the face of their own desperate angst.

Let's briefly revisit these three classic films.

Planet of the Apes (1968)

The tale of Taylor, the cynical interstellar astronaut who finds himself stranded alone on a planet where talking apes rule and humans are mute beasts, is culturally iconic; even those who have little or no interest in science fiction films are familiar with its stunning final visual – the Statue of Liberty protruding from a desolate ocean shoreline.

The film's impact (as well as Heston's characterization of Taylor) can scarcely be overstated. The story of Taylor's struggle to make sense of the insane world in which he finds himself, his efforts to connect with the benign chimpanzee intellectuals Cornelius and Zira, his bafflement at the emptiness of the humans around him – and, most importantly, his struggle against the machinations of the authoritarian Dr. Zaius, who seeks to suppress the truth of his situation from him – that story resonated with audience (and still does today) through its un-subtle themes of racial bigotry, revisionist history, and dark manipulation.

Taylor pieces together the inner workings of this strange ape society, aware that he is being handled by those in power, and that his friends Cornelius and Zira are just as much at their mercy. He connects, to some degree, with one of his kind – a young woman named Nova – and manages to escape to the Forbidden Zone, where the truth is hidden, and finds the statue, with its brutal, horrific message: he's been home, all along.

The Omega Man (1971)

Military scientist Robert Neville – Heston - is the only survivor of a virus that has swept the planet, killing most of humanity and turning the rest into nocturnal bloodsucking monsters. As the lone source of reason in an insane world, Neville defends himself against Matthias, leader of the Family, a vampire cult determined to destroy him because he clings to science, against which his cult rails with propaganda.

In a series of confrontations, Neville keeps madness at bay in his own mind as he continues his search, eventually discovering Lisa, a young woman unaffected by the virus. They become close, and he learns that she is one of several survivors, a group that includes a young intern and her own brother, who has the virus and whom Neville has a chance of curing.

Matthias rallies, attacking Neville and Lisa in his stronghold. They fend the attackers off, and the cure works. Lisa's brother, insisting that the Family are still human and can likewise be cured, returns to them and is killed by Matthias as a suspected spy. Neville, attempting to rescue him, is captured, as Lisa succumbs to the virus herself. There's a showdown, and Neville is mortally wounded; but Lisa's group, including the med student, find Neville before he dies, and he hands off his cure as they head out of the city.

Soylent Green (1973)

The world is desperately overpopulated and just barely holding together. Forty million people are stuffed into New York City, where police detective Frank Thorn (Heston) is investigating the murder of William Simonson of Soylent Industries – the company that is feeding the seething masses with its product Soylent Green, advertised as a food made from ocean plankton.

With the help of a concubine named Shirl, Thorn follows a shadowy trail toward the truth of who murdered Simonson and why. Things are not as the world is being told; for one thing, the ocean is no longer producing plankton. Soylent Green is being made from some other protein source, and Simonson was murdered at the behest of Soylent board members because he was on the verge of revealing this to the public.

Thorn's aging friend Sol, disgusted by it all, seeks assisted suicide; Thorn tries to stop him, but is too late. Sol's dying words to Thorn are to insist that he get to the truth of Soylent Green.

This he does, following Sol's transport to a recycling plant, where he realizes the horrific truth: Soylent Green is made from human bodies. He is spotted, there is a showdown, he is captured – and as he's being taken away, he calls out to the crowd:

"Soylent Green is people!!!"

Fanboys certainly cheer when Taylor wins out over Zaius; when Neville survives Matthias and hands off the cure; when Thorn realizes the truth and shouts it for the world to hear. And they cheer for good reasons; these three stories are much the same, and Heston presents a figure that binds them together, while shining through as the hero fanboys need. Let's break it down.

The world is going to hell

In all three stories, dystopia rules.

In *Apes*, the natural order has been overturned, and what remains is in poor working order. Taylor finds himself confronted with a twisted reality that is being held together through manipulation, lies, and brute force.

In *Omega*, the world has been very nearly wiped out, and the one organizing force that remains is malevolent, fanatical and chaotic. Neville is alone, holding back a new Dark Ages as the sole repository of reason.

In *Soylent*, the world hovers on the edge of collapse, teetering on a precipice with only a thin lifeline of deceit and horror to stave off collapse into madness. Thorn is determined to know the truth, whatever the cost.

There's a truth to be revealed

The truth in each case, pursued relentlessly by each Heston character, is existential; in each case, that truth cuts to who we are and how we got where we are and why it happened. The devotion of the Heston hero figure to get to the truth, against all odds, is the ultimate fanboy calling.

Fanboys, you see, are truth-seekers at heart, and Heston is volunteering himself as High Seer in all three films. He becomes the embodiment of the fanboy's deepest quest.

A hero archetype

Taylor, Neville and Thorn are the same guy – cynical, yet valorous; tainted, yet true; alone, yet still connected to his core humanity.

As we observed above, this had never happened before. Sci-fi had served up heroes by the score, to be sure, but we'd never had this many heroes conforming to such a fanboy-friendly profile – and played by the same actor! It's no wonder Heston became the fanboy generation's hero archetype.

Whither the Heston hero? What does all of this mean? Why does he, rather than any other hero, truly reign in the fanboy heart? Why didn't Harrison Ford end up succeeding him?

It's all to do with a *Mad* magazine send-up of *Apes*, where Taylor – roped by gorillas and being dragged to jail – shouts, in his biggest Moses voice, *"Let my people go!!!"*

And one of the gorillas says, "Boy! Once he gets hold of a hot expression, he doesn't let up, does he?"

Now, that's funny as hell, but what's really fun is that it doesn't just hilariously bridge Heston from *Apes* back to *The Ten Commandments* – it arcs across all three of his Seventies hero outings. In each of these movies, he's trying to liberate humanity with an essential truth.

That's the true nature of his fanboy hero appeal. Because liberating humanity with an essential truth is exactly what the fanboy longs to do.

We believe we see the world as it really is; we believe we have the inside scoop on the human condition. We believe we see the future more clearly.

And in our own hero fantasies, we're Charlton Heston, risking everything to get there, and take everyone we love along.

The Closet Scientist

The space program got me rolling in science.

Next came chemistry. My parents got me a chemistry set, augmented by a high school chemistry textbook from my Grandpa John. I started testing foods to learn the levels of this or that they contained. I got a book on rocketry and started designing my own.

Then came science fairs, two of which I placed 2nd in, county-wide; then came a book about how computers worked, and a radio I built from scratch. Then came homemade gunpowder (à la Captain Kirk in "Arena") to be used in my rockets, with which I easily could have blown off one or both hands (my parents never knew about that).

And from the New Wave science fiction I'd discovered at the town library – Samuel R. Delaney and Ursula Le Guin and Harlan Ellison and Roger Zelazny and Robert Silverberg and Joanna Russ (Philip K. Dick and Thomas Disch would come later) - I had begun gradually forming a new worldview, that the science and technology that hovered vaguely at the edges of my very parochial existence were in fact at the very center of the real world, propelling it in directions that would have society-altering consequences.[41]

Science would, in the long run, change human beings, and change them far more than religion could.

This dawning awareness remained shapeless for many years, but I voraciously prepared for it, all the same. I soaked up math and physics and took a computer course my first semester at the University of Kentucky, eventually majoring in it.

This was a severe heresy, but one easy to overlook so long as I did not say the E word; the notion that one can be religious and a believer in science was beginning to represent a convenient compromise in Evangelicalism, as technology was beginning to creep into the economy with the advent of affordable computers.

I didn't then, and don't now believe that one can be religious and a believer in science, and I've written extensively about why that is so; I'll not repeat it here.

---

[41] At the time, I was unaware that my cousin Kirk was paralleling me in this (see the chapter immediately following). I would learn many years later that he had discovered these far-sighted authors not long after I had. Had I known this at the time, I'd have had someone to talk to about all the ideas that poured out of those books; but at the time, my only thoughts where he was concerned was jealousy over the fact that his dad worked for NASA...

But neither will I cop to any cognitive dissonance on this point; as I said up top, my continued dalliance with the church wasn't a tug of war in my head; science, not religion, was worthy of my fealty - my mind was made up. My continuation in the church was a social concession. I knew no other way to live.

But as with music, the taboo side of science slipped right into me along with all the rest of it – and ended up defining me.

Parallel Universes

As I said at the top, I was born between the Mercury flights of Alan Shepard and Gus Grissom. I wasn't the only one.

My due date was June 16, 1961. But that date was usurped by my first cousin Kirk, the first son of my father's sister. I got bumped to July 6, like John Glenn waiting for a launch window.

Having experienced contemporaneous gestation, we proceeded – though we lived 1,000 miles apart – to live parallel lives.

We were both born into Fundamentalist Evangelical families, having been born of the children of one. We were both particularly brainy exemplars of brainy households. We both spent more time in churches than we spent in our homes, attending this event or that as many as five nights a week.

And we were both natural nerds.

We were jointly possessed of insatiable curiosity, making us voracious readers. We were both adventurous. We were both pensive. We both loved music, emerging rapidly from our forced piano lessons into self-teaching of other instruments, dissecting music in our heads before we understood it formally. We both had a knack for science.

We were both first-born sons with two younger brothers (I had a younger sister; Kirk had an older half-sister). We even looked alike, though in the end he grew four inches taller.

Why is he telling us this?

I'm telling you this because all the stories I've told thus far, all the things that happened to me to make me a nerd and a fanboy, happened to Kirk as well, all those hundreds of miles away.

To be sure, the nerd preceded the fanboy in Kirk's case. Though my father was a pastor and his was a computer systems engineer (working for NASA, via IBM Federal Systems Division, no less), his household was actually more strict than mine, regarding acceptable cultural content for young Evangelical minds. He and his brothers, for instance, were not permitted comic books, while I swam in them.[42]

On the other hand, he was growing up on the edges of the space program, so it was no surprise that his father not only had lots of nerdy tech books laying around, but a good deal of sci-fi as well. He just didn't know it yet.

---

[42] I hasten to point out the exception here – the Classics Illustrated series, which was allowed, and in which I, too, delighted…

But Kirk only became aware of the whole fanboy thing when our families met up in Anaheim in the summer of 1974 for our Evangelical order's annual convention. This was, of course, Cousin Heaven; the genetic brethren we hardly ever got to see, we now spent an entire week with, taking in Disney's California adventure, Knotts Berry Farm, and a big wide convention center to explore.

Remember that despite my own family's rigid adherence to right-wing culture, I was permitted TV sci-fi and comic books, because my parents didn't fully realize just how toxic they were to Fundamentalist thinking. Well, Kirk and his younger brother Jonathan were totally primed for a contraband fix! I bought up as many comics as I could in our hotel gift shop – issues of *Spider-Man* and the Gold Key *Twilight Zone* stand out in my memory – and allowed Kirk to devour the *Trek* paperbacks I had brought along.

We also discovered, together, the first video games ever. At Disneyland, we hovered in Tomorrowland, especially the arcade, where there were two electronic games – the first edition of the classic Pong, and a more sophisticated game called Computer Space, a missile attack simulator.

When he returned home to Texas with his family, Kirk went out and bought some of the James Blish *Trek* paperbacks. His father, noticing, mentioned that perhaps he might enjoy some similar fiction from his own collection – Asimov, et al.[43]

Now Kirk, already a nerd, was becoming a fanboy. To be sure, he never made his own Spock uniform, as I had done (as far as I know),- and I can't say to what degree he bonded with other fanboys at school, as I did – but he became (and remains to this day) a staunch devotee of classic *Trek*.

And not just *Trek*; though I don't know his feelings about *Space: 1999*, and understand that his commitment to *Star Wars* is decidedly casual, I can tell you that he is rabid for *The Prisoner* (which he turned me on to, returning the Blish favor), *Blade Runner*, the novels of Thomas Disch and Philip K. Dick, and other brainy confections.

We remained close through the years, despite the distances. We played a few games of chess through the mail. When he broke from our family's

---

[43] This really took hold, in ways that made me envious; my uncle Jerry and Kirk and Jonathan proceeded, over the next two decades, to hand around the latest Heinlein, or whatever other sci-fi novel happened to be of interest that month. I ended up enjoying the same kind of connection with my own two sons, passing around the Ender books and Ray Bradbury, years later (Kirk indoctrinated his own kids the same way) - but never had that experience with my own father, who didn't read much fiction. I did, however, have such an experience with my Uncle Billy – see "Aslan on Mars", page 157.

religious tradition in the early Eighties, I was the first person in the family he told.

Then came the Internet. In the early Nineties, the days of the earliest email services, we connected permanently, and have been in near-daily contact ever since. And though those thousands of exchanges contained more than enough nerd and fanboy to suffice (we still pass books back and forth through the mail), our connection grew into professional partnership – we have done a lot of research together, and today own a small AI company that develops social applications of predictive models.

Underneath that research was a core common interest. Having grown up in isolated communities so like-minded that deviation from tribal thought meant disassociation, and having both realized we were unfortunate square pegs in those round holes, we became fascinated with the nature of tribal thought. In 2007, we undertook a deep dive into the anthropological and neurological underpinnings of social cognition, working out an understanding of just how such communities come to be, and how they impact the world.

In the 15 years since, we've experimented with cognitive diversity in online communities, bringing together people from all over the world, with different backgrounds and different styles of thought, to learn how people can come to mutual understanding. To push back against our bumpy social barriers. To fix the world.

And all because of James Blish, at a 1974 church convention...

Published!

I shared earlier that my mom had cultivated in me an interest in creative self-investment. Little did I know at the time just now rapidly this would proliferate, or where it would ultimately lead.

The combination of creating things, my voracious appetite for books and my insatiable curiosity pushed me in a new direction: I started to experience ideas coming from within, rather than from the pages in front of me, and felt the urge to write them down. Still a pre-teen, I was becoming a writer.

I began to wonder if the things I was reading in Asimov and Ellison were possible. Could a robot truly pass for a man? Is it possible to build a computer that wipes out humanity? To communicate telepathically with a dog? To predict the future?

I started coming up with my own what-ifs and questions surrounding them. Writing them long-hand in a notebook, I filled page after page after page. Noticing this, my parents gave me a manual typewriter on Christmas, 1974.

And the following spring, my 8th-grade English teacher announced to the class that she was accepting original stories for an award given every year, the Florence Schultz Memorial Award. I didn't need to be told twice; I started a story that very day, while still in school.

Suppose, I wondered, that there was a power source up on the moon, abandoned because we decided to have a war back on Earth; suppose, I wondered, that an artificial intelligence had been left behind on the moon to look after this power source; suppose, I wondered, that over time, the AI went crazy...

That night, I struggled to finish my long-hand draft of the story, before typing it up. I was sitting on the steps leading up to my bedroom, rather than in the bedroom itself. Mom noticed me and sat down beside me on the steps, asking what I was doing.

I was a bit hesitant, but I was kind of trapped there, so I handed the story to her and explained about the contest and award. She quickly read through the story, then shifted into Project mode, asking me a few clarifying questions. She accepted the premise of the story without blinking, which astonished me; I'm confident she's never read a shred of science fiction in her life.[44] She immediately understood what I

---

[44] I say that with the condescension of hindsight, but here's an out-of-left-field surprise: In early 1995, I met my mom and her second husband John for dinner in

was shooting for, and made several useful suggestions that helped me improve the story's tone and flow – especially the ending, which I intended as a shock.

I won the Florence Schultz Memorial Award. It's upstairs on the wall in my music room.

And if I could do *that*...

Alongside *Trek* and Heinlein and Asimov and the New Wavers, I was taken with a paperback series imported by Ace Books from Germany – the Perry Rhodan novels. Shepherded in the US by sci-fi superfan Forrest J. Ackerman, the series doled out the adventures of Major Perry Rhodan of the US Space Force (I kid you not), who discovers a marooned alien ship on the moon and proceeds to exploit its technology to unite Earth and carve out a niche for humanity out in the universe.

The thing is, these books were based on stories in a German magazine,[45] and were novellas at best; Ackerman needed to pad the books out to get the page count up to what Ace Books expected in a paperback. So Ackerman solicited original fiction from Perry's fans.

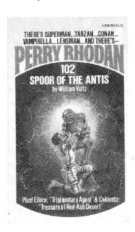

THERE'S SUPERMAN...TARZAN...CONAN...
VAMPIRELLA...LENSMAN...AND THERE'S—
PERRY RHODAN
102
SPOOR OF THE ANTIS
by William Voltz

Plus! Etlern: "Triplanetary Agent" & Coblentz: "Treasure of Red-Ash Desert"

Lexington, where they lived, and they both gushed over a new TV show they'd discovered and fallen in love with – a show I wasn't yet aware of. It was the last show on earth I would ever have expected my mother to watch – yet she just loved it, like I loved *Star Trek*. I began watching it, too, and it remains one of my all-time favorites. Ironically, it's a show about the tension between reason and faith. Have you guessed it? It was – wait for it! - *The X-Files*...

[45] The Perry Rhodan magazine is *still* published in Germany, to this day; the 3000th issue was published in 2019.

Helen O'Loy. Lester del Rey's unusual tale about a young engineer and a medical student who modify a household robot to develop emotions, resulting in the strangest love triangle of all time, is unexpectedly a tear-jerker.

The Roads Must Roll. This was my first encounter with the legend Robert Heinlein, who dominated the field for most of his life. This odd tale imagines a near future when moving sidewalks replace highways and train tracks, and he uses that unusual backdrop for one of his many emphatic social statements – that social status should be dependent upon one's function in society.

Nightfall. I'd already gotten to know Isaac Asimov in *World's Best Science Fiction*, and he'd impressed me greatly. But this story, taking place on a faraway world where six suns keep the sky bright constantly, explores a madness previously unimagined – a madness triggered when every sun goes down every few thousand years, and people see the stars for the first time...

Arena. This Fredric Brown tale of a military pilot who finds himself in gladiatorial combat with an enemy alien to settle the war between them – imposed by some more powerful alien referees – was adapted into one of *Star Trek*'s best episodes.

The Nine Billion Names of God. I'd read *2001: A Space Odyssey* by this time, but there was much Arthur C. Clarke yet to discover. Like "The Star", which I'll get to later, this is a story that blends science and religion, with a startling result.

The Cold Equations. Tom Godwin's tale of a pilot rushing desperately-needed medicine to a dying colony planet, discovering a young girl stowed away on his ship, is one of science fiction's true heart-breakers. So powerful was this story to me that I wrote a "reply" story decades later, to refute the story's cover premise.[47]

Flowers for Algernon. Twice caught on film, Daniel Keys' story of a mentally retarded man who undergoes an operation that makes him a

---

[47] That story can be found in my collection *Shadows of Shadows*, or read online at https://www.scottrobinson.online/post/the-wire.

genius, only to have the effects rapidly fade away, competes with "The Cold Equations" for the saddest in all of science fiction.

Those are just my favorites – there's much more going on here. The book includes stories by John W. Campbell, Theodore Sturgeon, A.E. van Vogt, Ray Bradbury, Clifford Simak, Judith Merril, Fritz Leiber, Richard Matheson, Damon Knight, Roger Zelazny, Alfred Bester, Jerome Bixby, and others.

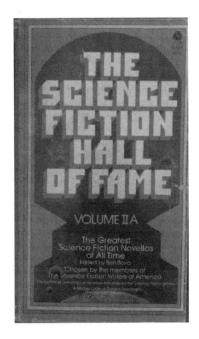

The second volume, edited by Ben Bova (who did the impossible job of replacing John W. Campbell as editor of *Astounding/Analog Science Fiction*) contains novellas, rather than short stories – pieces running more than 10,000 words.

Here are my favorites. But, like the previous volume, there is much more to be found: contributors include Poul Anderson, Lester del Ray, James Blish, Frederick Pohl, Jack Vance, H.G Welles, Algis Budrys and others.

Who Goes There? John W. Campbell's tale of a group of scientists in the Antarctic digging up an alien spacecraft in the ice, recovering and reviving its pilot and realizing they've unleashed a threat to the entire planet, is the basis of John Carpenter's classic sci-fi horror film *The Thing*.

The Martian Way. Asimov is back in this tale of "Scavengers", Martian-born humans who recover spacecraft parts, spinning one of the first explorations of terraforming while also getting in a few digs at McCarthyism.

Universe. Robert Heinlein creates a social microcosm in a generation spaceship where the passengers don't realize they're in a spacecraft, and the surviving crew must struggle against a competing tribe of mutants.

Though the contents are decidedly old-school by today's standards, both books are very much worth seeking out.

Run, Logan, Run!

There can be no survey of the nerd Seventies without an accounting of *Logan's Run*. Prior to *Star Wars*, it represented a giant step beyond the low-budget fare we'd grown so accustomed to.

But it needs to be pointed out up front that *Logan's Run* isn't just a movie; it started out as a novel written by William F. Nolan and George Clayton Johnson (a name I recognized from *Trek*, author of the episode "The Man Trap") in 1967. It was that novel – republished in paperback in the spring of 1976, in anticipation of the MGM movie version to be released that summer – that was my first exposure to Logan and company.

I found the novel on the rack at a tiny hole-in-the-wall bookstore in Frankfort, not long after my family had moved there early in 1976.[48] I read it in a matter of hours. I was fascinated with the premise: that several hundred years in the future, humans would be living in domed cities under computer control, because the surrounding countryside was uninhabitable as a result of war. Life inside the cities was perfect – but it ended at age 21. To maintain population control, that was all the living that was allowed.

If you tried to escape this fate, if you decided to run, a team of elite cops would hunt you down and terminate you. Logan is one of those elite cops – until he learns that he has been tagged for termination, as an incentive to seek out a place called Sanctuary, the destination of all those who try to run.

Loved the book. *Loved* it! It was filled with fascinating ideas and a truly breathtaking plot. I soon learned about the movie, due out in June, and saw it opening weekend (alone, I might add; this was months before I would meet a batch of nerds at school who would change my world).

The movie, starring Michael York, Jenny Agutter and Peter Ustinov, was nothing like the book. Huge sections of the book were missing, as the film sought to greatly simplify the plot and streamline the story as a straightforward chase film. I didn't mind; I found it thrilling, and enjoyed the performances tremendously.

Among the changes: in the movie, the cutoff age is bumped up from 21 to 30; Sanctuary is off-world; and Francis, Logan's friend-turned-pursuer,

[48] The relocation to Frankfort is a key part of the tale. My father, for a time, gave up church ministry to manage several small clothing stores. This meant not only a change of scenery, but a major social shift for my family: we were no longer the Preacher's Kids; we were suddenly just like everybody else, and the old rules began to relax, opening the door for me to explore new friendships, new interests, and new ideas…

is reduced to just that, rather than a covert agent of Sanctuary, as in the book. I happily accepted these deviations.

Next came an odd twist. Above, I mentioned that David Gerrold, the Tribble Guy, picked a fight with William F. Nolan in his *Starlog* column. To this day, it doesn't make sense to me, but there it was. Having enjoyed the novel, David's columns on the subject made me feel self-conscious; I respected his opinion tremendously, and he was saying some pretty ugly things about the entire premise of *Logan's Run*. I remember feelings of embarrassment and self-consciousness, as only a 15-year-old can experience them; was there something wrong with me, that I didn't see the novel as the waste of time that David did?

I shared these feelings with my buddy Joe. His answer: "Who cares?"

I considered myself cured. And when *Logan's Run* became a TV series the following year, with *Trek*'s Dorothy Fontana as story editor and both David Gerrold and Harlan Ellison contributing scripts, I became a loyal if short-lived fan, as the series only lasted one truncated season. I did pick up something useful from it, however; there was a new character, an android called Rem. A precursor to *NextGen*'s Data, he looked human and often acted human. He reinforced my interest in AI.

Logan's adventures continued, as William Nolan kept writing sequels (though none were filmed) - *Logan's World*, published after the TV show premiered, and *Logan's Search*, released during my first year of college. I dutifully bought and read them, though with less enthusiasm.

Womp

When I did begin making friends in my new school in Frankfort, they were exactly the right ones.

It started with a big, tall, geeky guy named Joe Lee, whom I met when I finagled a transfer from Boring English to Advanced Placement English in first semester of my sophomore year. Joe sat in the back – and, joining the class in the second week of school or so, so did I. We rapidly became the best of friends.

Then there was Chemistry, where I was the lone sophomore; most kids took Biology their sophomore year and Chemistry their junior year. And one of these juniors was a short, red-headed kid with bug-eye classes named Jim Wampler.

I met Jim when my labmate Tracy Huffman took note of the story I had published in Perry Rhodan (two chapters back) and chanced to show it to Jim, whom he knew to be the sort of kid who read such stuff. Tracy himself mentioned that it seemed to him that my story "Wings of Immortality" was pretty much just a rip-off of *The Fly*. True enough, but Jim's response – Tracy correctly informed me that I should call him "Womp" - didn't care so much about the story itself as he did the fact that I had undertaken to write it.

Womp, you see, was an artist – very specifically, a sci-fi-loving, comic-book-reading, *nerd* artist – and finding an equally sci-fi-loving, comic-book-reading, nerd writer was just perfect, as far as he was concerned. We began a collaboration – and a friendship – that persists to this day.[49]

Meanwhile, back in Advanced Placement English, Joe was telling me that Gene Roddenberry – *the* Gene Roddenberry, the Great Bird of the Galaxy, about whom I'd learned everything from David Gerrold's *Trek* books! - was coming to nearby Louisville later in the month to deliver a lecture and offer a screening of "The Cage", *Trek*'s original pilot episode, and the infamous Star Trek Blooper Reel.

"I'd give anything to go to that!" I declared, "but my folks would never drive me all the way to Louisville. They'd think it was silly."

"Oh, we have a ride," Joe answered. "I'm going with Bob Fields. His mom is driving. You should ask if you can go along."

---

[49] To that end, the astute Gentle Reader may be assured that Womp's cover cartoon of me on the front of this book is no leap of imagination, but built on actual memory.

I made it my immediate mission to meet Bob Fields. He, too, was a Trekker, so it was with no effort at all that yet another friendship was formed.

And yes, his mom would take me along.

I tell this to Womp, and he immediately wants in on it. He, too, meets Bob and becomes friends with him, and a couple of weeks later, the four of

Womp's pre-production sketch of a Bekorii warrior, from the script I wrote for our movie-making adventures described later on.

us and another kid named John crammed ourselves into Bob's mom's car and made our way to Louisville.

That was the beginning of a beautiful friendship. Over the next few years, into our early college days, we spent innumerable hours at one another's houses, watching TV and movies and listening to great music (I turned him on to the Beatles; he turned me on to The Alan Parsons Project). We began various creative enterprises – everything from collaborating on his school paper comic The Afghan to making parody sci-fi comics to filming Super 8 movies (read on).

Imperial Earth
Children of Dune
Man Plus
The Star Trek Concordance
The Gods Themselves
A World Out of Time
A Scanner Darkly
The 1977 Annual World's Best Science Fiction
Where Late the Sweet Birds Sang
The Early Pohl
The Best of Damon Knight
Millennium
The Bicentennial Man and Other Stories
Gateway
The Best of Leigh Brackett
Before the Golden Age
A Heinlein Trio (The Puppet Masters/Double Star/The Door into Summer)
The Hugo Winners, Vol. III
Mindbridge
Time Storm
A Canticle for Leibowitz
The Martian Chronicles
Michaelmas
Dreamsnake
The Silmarillion
The Far Ends of Time and Earth
The Fountains of Paradise

Whew! How's *that* for a nerd library?

I remember transitioning to Franklin County High School in the spring of that year, trucking my new introductory treasures with me. I hadn't made any new friends yet, but as I sat there in study hall, Arthur C. Clarke and Isaac Asimov and Larry Niven and Kate Wilhelm and "James Tiptree, Jr." and Ursula LeGuin and Ray Bradbury and J.R.R. Tolkien all kept me company.

It also became a pleasure to order books for the nerd friends I eventually accumulated; I remember getting Joe a copy of *Children of Dune*, and Bob a *Starfleet Technical Manual* (they paid me back, but it was a joy to be able to provide them, even so).

About 20 years later, I was sitting in a doctor's office as my daughter was having a routine audio exam. On a coffee table in the waiting room was a pile of magazines – and, lo and behold, someone had left their monthly SFBC catalog!

I had long since dropped my membership, but it was still a great pleasure to look at the recent offerings. The prices had increased – to $7.99, if memory serves – but everything else remained the same. It filled me with nostalgia.

Boucher's Treasure

In the magazine inserts that lured young readers like me to the Science Fiction Book Club, we were tempted by the offer of four hardback books for only $1 plus shipping and handling, as an enticement (it worked!) - and one of the offerings dangled as a temptation was Anthony Boucher's Treasury of Great Science Fiction.

Like the *Science Fiction Hall of Fame* volumes, Boucher's *Treasury* was packed to bursting with the very best the genre had to offer. And Boucher – for almost a decade the editor of *The Magazine of Fantasy & Science Fiction* – was the guy to compile such a volume.

All the names I'd already come to love could be found there. Here are the tales I loved best.

Pillar of Fire. I had found Ray Bradbury's work more poetic than terrifying, but this tale of a vampire being released from a grave in the year 2349 made very clear to me that there was more to Bradbury than I had yet fully grasped.

The Father-Thing. Philip K. Dick cannot go unmentioned in any book explicating my nerd roots. His endlessly inventive plot devices are well-represented here in this story of a young child who realizes his father has been replaced by a duplicate, which foreshadows *Invasion of the Body Snatchers*.

The Weapons Shop of Isher. A.E. van Vogt, whom I had discovered through his short story collection *Destination: Universe!*, imagines a civilization in political tension, with Weapon Shops arming a population that delivers an un-subtle discussion of the right to bear arms.

The Man Who Sold the Moon. I wasn't yet aware of Robert Heinlein's "Future History" continuity, which this story is part of, but I was deeply impressed with the near-future he imagined in this tale of a businessman - "the last of the robber barons" - who conspires, not only to travel to the moon, but to own it.

The Stars, My Destination. This was my introduction to Alfred Bester, who rolls out a lengthy adventure in which the solar system's inner planets are at war with the outer moons. It mixes revenge, teleportation, psionics and synesthesia against a quirky and riveting social universe.

As with the *Hall of Fame* books, Boucher's *Treasury* is well worth searching out.

Cousin Jimmy

When my family relocated in Frankfort, Kentucky in the spring of 1976, my father – having nurtured my interest in the guitar – arranged lessons for me at the local music store. And my instructor was none other than his own younger brother's sister's brother – a guy named Jimmy Boggess.

I had never met (or even heard of) Jimmy, who would have been in his early thirties at the time. He didn't look or act like a member of our Evangelical clan; he had long hair and a beard and very hip glasses, dressed in bell bottom jeans, and – *gasp!* – he smoked, which *nobody* in our world ever did.

He played the guitar like a badass, and I learned that he played in a band in a local lounge – *secular music*, which our family didn't indulge in, in a place where alcohol was served.

In hindsight, I would have thought my parents would have kept me far, far away from Jimmy. But my dad was quite enthusiastic, and didn't think twice about it.

I remember Dad introducing me to Jimmy by taking me to visit him at his home in nearby Versailles. And lo and behold, there in Jimmy's den is a wall of science fiction books – including Anthony Boucher's *Treasury*, which I just told you about. I remember my dad taking note of the two-volume set, and wanting to cry out, "I have those books, too!"

I only took lessons with Jimmy for about a year, and from time to time we would discuss the latest, greatest sci-fi novel he'd read, and I would rush out to buy it. When the lessons were over, I doubted I would ever see Jimmy again.

But I did. In 1982, he appeared out of nowhere at one of my parents' clothing stores, seeking me out because he'd heard through the family grapevine that in addition to guitar, I also played keyboards. Turns out his lounge band needed a new keyboard player, and I was now 21.

I was newly married and had just become a father, so I really couldn't see playing in a lounge band at night, when I was needed at home. But Jimmy and I had a great time talking about the latest Heinlein…

September 24, 1976

It's September 1976, and I'm a 15-year-old high school sophomore living in Frankfort.

And *Star Trek* is five years younger, an uncelebrated decade old this month - though no one is yet noticing that sort of thing, this early in Trek history.

And Gene Roddenberry – the Great Bird of the Galaxy himself! – is coming to a civic arena near me.

As mentioned previously, Joe and Jim and I got Bob's mom to drive us from Frankfort, Kentucky to Louisville's Freedom Hall, where we experience for the first time what we've only read about, up till now – Trek fandom, up close and personal. Those wonderful fan fests they'd had in New York, on the West Coast – we in the Midwest are now entering that amazing world for the first time!

Fans in homemade Starfleet uniforms.

Tables packed with *Trek* memorabilia for sale (I buy a poster).

A screening of a worn black-and-white print of "The Cage."

A screening of the infamous blooper reel.

And more than an hour of the Great Bird, pontificating on the future of - and the potential of – the human race.

Along the way, he serves up all his greatest hits from the college lecture circuit: how he fought to keep Spock in the cast for the second pilot; 'Letter from a Network Censor'; why he bailed on Season Three, all of it.

He talks about Questor,[50] and his belief that technology will one day deliver us from our weak, frail meat bodies. And how *Star Trek* is a watered-down version of what he *really* believes the future will be like.

He doesn't talk about starships and Klingons and phasers, or even the cool tech awaiting us in the future – tricorders, transporters, warp drive. Oh, in passing, a bit, but that isn't his focus.

His focus is *us*. Human beings – what we are, what we can be, what we are becoming. *Star Trek*, the glitzy nacelles of our imaginations, isn't the thing – it's just a hailing frequency for something much bigger, much grander, much more important.

---

[50] Questor was the protagonist in Roddenberry's 1974 TV pilot *The Questor Tapes*, the last of a long line of androids planted on Earth to guide humanity to maturity. See "Roddenberry Theater", page 132.

I stand in line later than evening, clutching my overpriced poster, and I find myself in front of the man himself – imposing in stature, yet congenial – and shake his hand after he autographs my poster.

I'm a 15-year-old high school sophomore, and it will be years before I truly absorb and fully understand what I've seen. It will become more clear in the decade to come, as Roddenberry goes to war with Paramount and Harve Bennett and Nick Meyer, fighting for his humanistic vision as the *Trek* films unfold – and again as *The Next Generation* emerges, and the tussle over the vision of *Trek* begins anew.

My First Cognitive Clusters

I mentioned earlier that my cousin Kirk and I had lived near-identical lives, despite great distance between us, owing to our shared Evangelical upbringings and family traditions. I also mentioned that we had, as adults, entered into deep and persistent research into the nature of social cognition, seeking explanations for how ideological tribalism takes hold in the human mind.

It took years. We were determined to tackle the problem from many sides, to take a cognitive view, a sociological view, a neurophysiological view, an anthropological view – and seek an explanation that was harmonious between them all.

We call the result "Octant Theory", and it goes like this...

Social cognition in the human brain presents a vast range. It is possible for any two people to think very differently about themselves, about others, about the world, because there are certain aspects of our worldview (particularly where people are concerned) that rely upon how any one person's particular brain processes social information. And that, in turn, relies upon the amount of tissue that person happens to have in certain areas of the brain (we won't go into that here).

This brain tissue thing ties to three deep aspects of thinking about other people:

- Some prefer to follow a leader; others prefer to have the group decide;
- Some prefer to explore the world; some feel the world is full of danger;
- Some seek out the new-and-different; some are more comfortable with consistency and the familiar.

Of these three scales is the social universe constructed.

Now, of course, none of those three ranges of preference are absolute; every person falls somewhere on a spectrum between each extreme. But if you map them out, these three scales offer up eight general models of the human personality. Those are our "Octants".

Here's the thing: it is a natural human tendency for any one person to gravitate toward other people who share their preferences in these three areas. They cluster together, seeking out others with their own social cognition biases.

And that's what Kirk and I have explored: to understand the various cognitive clusters, how people end up in them, and how such clusters affect the world, for better or worse.

Why is he telling us this?

I'm telling you this because, in hindsight, the world Kirk and I grew up in was (is) a cognitive cluster: whatever the individual differences between the members of our respective churches, they were all people who 1) preferred to follow a leader (in an authority hierarchy of God->Male Church Leadership->Husband/Father->Wife->Kids); 2) felt the world to be a dangerous place, where Satan and evil influences held sway, and were thus perpetually wary; and 3) were very uncomfortable with change, preferring the comfort and safety of uniformity, suspect of anything new.

In hindsight, of course, this is all very obvious, and the restrictive parameters of the world of my youth are astounding to me, when I consider all that I didn't see around me. But then, it was all I'd ever known; the Evangelical world was *the* world; the only social universe I had experienced was made up of people who lived in that one Octant. That one cognitive cluster.

But now we had moved to Frankfort, and I had met Womp and Bob and Joe and Ruby and Heidi and so many others – and they thought very, *very* differently.

I had, for the first time in my life, *entered a new cognitive cluster.*

In this cluster, there was more variety; though socially bonded, its members didn't think alike on all three Octant scales. This was a very new thing for me, and very revealing.

To be sure, we were all seekers of the new-and-different, as all nerds and fanboys/girls necessarily are. We all had our minds on the stars, and couldn't wait for the next great novel or movie or comic book title. You can't really love *Trek* or its cousins without having this particular tendency.

And most of us were explorers, seekers of opportunity – we mined the world for ideas and beauty and wonder, the riches of the mind and heart. I was a writer, Womp was an artist; our buddy Todd was a photographer. Ruby was very visual, with a strong fashion sense. Bob was tactile; he had a brain for engineering. Only Joe tended to view the world as an inherently unsafe place, preferring risk aversion to exploration (though he was certainly a friend of scholarship and the pondering of big thoughts).

Where our biggest Octant variety emerged was in our social hierarchy thinking. Most of us were egalitarian; we had a strong preference for group decision.[51] In adulthood, we became progressives, or moderates at the very least.

Here again, Joe was the exception. The son of two parents who leaned right and the younger brother of a military officer, he saw the world as most orderly when everyone was part of an authority hierarchy. This was to some degree ironic, as his family was decidedly non-religious.

Heidi, too, whose father was an Army colonel, may have leaned toward the follow-the-leader end of the scale; but I never came to know her well enough to know for sure.

Probably the most egalitarian among us was Ruby, who had been raised by an aunt and who was the one among us who broke free of childhood with the greatest propensity for exploration, novelty-seeking, and fierce life-long learning. While I got to know her very well, our time in close friendship ended all too soon – so I don't know what she ultimately made of her strong independent tendencies.

In migrating from my original cognitive cluster into this new one, I couldn't have experienced a more extreme social swing. It literally changed my brain, leading me to think in new ways about the world, about the people around me, and about myself.

---

[51] In an embarrassing exception, I (the life-long wallflower) turned out to be too pushy and insistent on my own way in our joint creative endeavors, to be described shortly. My early college experience as a writer in a newsroom taught me that it is far better to remain open to the ideas of others than to be bossy, and I saw the error of my ways.

Fake Beatles in Space

Two high school friends informed this next great nerd discovery, one that merged my two great lifetime loves: science fiction and the Beatles.

One was my *Trek*/HAL buddy Joe; the other was a mutual friend named Ann Victor, and they both had an album that just blew my doors off – *3:47 EST*, by the Canadian band Klaatu. They both thought it was amazing, and insisted I check it out.

Hearing it, I knew that it must be mine. It was pop-rock that just burst with creativity and novelty, quirky and offbeat and – uniquely, in my experience – as nerdy as music could be.

This album, released in 1975, was the band's first. It started off with a track that was unmistakably science fiction in theme: "Calling Occupants of Interplanetary Craft", a paean to first contact between humankind and whatever's out there. Though *Close Encounters of the Third Kind* would not hit theaters for another two years, the song retroactively threw off the same vibe, with its footsteps-in-the-woods opening sound effects and Mellotron intro. I was hooked.[52]

Other tracks stood out. The raucous "Anus of Uranus" is open to multiple interpretations, but its tone and humor and clever production unquestionably added color to the album. "Doctor Marvello" and the

---

[52] The Carpenters, of all people, would do a mediocre cover of the song two years later, hoping to cash in on the *Close Encounters* wave.

lovely, ethereal album closer "Little Neutrino", with its extended outro, just wrapped the whole album up as a nerd treasure trove.

The last track of side one of the album, all the more so: "Sub Rosa Subway", an ultra-nerdish trivia fest that serves up the real-life story of Alfred Beach, who built the world's first subway in New York City in 1870, sounded so much like the Beatles that the world decided that Klaatu – who were never individually named and of whom no photographs existed – were in fact the reunited Fab Four.

First, the story of that song – then a look at Klaatu going full interstellar.[53]

Sub Rosa Subway

"Back in 1870, just beneath the Great White Way
Alfred Beach worked secretly, risking all to ride a dream
His wind machine..."

One of the most interesting cases of mistaken identify in rock history happened in 1977, when music journalist Steve Smith suggested in a review that Klaatu, a Canadian progressive rock trio, might actually be the Beatles, secretly reunited.

It's an easy case to make: the perpetual inventiveness, strong musicianship and expansive themes owed much to the studio-era Beatles, conveying an influence possibly underscored by outright worship. John Woloschuk, Dee Long and Terry Draper may not have been the reunited Beatles, but they clearly were among the Fab Four's biggest fans.

This was especially obvious on "Sub Rosa Subway," the last track on side one of the band's 1975 debut album, *3:47 EST*. The lead vocal (by Woloschuk), near-perfect Paul before you even get to the inflection, is only the start: from the song's Victorian theme to its sweeping arrangement to the punchy horns and soaring strings to the totally-Paul bass line, this song is vintage McCartney, a masterpiece in the same sense that the successful forging of an acknowledged classic is itself a work of art.

On top of all of the above, we have the jacked-up guitars over cinematic orchestration, embedded voice-over-the-phone, a key change out of nowhere. A more McCartney-esque facsimile is hard to imagine; Smith's suspicions that the Beatles had reconciled were completely understandable.

[53] From *Uncle Scott's Treasure of Useless Knowledge*, by the author.

Capitol Records, Klaatu's label and the Beatles' distributor, milked the reunion rumors for all they were worth. The band eschewed live performance and used the songwriting credit "Klaatu," rather than their names, so the 'Beatles Reunion Hoax' ended up going on and on, until a Washington D.C. radio program director tracked down their actual names in the U.S. Copyright Office.

The band suffered for it in the end. The whole thing, now a hoax in the minds of the record-buying public, tainted them as frauds – even though none of it had been their doing. Though they recorded several more albums, Klaatu disbanded, even in the face of such a promising start, only a handful of years later.

Hope

It was Klaatu's follow-album – *Hope*, released in 1977 – that cemented them forever in geek history.

A concept album on a par with progressive rock's best, *Hope* was an integrated suite of songs that told the tale of a faraway civilization gone wrong. Its musical invention was pervasive, its production pristine. The narrative, though somewhat simplistic, was excellent pop fare while also teasing at possibilities as yet unexplored in the genre: it seemed to be an album that David Bowie or Yes might have undertaken, but more accessible.

Side One of Hope takes us to a civilization in a faraway star system. The opening track, "We're Off You Now" sets up the journey to come; "Madman" intimates, with some subtlety, that this world fell to a leader who led it to ruin; "Around the Universe in 80 Days" echoes the hopefulness of the previous album's "Calling Occupants", almost bookending it, setting up some hint that the horror to come isn't absolute; and Side One wraps up with "Long Live Politzania", a national anthem that is, in context, being scrutinized by archaeologists long after the fall of the planet.

This is all great fun, and it surges with unapologetic novelty. But it's Side Two that really reaches out and grabs the inner nerd, as the narrative shifts to the aftermath of this civilization's collapse. "The Loneliest of Creatures", with its children's sing-song pianet and operatic chorus, reveals that the lone survivor of this planet is an astronomer, the Lighthouse Keeper, who spends his final days scanning the stars for with his laser flare for some sign of remaining life:

"Suppose I'm not the loneliest of creatures," asks the singer, *"Then tell me who this wretched soul might be?"*

"In the dark of night, there lives a lighthouse keeper," comes the answer, *"And the lone survivor of his world is he..."*

"Prelude", featuring a bombastic London Symphony Orchestra, summarizes the civilization's fall, leaving us with "So Said the Lighthouse Keeper", which chronicles the lone survivor's final day:

So said the lighthouse keeper, as he wiped a teardrop from his nose
Upon which his spectacles rose and gazed out to the stars
And like a portrait still he stared, and sighing to himself declared,
"I must invent the perfect prayer, not yours, not mine, but ours
Which in the name of charity, might lead us to eternal peace
The ultimate philosophy some simple, single phrase..."

The old and much encumbered man
Then came to rest with head in hand
He thought and thought and thought away
His last remaining day...

"Hope" summarizes the album's message, that it need not all come to this – making the album a parable for the modern world.

This is all very simple and pop, to be sure, and its cleverness doesn't overreach; *Hope* doesn't try to be more than it is, as much progressive rock of the era was certainly guilty of. It allows the listener to let it lay claim to greatness *for existing at all*, in an era before such themes and modes of expression were considered cool.

Many years after my discovery and embrace of Klaatu, I unpacked these two great albums – essential entries in every nerd's collection! - for my kids. My younger son, Trey, took to it in particular. I burned him a CD of *Hope* to use as bedtime music, alongside *90125* and the Beatles No. 1s. When he was six, I'd ask him what music he wanted as I tucked him in, and true to form, he'd say, "SometimesIFeelLikeI'mTheLoneliestOfAll-CreaturesInTheUniverse!"

Nerd Theory: Monty Python

Not all nerds are fanboys, but all fanboys are nerds.

Similarly, not all people who love Monty Python are nerds – but all nerds love Monty Python.

By extension, then, many if not most fanboys/girls are Monty Python fans. Basic set theory!

I learned this in the mid-Seventies, when my family had moved to Frankfort – but before I'd discovered that *Star Trek* was on every morning at 11 a.m. and I could catch it if I ditched church. In those days when I still sat through Sunday morning services, I sat with a kid named Keith from school – and he asked if I had seen Monty Python the night before.

I'd never heard that name. What was it?

He went on to describe *Monty Python's Flying Circus*, the British comedy from 1969-1973 that was burning into the US cultural landscape like wildfire. It was on late Saturday nights on our local PBS channel. Keith described it as nothing like I'd ever seen on US television – rude, chaotic, staggeringly intelligent, and laugh-til-you-choke funny.

I started watching. My parents would not have approved (there was actual nudity, right there on television!), but they never caught me.

Then *Holy Grail* came to town, and Python became a whole new thing.

My memory is that it was Joe who was most enthusiastic, but there was no one in our entire nerd gang who didn't fall in love with Python.

Joe and I got to the point, thanks to my cassette recording of a television airing, of memorizing entire scenes and being able to perform them for others on demand: we could do Constitutional Peasant. Bring Out Your Dead. The French Taunter.

And we did some classic Python, too – Wink! Wink! Nudge! Nudge! The Parrot Sketch.[54]

My friend Steve Fry turned me on to the Python albums. We soaked those up, too.

Why is he telling us this?

I'm telling you this because the fanboy universe, in all its nerdy glory, wasn't limited to sci-fi/fantasy; every aspect of our cultural lives followed these patterns, and that included humor: we took it to the same extremes

---

[54] In later years, all my kids would come to love *Holy Grail*, but none so much as my youngest daughter Josie, with whom I would perform the scenes at the local playground.

that we took everything else – memorizing it, performing it, worshipping it.

There was also Tom Lehrer. But I digress...

Interstellar Rock

As my mind drifted further and further into space, the jukebox at my junior high school became my friend.

It sat in the school gymnasium, convenient for use at dances, and was rigged so that no quarter was needed to play a song. During lunch hour, when we were done eating, we were allowed to hang out in the gym until the bell, playing songs.

One of those songs was David Bowie's "Space Oddity". I would race to the jukebox and punch it in.

Ground control to Major Tom...
Ground control to Major Tom...
Take your protein pills and put your helmet on...

Thus began the dialog between the two, in Bowie's moving tale of isolation and alienation. I didn't think I could get away with buying the single and playing it at home – rock music wasn't allowed in our Fundamentalist home – but I had the jukebox, and I rapidly memorized the song.

It was very much a nerd song, and yet it had depth and substance.

And sound effects!

There's the moment after the "countdown" section, in which one David Bowie utters a rhythmic *"Ten...nine...eight...seven..."* while another David Bowie remains the voice of Ground Control: *"Check ignition and may God's love be with you..."*

At that moment just after, there's an instrumental transition where a single guitar note wavers, then bends upward, as a rising flute note ascends above it – a musical rendition of *liftoff.*

Making a guitar sound like a spacecraft launch! That just rocked me. (There were also the spacey synthesizer notes by Yes keymeister Rick Rick Wakeman.)

I didn't buy the album until my second year of college. But the song has never left me, and I raised my kids on it.

And soon after, Elton John, with "Rocket Man".

This is very much the same song, though musically it's very different. It's another portrait of isolation and alienation set against the backdrop of the stars, with an added layer of self-doubt. The guitar effects are more prominent, as Elton's guitarist Davey Johnstone does long upward glissandos at the beginning of each chorus, as Elton begins to sing, *"And I think it's gonna be a long, long time / Till touchdown brings me 'round again to find / I'm not the man they think I am at home / Oh no no no / I'm a Rocket Man / Rocket Man, burning out his fuse up here alone..."*

Then there's Boston, the mother of all interstellar rock bands.

It starts with the cover of their 1976 debut album, which depicts starships departing a disintegrating Earth. Each starship is guitar-shaped, and each is transporting an Earth city.

This interstellar visual theme sets the tone for what's inside. There are the themes of loneliness and isolation heard in the earlier songs, right up front in the song's opening track. But there's also the beginnings of what would become a long-term Boston staple – those guitars that sound like spaceships. And layered underneath, a unique wash of sound created by band mastermind Tom Schulz that is meant to suggest deep space.

We first hear this toward the end of Side One of that debut album. There's a dual track called "Foreplay/Long Time"; the first half is pure in-your-face instrumental, featuring a blazing Hammond organ lead run of almost a thousand notes in under two minutes. This triumphant instrumental – one of the most breathtaking and noteworthy in all of rock – then bridges into "Long Time", an energetic but wistful song about an amicable breakup.

The music snaps off suddenly, leaving a single lonely Hammond organ tone, reverberating as though from orbit. As that note is joined by another, building a chord, which morphs into another chord, and another, and another, a series of distorted sweeps swirl beneath – the toneless edging of a pick against a guitar string, delayed and chorused and reverberated with analog signal processing. These sweeps overlap and double back on each other, suggesting the void of space. It's a first-ever use of such technology in rock music, though Schultz will deploy the technique again and again. It's hypnotic, highly effective, and perfectly receptive of the rising pulse of "Long Time" which erupts seconds later.

This overall theme of seeking and finding, played out in the guitar-starship metaphor, continues over the next two albums, *Don't Look Back* (1978) and *Third Stage* (1986). Both of those album covers feature the same *Starship Boston*; the first is shown hovering over an alien landscape, the second descending to a new world from orbit.

Schulz is truly a Baby Boomer Fanboy, milking this theme until it screams for mercy. He gives us the sweep of deep space again in "The Journey", track two of Side One of *Don't Look Back*, a simple instrumental that juxtaposes Hammond organ and lead guitar in an extension of the "Foreplay" break. It is hypnotic, as was the first version, and is notable for its endless-loop structure; the musical phrase never resolves. That is surely intentional and meaningful.

Then Schulz gets as up-front as he can. Track three of Side One of Third Stage is a three-part instrumental that directly parades his space travel metaphor: "The Launch". Part one of the track is titled "Count-down"; then comes "Ignition", then "Third Stage Separation".

The track begins with a rumble – once again, Schulz's clever analog processing of toneless low-end guitar noise, with an organ part layering quietly in above it. Drums and bass and power chords crash into this sonic backdrop, and an instrumental theme – heavier and more emphatic than the one in "The Journey" - rises and roars.[55] Finally, the music shuts off abruptly, and a rising swirl of guitar tones climbs and climbs and climbs like a rocket, then smashes into the spaceship-themed "Cool the Engines", a straightforward rocker that leverages the rocket metaphor to underscore a message about steady but aggressive forward motion in relationships.

---

[55] Schulz took great satisfaction in declaring, in the album's liner notes and in interviews, that he never resorted to synthesizers to get these sound effects, which would have been the easiest thing in the world in the very digital Eighties. Instead, he began to take pride in being a technological Luddite, able to do more with ancient gear than more modern musicians could manage with the latest-greatest tech.

Honorable mention to the track "Rock and Roll Band" from Side Two of the *Boston* debut album. At the end of the second chorus of that song – a faux-autobiographical celebration of the joys of music – Scholz plants a rising unidentifiable something under the guitars and lead singer Brad Delp's rising voice that bends rapidly upward, stretching reaching, then exploding with a downward burst of toneless sound as the song's key changes and the lead guitar break begins. Swear to Zeus, it sounds exactly like the *USS Enterprise-D* going to warp – 11 years before that show existed.

What difference does all this make? Not a lot, I suppose, in the big picture – but it was seamlessly of a piece with my emerging fanboy sensibilities. I'd found a band that spoke my language.[56]

---

[56] I've recently demonstrated fealty to this childhood love, through my two books *Rock Candy: Boston* and *More Than a Feeling: Analyzing the Music of Boston, 1976-1988*.

TV Sci-Fi of the Seventies

The television sci-fi of the Sixties, while not particularly brainy or imaginative, was nonetheless interesting and fun.

The television sci-fi of the Seventies? Not so much.

It's hard to say why this is so. Certainly science fiction was more mainstream in the latter decade, after *2001* and *Planet of the Apes* had made it more palatable to the public at large; but *Lost in Space* and *Star Trek* and *Time Tunnel* and *Land of the Giants* and *Voyage to the Bottom of the Sea* had been a big deal in part because they were visually dazzling; they were in color – and that alone made them fun and interesting at the time. A decade later, *everything* was in color.

This isn't to say that there weren't any real gems; there were several, but they were the exception, rather than the rule.

Here's a sampling, from best to worst:

Kolchak: The Night Stalker

Twenty years before the *X-Files*, there was Kolchak.

This gem was born of two television movies – *The Night Stalker* and its follow-up, *The Night Strangler* – both of which centered on the investigations of Carl Kolchak (Darren McGavin), a tabloid reporter with a nose for the paranormal. The TV movies were such a hit that he got his own regular show, which sadly only lasted one season, wherein Kolchak would face down zombies and vampires and werewolves and demons in (then) present-day Chicago. Kolchak's rumbled demeanor, straw hat, tenacity and impetuous nature made him an irresistible character, entertaining and even humorous under the most horrific circumstances.

The show was a huge influence on *X-Files* creator Chris Carter, who created a character on that show for McGavin to play. Almost 50 years on, it is still considered a cult classic.

Planet of the Apes

Cashing in on the success of the Apes movies, CBS launched a short-lived variation on the theme in 1974. Starring Ron Harper and James Naughton as astronauts Alan Virdon and Pete Burke, with Roddy McDowell returning to the franchise as the ape Galen and Mark Lenard (Spock's father) as General Urko, a gorilla, the show wasn't particularly imaginative and was basically *The Fugitive* with apes. It only lasted 14 episodes.

But yes, I watched it, and yes, I have it on DVD.

Buck Rogers in the 25ᵗʰ Century

Fresh off the failure of Battlestar Galactica (see below), producer Glen Larson created this contemporary take on the classic cartoon strip character, a 20ᵗʰ century astronaut relocated five centuries in the future. Gil Gerard played Rogers with charm and humor, with Erin Gray appearing as Wilma Dearing. The stories were dumb, but there was a level on which the show was fun. It lasted two seasons.

The Fantastic Journey

This show gave Roddy McDowell something to do after *Apes* was cancelled. It ran for 10 episodes in the fall of 1977, and had to do with five travelers trapped on an island in the Bermuda Triangle, a place where time is broken into zones, and it is possible to pass from one zone to another. Two of the group are contemporary folk from the US mainland who just got lost; one is a man from the future with unusual powers; one is a woman born of a father from Atlantis and a mother from another world; and the last (McDowell) is a rebellious scientist from the Sixties.

Dorothy Fontana was on board for this one, too, and did her best to inject some integrity into the mix, and there were visits from Joan Collins ("City on the Edge of Forever") and John Saxon (*Planet Earth*).

The Man from Atlantis

Though *The Man from Atlantis* ran three episodes longer than *The Fantastic Journey*, it was by no means a better show.[57] It was built around the character of Mark Harris, an amnesiac who washes up on a beach and gets taken in by oceanic researchers. The strange man has gills and webbed appendages, can breathe underwater and swim like Aquaman.

---

[57] There were actually four TV movies produced before the series began.

Thus begins a series of adventures in the ocean aboard a submarine, the *Cetacean*, until people got tired of watching. Which wasn't long.

Battlestar Galactica is part of this round-up, but it's special enough to have its own chapter (See "Babbatar Gaggita", page 192). *Land of the Lost*, likewise, even though it was a Saturday morning children's program. And *Logan's Run* was a TV show briefly, after it was a movie.

See what I mean? Not much going on. It's no wonder that nerds everywhere looked to the movies, rather than the boob tube, for their thrills...

Roddenberry Theater

Star Trek creator Gene Roddenberry, in giving us Kirk, Spock, and the crew of the starship *Enterprise*, truly turned out to be one of those creative voices in media who changed the world. As yet another *Trek* series (*Star Trek: Discovery*) has launched following three new motion pictures, in the wake of four other TV shows and 10 films, it's safe to say that no other franchise has even come close to its popularity, ubiquity and cultural influence.[58]

Roddenberry postured for fifteen years as a visionary whose humanist conceptualization of his own species was his driving artistic force, but there is much reason to doubt this: his schooling in humanism came from sci-fi pal Isaac Asimov, a true humanist apostle, and Roddenberry's own me-too claims in this domain emerged more than a decade after *Star Trek* had debuted.[59]

Even so, his multicultural characters and high-sounding themes make a good case for the humanist shadow that *Trek*, in all its incarnations, came to emulate in later decades. The best argument that Roddenberry was, at best, an accidental philosopher exploiting a fortuitous sweet spot in the perceptions of his fans is made by his subsequent canon: *Trek* was his only true hit, and his many follow-up attempts display a muse that is less than virtuous, and often openly dystopian...

Pretty Maids All in a Row

This 1971 theatrical release was based on a 1968 novel of the same name by Francis Pollini, and starred Rock Hudson, Angie Dickinson and Telly Savalas (*Trek* veterans James Doohan - Scotty - and William Campbell - Trelane and the Klingon Captain Koloth - were also in the cast). Roddenberry produced and supplied the screenplay.

The plot centered on the serial killing of high school girls, the school counselor/football coach (who has sex with some of them), and a frustrated teenage boy. Hudson is the coach, Dickinson is a substitute teacher whom

---

[58] ...with the obvious exception of *Star Wars*.

[59] See the entire story in *Chasing the Enterprise: Achieving* Star Trek's *Vision of the Human Future*, by the author.

Hudson fixes the frustrated boy up with, and Savalas is the police detective looking into the murders.

The whole thing is supposed to be dark comedy, and on some level it is, but ultimately it's even more ludicrous than it sounds. It's right up Roddenberry's alley, filled with misogynist attitudes, cliché characters and gratuitous (and adolescent) sex. It is noteworthy only in its boldness to challenge contemporary sensibilities with no trace of self-consciousness.

Oddly, Roddenberry didn't originate the project (unlike those that followed); originally another producer, director and screenwriter had the project. When Roddenberry came on board, he rewrote the earlier screenwriter's script, and directing chores were handed over to Roger Vadim, the French director of genre hit *Barbarella*. The gig came to Roddenberry by way of Herb Solow, former executive of Desilu Studios, which had produced *Star Trek*. Roddenberry was paid $100,000.

Nor was Hudson a first choice: football great Joe Namath was originally to have played Hudson's role, and Brigette Bardot (Vadim's ex-wife) was to have played Dickinson's.

The film made no splash, despite a nine-page pictorial of Dickinson and all the pretty maids in *Playboy*, and Roddenberry had no non-*Trek* success in film after that. Said *Variety*: "Whatever substance was in the original [novel] or screen concept has been plowed under, leaving only superficial, one-joke results."

Quentin Tarantino, of all people, rates it one of the Top 10 Greatest Films of All Time (in a list in *Sight & Sound* magazine, 2012).

The film is Roddenberry's only feature film credit, though he did write other feature film scripts.

Genesis II

Back to television, where Roddenberry spent several years cranking out failed pilots for new sci-fi series. The first of these, *Genesis II*, was set on Earth many decades in the future, after a terrible apocalyptic cataclysm that left humanity split into two groups – a scientific community attempting to preserve humanity's knowledge, and mutants who live in the US Southwestern desert.

Into this mix arrives Dylan Hunt, a NASA scientist who is buried alive while conducting a suspended animation experiment for possible application in space travel. Upon being rescued by the scientists, he is courted by the mutants, who want him to repair a nuclear reactor – but *really* want him to reactivate a missile system that they can use to dominate everyone else - so Dylan destroys their reactor and sides with the scientists. From these beginnings, a weekly series was to have taken off.

Produced in 1973, the pilot starred Alex Cord (later of *Airwolf* fame) as Hunt, with *Trek* veterans Mariette Hartley ("All Our Yesterdays") and Ted Cassidy ("What Are Little Girls Made Of?"). Majel Barrett, who played Nurse Chapel in *Trek* and was by this time Roddenberry's wife, had a bit part.

Roddenberry scripted the pilot and wrote a 45-page writing guide for the proposed series, including some story ideas for exploitation as scripts. When the pilot aired in March of 1973, it set a viewership record for the CBS *Thursday Movie of the Week*, and should have then gone to series. But CBS soon aired the 1968 film *Planet of the Apes* and got even greater ratings, so it scrapped its order for a *Genesis II* series and went with a *Planet of the Apes* series instead, which lasted half a season before being unceremoniously cancelled.

The Questor Tapes

A better concept emerged in *The Questor Tapes*, about an android constructed by an international consortium using the notes and schematics of a renowned but somewhat mysterious scientist, recently disappeared. The android, known as Questor, goes missing after a bumpy birth, with the activation tape left by his designer partially erased and clumsy substitutions inserted by the consortium.

Questor hijacks a young engineer from the project as he sets out, super-competent in most areas but not so much in human relations, to find his creator. With all sorts of people hot on their tail, Questor and his reluctant accomplice run down clues to discover his real purpose.

With Robert Foxworth (*Star Trek: Enterprise*) and Mike Farrell (*M*A*S*H*) as Questor and Jerry Robinson, the engineer, would probably have made a terrific weekly series in the Seventies; but NBC, after ordering the pilot to series, wanted Farrell's character dropped, and was planning to put the series on Friday nights at 10pm, where *Star Trek* had died. Roddenberry backed out, and the whole thing was dropped, despite the quality of the concept and pilot episode.

Even so, the pilot left a legacy. The character Data, appearing 15 years later on *Star Trek: The Next Generation*, was overtly based on Questor (both were "fully functional").

Dorothy Fontana, who scripted many of Trek's best episodes, wrote an excellent novelization of the pilot. Herbert Wright, a Roddenberry friend and *TNG* producer, tried to get a remake of *Questor* made when the rights to the characters reverted to the Roddenberry family n 2000, but died before he was successful. Roddenberry Productions has since announced an effort with Imagine Television to produce a *Questor* series, but nothing further has occurred.

A final bit of trivia: Leonard Nimoy was originally courted to play Questor, and Nimoy actually became enthused about it, after initially fearing the character was too Spock-like to be a good career choice. It fell through, however, when NBC chose Foxworth instead, and Roddenberry misled Nimoy about it. It added to the bad blood that accumulated between them over the years.

Majel Barrett made her token appearance as a member of the scientific consortium constructing Questor.

Planet Earth

One magic touch Roddenberry seemed to have was the Gift of the Second Pilot. *Trek* itself had gotten two shots - "The Cage" and "Where No Man Has Gone Before" - unheard of in the industry. Now *Genesis II*, which had actually been successful by many measures, got its own second shot – this time from ABC.

The new version was called *Planet Earth*, but it carried over many elements of the original. The main character was still Dylan Hunt (played this time by John Saxon); the setting is still post-apocalyptic North America; and there's still a scientific community called PAX. Ted Cassidy returns, and this time *Trek* guest star Diana Muldaur ("Return to Tomorrow" and "Is There in Truth No Beauty?") is the female lead. Majel Barrett once again makes her obligatory appearance.

Saxon is more Kirk-like than his predecessor Cord, and the action in *PE* is less cerebral, while at the same time more filled with scientific concepts and buzzwords (a skilled surgeon must be found in time to render a life-saving surgery), and Roddenberry offers up a race of domineering Amazon women, another favorite theme of his ("Spock's Brain" from original *Trek*, "Angel One" from *TNG*). The pilot was directed by *Trek* veteran Marc Daniels.

Alas, despite good reviews, ABC did not pick the series up: they were not pleased with the women in the show. They did, however, try to rework it on their own, as *Strange New World* (cribbed from *Trek*'s opening credits), keeping Saxon, the post-apocalyptic setting, and PAX. This version did no better.

Spectre

Roddenberry made one last effort before returning to the world of *Star Trek* in late 1977: *Spectre*, an occult-based series about a criminologist and his sidekick, loosely based on Sherlock Holmes and Dr. Watson, played by Robert Culp and Gig Young.

Culp's character William Sebastian is concerned with the puzzles of human evil and studies the occult for answers; sidekick Amos Hamilton, a colleague, joins in, but does not believe in the supernatural. Lilith, Sebastian's housekeeper (who is also a witch),
is played by Majel Barrett (probably her most substantial role in any of these Seventies pilots).

The pilot concerns a family Sebastian is investigating who turn out to be in thrall to the demon-king Asmodeus, with whom Sebastian and Ham do battle. All quite exciting for Seventies television, but this, too, wound up rejected.

A lengthier version was released in the UK as a feature film.

* * *

At this point *Star Trek* came back to Roddenberry's attention, first as a proposed syndicated television series, then as a feature film. These, along with *Star Trek: The Next Generation*, dominated Roddenberry's career until his death in 1991.

But television wasn't done with Gene Roddenberry: six years after his death, a Canadian series - *Earth: Final Conflict* – was produced, based on ideas found in Roddenberry's notes by his widow, Majel Barrett, who went on to be an executive producer of the series. This show, about an alien race that benevolently settles on Earth, offering new and wondrous (but ultimately suspect) technology, ran for a full five seasons.

Then came *Andromeda,* a joint Canadian-US syndication venture that borrowed heavily from *Genesis II/Planet Earth* (the hero is named Dylan Hunt). It takes place in the far future in a heavily-populated galaxy, and also ran five seasons.

Roddenberry found, then, in death, the post-*Trek* success in television that had eluded him in life.

Sci-Fi Cinema in the Seventies

If television was a relative sci-fi wasteland in the Seventies, the cinema – pre-Star Wars – at least had the virtue of being varied and interesting... and, on occasion, intelligent.

We've covered the *Apes* movies, *Logan's Run* and the Charlton Heston films already. The following list represents most of the rest. All of them have some merit.

The Andromeda Strain (1971). Michael Crichton wrote the novel this movie was based on, while Robert Wise – later to direct *Star Trek: The Motion Picture* – helmed the effort. Smart and scary, *The Andromeda Strain* is a modern-day disaster story about a space-borne virus loosed on Earth by a fallen satellite, wiping out a town. A team of scientists converge on an underground government laboratory designed for just such a crisis. Their job: figure the virus out before it spreads, and hope they can contain it themselves.

Silent Running (1972). This unusual film stars Bruce Dern as a loner astronaut, tending domed forests on a long-orbit space freighter tasked with preserving what might be the last arboreal plant life in the solar system. Intended as a statement of environmental conscience, it pits Dern's character against his shipmates when they are ordered to jettison the domes. He kills them, and now must find a way to save the last forests before his crime is discovered.

Slaughterhouse-Five (1972). Kurt Vonnegut's quirky time travel tale, directed by George Roy Hill of *Butch and Sundance* fame, follows an aging Billy Pilgrim, who has become "unstuck in time," bouncing between his own past, his present, and the planet Tralfamadore. Funny, poignant and a little disturbing, including as it does Billy's time as a young POW in Dresden in World War II. Oddly philosophical, the film is a real treat, and features Valerie Perrine of *Superman* fame.

Westworld (1973). Michael Crichton's Frankenstein spin was the first of several (*Jurassic Park* stands out among them); he just loved to write scare stories about technology run amuck. In this take about a futuristic adult amusement park populated by androids, two businessmen in need of recreation find themselves trapped in the midst of a massive systems failure as the androids begin killing all the guests.

Dark Star (1974). This riotously funny partnership between John Carpenter (*The Thing*) and Dan O'Bannon (*Alien*) is basically a student film gone viral, made for a paltry $60,000. It became a campus cinema favorite[60] in the Seventies and has been a cult classic ever since. The *Dark Star* is a starship tasked with blowing up unstable planets that threaten the orbits of habitable ones by means of planet-killing bombs. It has been among the stars for almost 20 years, while its time-dilated crew of four have slowly started going bonkers. When the last bomb malfunctions and becomes contrary, threatening to explode in the bomb bay, things get tense.

Zardoz (1974). See "Fanboy Reviews – Pay No Attention to the Man Behind the Curtain!"

Doc Savage: The Man of Bronze (1975). The Seventies winner of the So Bad, It's Wonderful Award has got to be *Doc Savage*. And there's some irony: based as it was on the wondrous pulp action hero of the Thirties, it had going for it beloved source material that predated *Trek* and all its kin, the sci-fi films of the Fifties, even science fiction's Golden Age print stories. Produced by the legendary George Pal (*War of the Worlds*, *The Time Machine*) and directed by Michael Anderson (who would go on to *Logan's Run* the following year), it starred Ron Ely of Tarzan and Miss America fame as Doc Savage, adventuring in South America with his buddies Monk, Ham, Renny, Johnny and Long Tom.

It is beyond horrible. It's one long cringe. But it's so bad, you can't take your eyes off it, and you wind up endlessly entertained.

"Execrable acting, dopey action sequences, and clumsy attempts at camp humor…" *~Variety*

"…demonstrates none of the charm or thrills of Pal's classics…" *~A.V. Club*

"Just terrible. Ron Ely is in it, and he doesn't even take off his clothes." *~Amazon review*

King Kong (1976). The value of this remake of the 1933 classic is really in the filmmaking innovations that updated Kong himself. A life-size

---

[60] My own first viewing was at the University Kentucky Student Center in 1980.

animatronic arm and hand were constructed to grab and hold Jessica Lange, this version's Fay Wray. The new Kong is far more convincing than the old one as he scales the World Trade Center, and his actual-size corpse in the plaza below truly conveys tragedy.

Wizards (1977). See *"Wizards!"*, page 166.

Damnation Alley (1977). It will come as no surprise that I read the 1969 book by Roger Zelazny before seeing this one – and, as with *Logan's Run*, the two were very different experiences. Starring George "A-Team" Peppard, *Airwolf*'s Jan-Michael Vincent and Paul Winfield of *Star Trek* fame, it's the story of a cross-country excursion across a radioactive United States by a handful of survivors in search of a surviving community. The star of the movie is really a spectacular vehicle called a Landmaster (the filmmakers built one for real, at a cost of $350,000), designed to take on any terrain.

I have all of them on DVD, of course.

Nerd Theory: Nerd Rock

Nerds are virtually united in their love of music. You'd be hard-pressed to find an exception. And, almost as universally, nerds like music that is different.

As aficionados of the esoteric by definition – and, often, as lovers of complexity – nerds go for music that's unusual.

That most often means (but is not limited to!) progressive rock.

The aforementioned Klaatu qualifies, as does The Alan Parsons Project's *I, Robot*. The former has a big progressive attribute going for it: it's an epic narrative, and epic narratives go over big with nerds!

David Bowie of "Space Oddity" went there with his *Ziggy Stardust and the Spiders from Mars*; Peter Gabriel of Genesis not only wrote epic but did the on-stage costumes, just like Bowie.

Progressive rock is a big space; and, as with Monty Python, it's a domain inhabited by millions who are neither nerds nor fanboys.

But nerds and fanboys do love progressive rock.[61]

There's Yes – by far prog rock's most cosmic band; there's Emerson, Lake, and Palmer, who ooze epic on their masterpiece Brain Salad Surgery; there's Pink Floyd and *Dark Side of the Moon* – one of the greatest albums of all time; there's Dream Theater and Spock's Beard (how perfect is that?), lesser-known bands that deep-dive sci-fi themes.

A more contemporary entry is Coheed and Cambria, a prog rock band whose canon is built on a sci-fi storyline called the Amory Wars. And the lead singer of the band My Chemical Romance, Gerard Way, is the writer of the *Umbrella Academy* comic.[62]

[61] In later years, I got some pushback on the progressive rock from Trey, my younger son. We're walking out of Wal-Mart one evening (he's about 13 in this story) and we can't find our van, which is dark green, like about 12 others in the parking lot.

"Dad, you know those buttons on keychains that make your horn honk?"

"Sure ..."

"Well, we could get one, and rig it up so that when you press it, it would turn your van stereo on, really loud ..."

"Okay ..."

"So, when you're lost and you press the button, and you hear MUSIC THAT NOBODY ELSE *EVER* LISTENS TO, EVER! - we'll know it's your van."

Then there are the one-offs: Queen's "39", about a time-dilated interstellar mission; Rush's masterpiece *2112*; "Mr. Roboto", from Styx's sci-fi theatrical epic *Kilroy was Here*. Black Sabbath's "Iron Man".

And nerd rock is not all about the epics or the complexity. If it's brainy and funny, nerds will love it (see They Might Be Giants[63]).

That's not to say that nerds don't go for more conventional fare – we certainly do! – but this is one of those domains where fanboys and fangirls find reliable common ground, wherever you find them: all nerds rock, and they rock to the same tunes…

---

[62] My son Trey is a huge fan of both My Chemical Romance and *Umbrella Academy*, and turned me on to both.

[63] While all my kids love They Might Be Giants, my daughter Josie loves them most.

Space: $19.99

It's hard to convey to Millennials, let alone Zoomers, just what it was like growing up in a world where *Star Trek* was just a single TV show, rather than a billion-dollar franchise with more spin-offs than *NCIS*, *CSI*, and *All in the Family* combined. We felt lucky to have even that much to run with; it was an era when cops, detectives and lawyers sucked up all the airwaves, and science fiction hardly ever made it to the television.

The arrival of Britain's *Space: 1999*, then, was most welcome. Syndicated across the Western world, it was (like *Trek*) off the prime-time path, and that suited fans like me just fine. My memory is that it was on early Saturday evening – perhaps 6 or 7 – when no one else in the house was watching TV.

I remember learning of the show's impending arrival from the fanboy magazines I ponied up my hard-earned allowance for – magazines that were mercifully uncritical, really just publicity tools to keep viewers like me up to date on the latest nerd offering. I remember the day and time the show was to debut varied from market to market, so I dutifully bought TV Guide each week in the late summer of 1975, as September approached, so I wouldn't miss it.

My family still lived in Crawfordsville that fall, and I was a freshman at North Montgomery High School - a new, ultra-modern high school that was decidedly anachronistic in a perfectly square Indiana county that looked for all the world just like Gene Hackman's *Hoosiers*. It had been there in the library of that high school that I had discovered Arthur C. Clarke's "The Nine Billion Names of God", "The Cold Equations" and other sci-fi classics.

My point in sharing that detail is that, alas, I had no one with whom I could share my excitement and enthusiasm for this new show. It would remain my private treasure until the following year, when my family would repatriate to Central Kentucky.

Even veteran Gen X nerds may be unaware of *Space*, so brief was its blip. Produced by Gerry Anderson, who had also done *UFO* five years earlier, it had originally been conceived as a follow-up to that earlier show.

The premise was as simple as it was silly: in late 1999, humankind has a huge city on the moon – Moonbase Alpha – which is basically Clavius Base from *2001*. An international astronautics consortium oversees the base, which among other things is in charge of managing Earth's nuclear waste disposal in a lunar crater. When this nuclear waste dump explodes, the moon is blasted out of orbit and begins a lengthy carom through the galaxy, encountering all manner of adventures and perils.

John Koenig, played by Martin Landau, is the commander of the base. His sidekick is the scientist Victor Bergman, played by Barry Morse; his kinda-sorta love interest is Dr. Helena Russell, played by Barbara Bain.

Landau and Bain, of course, were married at the time, having just come off several years on *Mission: Impossible*; Morse had played the detective pursuing *The Fugitive* on that show. They were joined by other actors from all around the world - notably the Australian Nick Tate[64] as Alan Carter, captain of the base's Eagle fleet.

Though there was excitement and adventure to spare, *Space* wasn't at all like *Trek*; it was a moody, ethereal show, as much philosophy as it was action. Koenig had more in common with *Trek*'s somber Captain Pike than the dashing Kirk; Russell was downright morose at times. The inhabitants of Alpha rarely smiled and were seldom shown enjoying themselves.

Where Kirk, Spock and Bones would wrap up an episode in the center of the bridge with a laugh or a poignant reflection, Koenig would bring the curtain down with some mournful contemplation or weary recapitulation. Where Spock served up data, Bergman served up bad news; where the *Enterprise* radiated the joys and thrills of exploration, Moonbase Alpha was a graveyard of tormented expectations and dashed hopes. The two shows really couldn't have been more different.

And those differences invited endless comparison. Commander Koenig was a tall, handsome fellow who projected the required *gravitas*, to be sure, but he didn't have Kirk's bravado; on the other hand, Kirk wasn't the type to optimistically grapple with the existential, which Koenig had no trouble doing.

Victor Bergman, Alpha's science officer, was Spock-smart without the detachment. He had an artificial heart, foreshadowing Jean-Luc Picard, but was possessed of McCoyish warmth and empathy. Dr. Helena Russell lacked these qualities, but on the other hand she was not only a woman in authority but able to get up in Koenig's face and tell him how wrong he was – something *Trek* wouldn't do for another 15 years.

Part of *Trek*'s charm was nested in its props, I think: the phaser, communicator and tricorder were identity markers. *1999* managed to follow suit here as no other sci-fi show ever would. Moonbase Alpha's version of the phaser looked like a damn staple gun, and had not one

---

[64] Tate would later make memorable guest appearances on *Star Trek: The Next Generation* and *Deep Space Nine*.

but *four* beam emitters – what the hell? Was that supposed to make it cooler? It was goofy - but admittedly distinctive.

Then there was *1999*'s communicator, the "commlock" - another utterly distinctive piece, both cooler and more interesting than the *1999* stun gun: it was a personal communicator and a security device bundled together, Apple-style. Square on one end and cylindrical on the other, this hand-held device provided a visual of the person on the other end,[65] which *Trek*'s communicators did not, and its cylindrical tail would open doors at which it was pointed, provided the owner had security clearance. Again, distinctive.

The Eagles – Alpha's fleet of 28 all-purpose transports – fell far short of anything like a starship or a *Star Wars* X-Wing or even a *Battlestar Galactica* Viper – but they had it over all of those because they were *real* – they are honestly what we're going to be using up there in the next 50 years. They'd have been cooler if the damn landing struts had been retractable – they looked kind of stupid, hanging down like that when the ship was blasting through space at top speed – but the overall look and feel of the Eagle just felt very day-after-tomorrow.

Then there was Moonbase Alpha itself. Okay, yeah, it was a direct lift from *2001*'s Clavius Base, but so what? Steal from the best, right? It was an *awesome* place! Like the Eagles, it felt *real* – nothing over the top, nothing too far-reaching, just a very authentic snapshot of what our bases on the moon will actually be like, when we're there to stay.

Its un-Trekness aside, the tumbling of the moon through the dangers of the void was so thrilling that it couldn't be missed; I looked forward to the show every week, and when paperback novelizations began to appear at the bookstore, I gobbled them up.

It would be difficult to overstate just how goofy the whole concept was, beneath the stories themselves (many of which were on a par with *Trek*); an explosion powerful enough to remove the moon from its orbit occurs, and the moon isn't shattered? It floats from star system to star system, within reach of several dozen planets, in just a few years' time? Really?

Well, quibbling was pointless; if the moon coasting between star systems in a matter of months was silly, it was certainly no more so than warp drive and transporter beams.

---

[65] This seems passé in the era of the digital Internet-connected smartphone, but what was cool about the commlock video screen in 1975 is that it was *real: 1999* had several working models, with actual 2-inch video monitors embedded in them. They worked in real time, used often in actual episodes, by means of a video cable plugged into the tail of the commlock where the door-opener beam was supposed to be.

In any case, I was thrilled to have it; and when I learned there would be a second year of the show, I was – wait for it! - over the moon.

By the time that second season began, we had relocated to Frankfort, Kentucky – and this time, I could share the love. I had met several nerds as I started my sophomore year at Franklin County High: Womp, Joe, Bob, and a few others. And they, too, were on the *Space: 1999* bandwagon.

The second season of *Space* was, oddly, nothing at all like the first. Seems the brass at ITV, who produced the show, were underwhelmed by its performance, and were only willing to give it a second chance if it were retooled to be more like – well, like *Star Trek*.

So the Andersons brought in Fred Freiberger, who had presided over the final season of *Trek* itself (see "The Showkiller", page 184). Freiberger let most of the cast go – Morse was only too happy to – and brought in some new, exciting characters: Maya, played by Catherine Schell, an alien shapeshifter; and Tony Verdeschi (Tony Anholt), Koenig's second-in-command. Nick Tate's Alan Carter, a fan favorite, was kept on.

The show did get more exciting, certainly, but it got reciprocally dumber. Its moody, philosophical edge was gone; in its place were more special effects. That didn't trouble me overmuch, because those were days when fanboys were beggars, not choosers.

So great was my enthusiasm that I generated piles of blueprints of Moonbase Alpha, as well as tech drawings of the Eagle and various other vehicles.

To its credit, *Space* had plenty of guest star power going for it: Christopher Lee appeared, as did *Trek*'s Joan Collins and Jeremy Kemp (Picard's older brother); Darth Vader himself, David Prowse, did a monster turn, and Peter Cushing did an episode. (It should be noted that *1999* perpetuated *Trek*'s premise that our galaxy is populated primarily by humanoids, but in *1999*'s case, they all have British accents). Special effects wizard Brian Johnson kept the Eagles flying, and went on five years later to do *Alien*[66] for Ridley Scott.

It goes without saying that the entire series is across the room, sitting on the shelf. I haul it out every five years or so for a re-binge, but have never managed to get any of my zygotes to sit in.[67]

---

[66] Johnson had also done model work for Stanley Kubrick on *2001*.

[67] The chapter title, "Space: $19.99!" is a Womp idea. We did several sci-fi parody comics together, a la *Mad Magazine*, and he thought up that title for our *1999* spoof.

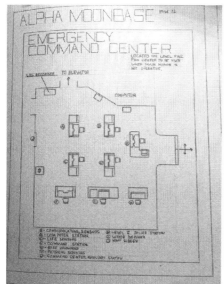

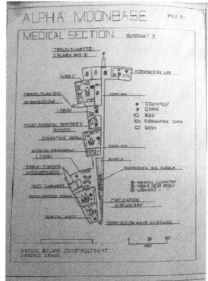

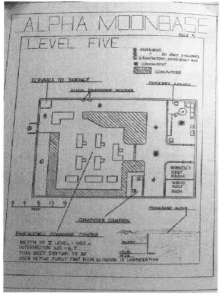

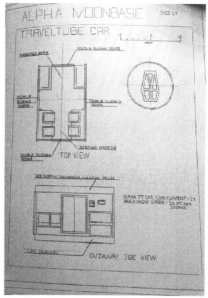

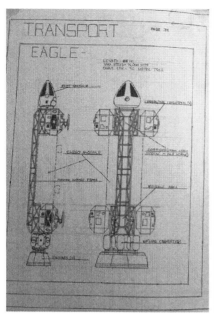
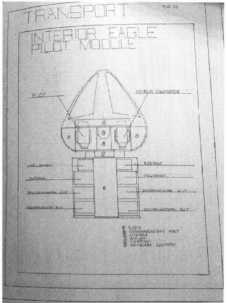
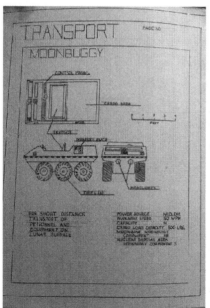
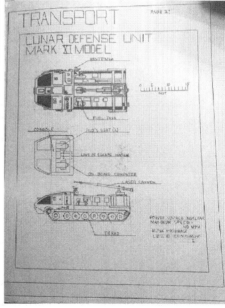

Are We Alone in the Universe?

In fandom, this chestnut arises from the portrait painted by *Trek* and *1999* and *Babylon 5* and other shows that offers up a Milky Way galaxy bursting with humanoid civilizations; life is ubiquitous in space, according to this portrait, and most of it is humanoid. Well, we know that last bit is ridiculous. Carl Sagan, Arthur C. Clarke and Neil deGrasse Tyson have all assured us that if there is intelligent life out there, it is utterly unlikely to look like us, or be in the same stage of development as we are – the niggling details of evolutionary environs will be far too varied, and cosmic time scales are just too vast. Whatever might be out there, intelligent-life-wise, will be very different from us.

But that's okay with us fanboys; we'd be quite content to know that there is any intelligent life out there at all, whatever form it might take.

And so we argue it endlessly, as do our fanboy and fangirl below, prompted by Dr. McCoy's "Don't Destroy the One Named Kirk" speech in "Balance of Terror":

> *"In this galaxy, there's a mathematical probability of three million Earth-type planets. And in all of the universe, three million million galaxies like this one. And in all of that – and perhaps more – only one of each of us…"*

FANBOY   **FANGIRL**

The good doctor is out of date; the latest numbers say
there could be as many as 11 billion Earth-like planets
in our galaxy alone.

I love it when you try to do math.

The 11 billion assumes 200 billion start in this galaxy – that's twice what we estimated back in the Sixties – and that about one in five G-type stars (like ours) have a goldilocks planet. (That's a planet that's not too hot and not too cold to have liquid ware on its surface.)

I know what a goldilocks planet is.

Of course you do. The one-in-five is based on our current survey of exoplanets – we've catalogued over 4,700 planets in over 3,500 star systems.

Somebody's been reading Wikipedia!

I'm just sayin' - it's even *more* likely than we thought, even then, that there's intelligent life out there.

Ah- the "We Are Not Alone" bit.

We *aren't* alone! It's mathematically impossible.

You mispronounced 'improbable'.

Suit yourself. There's *definitely* life out there.

Klingons and Vulcans and Gorns – oh my!

I didn't say *humanoid* life. Both Sagan and Arthur C. Clarke said that is definitely impossible.

…and I so had my heart set on touring Kronos…

If only one in a thousand of those 11 billion Earths has life- and if only one in a thousand of those has *intelligent* life – then there are *still* more than 10,000 potential Federation member worlds out there!

And you did that right there in your head, without a calculator!

Prove me wrong!

Pause the episode.

Paused!

Okay, lots to cover here, but in a nutshell – by your own math!
– you're wrong. The numbers tell us it's extremely *un*-likely
that there is any life at all out there, let alone intelligent life.

You wanna go fetch a calculator?

Get on with it!

Let's start with the Drake Equation –

-which isn't accurate!

No, it's not, but we have to start somewhere.
The Drake Equation gives us a number of
probable extraterrestrial civilizations by multiplying

- the rate of star formation in the galaxy;
- the percentage of those stars that have planets;
- the average number of life-capable planets around stars with planets;
- percentage of *those* planets that actually develop life;
- percentage of *those* planets that develop intelligent life;
- percentage of *those* planets that develop the tech to make themselves heard;
- how long civilization on those planets lasts.

As I'm sure you already know,
some of these factors are all over the place.
For instance, estimates on that last factor –
how long a techy intelligent civilization might survive –
range from a thousand years to a hundred million years.

Let's start with the median for the classical estimates.

Fifty million!

You had that memorized! I'm impressed.

It's in Wikipedia.

Of course. Now, that's more than the 10,000-plus
you were suggesting earlier, but it's also faulty because
the Drake Equation isn't just vague; it's seriously incomplete.

How do you figure?

In the decades since Drake scribbled his thing, lots of new factors have been identified.

Such as...?

Well, you know about the goldilocks zone around a star – a limited range that results in mean temperatures allowing liquid water. Turns out there's a zone like that for the Milky Way as a whole – you have to be a certain distance from the galactic core for interstellar radiation levels to be tolerable. That knocks the number of candidate planets to roughly five percent of all the stars in the galaxy.

Okay.

And to develop life, you need some shake-n-bake in your candidate planet. In our case, we've got an oversized moon, proportionally far larger relative to the planet than any other moon in the solar system – big enough to churn the oceans, which is one of the causal mechanisms of early life.

And you need a nickel-iron planetary core like ours, or something like it that will generate the magnetic field that keeps the solar winds from stripping our atmosphere away, as it did Mars.

And you need the planet to be tilted on its axis, as ours is, in order to get seasonal variation in weather, which drives the both the evolution and dynamic processes of both plant and animal life.

Finally, you need plate tectonics – the floating of the continents. Experts now tell us that this stimulated the emergency of biodiversity, without which any one of the five mass extinctions in our past could have ended life on the planet altogether.

That seems like a lot of guesswork.

On the contrary, that's the part of any new Drake Equation that's *not* guesswork; the guesswork is in Drake's original factors. And every one of these additional factors (and there are others) reduces the number of candidate worlds for actually producing life.

So at this point, we take your fifty million planets and we eliminate all the ones that don't have a moon big enough to churn its oceans; all the ones that aren't tilted, and thus don't have seasons; all that don't have a core that creates a radiation shield around the planet; and all the ones that don't have plate tectonics.

Let's say, even so, that these new factors only cost you two orders of magnitude, leaving you with 500,000 planets with the potential for life. Now we have to figure the odds for that life rising to intelligence - we have to bring in a whole new set of factors Drake never considered – factors in our own history that led to the development of our own intelligent species.

The axial tilt of the Earth gives us seasonal variation, and floating continents for geological diversity; even so, there needs to be ecological differentiation, which results from things like mountain ranges and other large-scale geophysical features. Our own species, and our two cousin species (and who knows how many others) emerged because the Great Rift Valley exists in Africa, generating several contiguous ecological extremes in the same general area. It's pure chance that the rift formed at all.

Bipedalism played a big part, because we and our cousins, with our opposable thumbs, had the potential to become toolmakers – a big component of the emergence of intelligence. Because life in the Great Rift Valley nudged our particular tribe out of the trees onto our two legs, our thumbs went into overdrive.

Mastering fire and learning to cook meat made a huge difference; our brains are the size they are because our distant ancestors had a huge spike in their protein intake because of cooked meat.

Then there's face-to-face mating, which only humans and bonobos engage in, among all of Earth's mammals-

Oh, come on! You're telling me human beings are intelligent because of the *missionary position???*

Yup. We are the only two species that gaze into each other's eyes; even chimpanzees track head and shoulder movement, not eye movement. This difference gives us the Theory of Mind – the realization that others of our kind have an inner life comparable to our own. That realization is likewise a cornerstone of our intelligence.

All of these amount to chance-defying accidents, or at least utterly circumstantial events – random chance, not inevitable design – big, game-changing episodes that came out of nowhere.

And if *any* of them hadn't happened, we wouldn't be here now.

So – on top of all the odds-defying celestial and planetary conditions we've already identified, we now have this long series of accidents our existence depended upon; and our number of candidate planets is now reduced to those where *every one of those random chance events, or something very like them, occurred.*

Well, now you're basically claiming that intelligent life could only evolve if it happened exactly the way it happened on Earth!

Not at all. There could be many variations of the factors we've listed that could also work. The point is that life, and more importantly, intelligent life, has many ingredients, many more than Drake supposed – and the absence of any one ingredient greatly reduces the number of potential civilizations.

When you think about it, I'm actually arguing for Hodgkin's Law of Parallel Planet: similar conditions yielding similar development.

"Bread and Circuses"!

Yes. That might be even more true than we already suspect; there's a final factor that makes a world exactly like ours essential for the development of life, let alone intelligent life.

And what's that?

It's called the Theory of Dissipative Adaptation, and it's only been around a few years. A young physicist named Jeremy England came up with it, and it makes Earth-like conditions of the kind I've described essential for life of any kind.

England points out that all physical systems are configured in such a way as to optimize whatever distribution of energy they perform. A snowflake crystallizes into the best shape for dissipating light (so does quartz); tornadoes form to disburse energy when heat goes into disequilibrium in the atmosphere, as lightning erupts to shed accumulated electrons. Matter is condensed energy, according to Einstein; England is suggesting that all matter wants to become energy again, and organizes itself in the most energy-friendly way it can.

That's interesting, but it doesn't explain life.

It's the first thing *ever* that explains life! The point here is that the ultimate configuration of matter that is optimized to disburse energy is *life* – organic molecules! Life on Earth is the ultimate expression of matter organizing itself to dissipate energy.

That's our ultimate purpose? To be thermostats?

Think about it: all the things we listed earlier that make Earth special – the ocean churning, the axial tilt, liquid water – all of these things make Earth a vast network of energy traps. We absorb energy from the sun constantly, and it escapes one trap – the atmosphere – just to get stuck in another one – the ocean. And the surface. And there are hundreds of smaller traps nested in all of them. Energy doesn't just flow from the sun onto the day side and out into space from the night side; it's constantly flowing from one thermal system to another, because our planet is so complicated. And the greatest energy trap of all is –wait for it! – life.

It's a cool idea. But it seems to me the only way you could prove it would be to model it, and wouldn't it be the world's most complicated model ever?

Yes. You'd need Spock working with Richard Daystrom to model it.

But you buy it.

I do. It fits with everything else we've talked about. And there's one more thing to consider.

What's that?

All you fanboys who are so in love with the idea that the galaxy is full of intelligent species are speaking from the Principle of Mediocrity – that life is abundant in the galaxy because there's nothing particularly special about

Earth, so if there are millions or billions of Earths, there must be millions of extraterrestrial civilizations.

But there's a *great deal* that makes Earth particularly special! It's a one-in-a-hundred-billion shot that our planet turns out to be so astoundingly special. And that is why we're here, and nowhere else – the Principle of Mediocrity doesn't apply to us.

You don't know *any* of this for sure.

I'm more sure of my facts than you and your pals are of your guesses and wishful thinking. And I've got one more thought to share, before we un-pause the episode…

By all means!

What Clarke said-

"Two possibilities exist: either we are alone in the Universe or we are not. Both are equally terrifying."

Yes! You knew that one by heart, too!

I've got another one for you.

By all means!

"The universe is a pretty big place. It's bigger than anything anyone has ever dreamed of before. So if it's just us… seems like an awful waste of space."

Contact.

The movie, not the book.

The book was better.

I cannot disagree.

Sagan wanted to believe in extraterrestrial life. But he also emphasized that if we're all there is, it's that much more important for us to do a good job with this planet before we hurry off to any new ones.

I cannot disagree with that, either.

Consider: maybe we will one day be the Preservers-

-from "The Paradise Syndrome"!

    -yes, the species that spreads intelligence throughout the galaxy. There may one day be Vulcans and Klingons and Andorians and so on – but they would be *our children*.

That's an idea I can get behind. But I'm going to keep believing there's already somebody out there.

It makes you feel good, doesn't it?

What if it does?

Roll the episode, Wikipedia Boy…

Aslan on Mars

Earlier, I wrote about my family\s ancestral farm in Northern Kentucky, where once I built myself a robot.

That farm was a very special place for all the kids in my generation who would visit it, this summer or that, climbing the hill behind the house or playing in the loft of the barn (against parental instruction) or wandering down the sleepy, just-barely-paved road into town to dangle our feet in the creek.

My parents, and those of my cousins (Kirk included), had grown up here. And there was one uncle in particular who plays a part in my nerd memories.

This was my Uncle Billy, younger son of my dad. Youngest of four, Uncle Billy was very different from his siblings. Less straight-laced, he had an adventurer's spirit, and became a professional pilot. This was quite exciting to me and my cousins, as he was not only into people-sized planes, but tiny remote-controlled ones, too.[68]

He was also, by far, the most adventurous reader. While most of the family focused on religious periodicals and safe, classical writings, my uncle leaned *wayyyyyy* toward adventure:

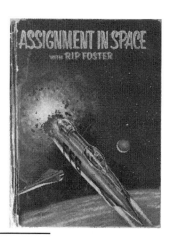

---

[68] Alas, my Texan cousins got the lion's share of the remote plane play; however, I still had some personal overlap with Uncle Billy; when I took up the guitar in my early teens, he took up the bass. This may seem inconsequential, but in our Fundamentalist family, it was very close to scandalous. I remember several evenings when he brought his bass over to our home in Frankfort and we jammed.

Kid's book? Sure! But *what* a kid's book! This was right in my wheelhouse! Rip Foster was straight out of Robert Heinlein, and when I discovered this Uncle Billy remnant in the attic of the old farmhouse, I committed myself to treating it with endless loving care. It exists today, holding a treasured place in my collection.

But Uncle Billy went a step further. In my early teens, he happened to be at the farmhouse one summer evening at the same time my family was there. And he took me aside, telling me he had something he wanted to give me.

It was C.S. Lewis's Space Trilogy – three novels by the famous 20th century Christian apologist, more famous for his *Chronicles of Narnia* series.

The three books are *Out of the Silent Planet, Perelandra,* and *That Hideous Strength.* The three books concern themselves with a Professor Elwin Ransom, patterned after Lewis's pub companion J.R.R. Tolkien of *Lord of the Rings* fame.

In the novels, Ransom is a Cambridge linguistics professor of the early 20th century, a solitary man who just enjoys being alone. Kidnapped by two nefarious rogue scientists as a sacrifice to allow them access to Mars (Macalandra), he is taken to that world and manages to escape, initiating a series of wondrous and perilous encounters that persist through the three novels.

As with Narnia, the books are bursting with Christian symbolism, more subtle in this series than the other. The books are written more as mythology than as science fiction, eschewing technical detail, but that's what one would expect of the author of the *Chronicles*.

It's noteworthy that Lewis introduces himself as a peripheral character in his own novel in *Out of the Silent Planet*, where he is a professor writing a letter to Ransom.

I won't deep-dive the story, except to say that it is surprisingly epic in scale, encompassing the entire solar system. It boasts an imagined ecology and geography on a Narnian scale, richly describing the creatures and plants and humanoids and aliens to be found in Lewis's universe – not on a par with Tolkien, but certainly entertaining and intriguing.

The books present challenging alternatives to the views of intellectuals such as J.B.S. Haldane, who would become part of my professional bibliography, and fascinates even those unconcerned with its metaphysical insights.

doug gifford's madcoversite.com

Though Uncle Billy visited our Frankfort home a number of times during my teenage years, I honestly don't recall whether or not we discussed the Space Trilogy books in depth. Instead, he indulged my Star Trek leanings: I remember him surprising me with *MAD Magazine*'s *Star Trek* Musical issue in 1976. I still remember by heart the alternate lyrics to the Beatles' "Yesterday":

Pinkus East
That's where budget-conscious spacemen feast
Where you'll buy the most and spend the least
So beam on down to Pinkus East...

I've re-read the Space Trilogy countless times, as I have *Narnia* and *LOTR* and *Dune* and all the others. I'm sure I thanked Uncle Billy at the time, but the thanks I'd muster if I saw him today would be far greater...

Nerdy Grrls

I've spoken of the nerd pals I connected with upon moving to Frankfort in 1976. But I made a discovery that year, one that changed my life: some nerds were *girls*.

Girls. In my very isolated world, where I had spent my fanboy life virtually alone to begin with, I had felt lucky to have *any* friend who shared my nerdy interests. And now – *girls!*

Fanboy, fangirl. That suited me just fine!

The first was Heidi Myfelt. She went to my school and was in the same grade, but more importantly, she was my neighbor: for about a year and a half, I was her family's paperboy, and it was a two-minute walk to her house to hang out, listen to records, watch *Space: 1999*. Heidi had brains, and we discussed required-reading books assigned by Mr. Schenk before being tested on them. The first time I saw *Star Wars*, it was with Heidi (that story follows).

Alas, Heidi was in a military family, and her dad, The Colonel, was reassigned to Germany after our sophomore year. So she missed out on all the fun I'm about to tell you about shortly.

Heidi's best friend was Susan Rossen. Equally smart and funny, she was just as big a nerd and just as into *Trek*; her big obsession was Chekov, whom she referred to as "Meester Chekove!" in the most Russian of accents. I think she wanted to marry him. When I went with Heidi to see *Star Wars* for the first time, Susan went along, too.

Remember Ann Victor, who turned me on to Klaatu, the Fake Beatles in Space? She wasn't along for *Star Wars*, but she was nerd to the core, and we all collectively embarked on the creative mission you'll read about shortly, she signed up right away.

And that leads us to Ruby Vansant, who had by far the greatest impact on my life of any of the four. Ruby was brilliant, perhaps the brainiest person in our high school, and tremendous fun to be around. We became instant friends, and she, too, became part of our creative collective. She was so smart that she got out of high school a year early, and made it to the nearby University of Kentucky while we remained seniors. She and I remained close for several years afterwards.

These were the first girls in my isolated world that had been real friends, rather than just church youth group acquaintances. They were the first I ever spent hours on the phone with, or talked nerd talk with, or enjoyed for their brains as well as their humor. That in itself gives them a

Baby Boomer Fanboy

prominent place in my memories of my youth, but also caused me to adjust my perspective on gender – which, having grown up Funda-mentalist, was in serious need of adjustment.

Women could be nerds. And they could certainly be smarter than men.

162

HAL and Me

My relationship with HAL 9000 goes back a long way, and has been... complicated.

It began in the summer of 1969, when my family visited the Donaldson family, members of my father's church in Lexington, Kentucky. The Donaldsons had three sons – Stone, Bobby and Joe – all older than me (though Joe was only a year past me). I loved visiting them, because they were funny as hell.

On this particular occasion, I noticed a plastic model on Bobby's desk in their shared bedroom. It looked like this:

Fascinated, I just had to ask: "What's that? Where's it from?"

"That's a moon bus," Bobby explained. "It's from the movie *2001: A Space Odyssey*." That was the first time I'd ever heard the movie mentioned.

"It's so cool!" I had to say.

"Oh, there are other ships that are a lot cooler," Bobby went on. "The main ship in the movie is like a mile long."

"What's *2001* about?"

"They go on a mission to Jupiter because there's this strange black thing shaped like a domino that they dig up on the moon. But there's an intelligent computer on the ship named HAL and it kills most of the crew."

"Just tell him the whole movie, Bob," Stone said.

"It doesn't matter," Bobby said. "His folks will never let him see it"

I puzzled over that for years, wondering what he meant.

I went on to check out a paperback copy of *2001* from the Crawfordsville Public Library in 1975, and finally realized what Bobby had been talking about: the whole "Dawn of Man" sequence with Moonwatcher and the African monolith are very firmly built on the concept of evolution – a dirty word in our Fundamentalist home.

Aside: not long after I had checked the paperback copy of *2001* out at the public library, my family moved to Frankfort, Kentucky. I never returned the book. It's now 45 years overdue. Here it is:

The book was my first exposure to HAL 9000, and I began a life-long fascination with the concept of a sentient computer. *Trek* hadn't really offered much in that department: until the character of Cmdr. Data in *NextGen*, which wouldn't happen for another decade or so, all the digital minds on *Trek* were really quite dull.

But HAL – HAL wasn't just interesting; he was terrifying. He was as much a monster as any big slimy creature that ever inhabited a sci-fi movie.

I proceeded to buy a hardback copy of *2001* when I joined the Science Fiction Book Club[69] and read it many times. So when MGM re-released the film to theaters in February 1976, on the upcoming occasion of its first-ever network broadcast, I was very ready to see it.

Joe and Bob and Womp, it turns out, were equally ready. I learned that Joe was a huge *2001* fan, though I can't imagine how he'd ever actually seen it. HAL was by far his favorite character, and he teased as much as he

---

[69] See page 108.

could about the events of the movie without ruining it as we made plans to see it.[70]

All of this turned out to be hugely inspiring, as it motivated us into the movie business – giving Joe the chance to play HAL, after a fashion (see "Move Over, Spielberg!", just ahead.

Why is he telling us this?

I'm telling you this because it pretty much set the course of my professional life. Though my studies included deep dives into journalism and behavioral science, I have been a systems engineer and a technologist throughout, making robot widgets for the Department of Defense and NASA in the Nineties, and doing AI in the business world since then. HAL basically inspired me to pursue the mysteries of living machines back in my high school days – and here I am, four decades on, a part of that world.

Cover art by Womp. On the back cover, he serves up the screen HAL used to offer readouts to Dave and Frank, and he actually tracked down the original fonts on the Internet.

---

[70] This viewing of *2001* at Franklin Square Cinema in early 1977 was the first of several times I snuck a cassette recorder into the theater so that I could record the movie audio. Subsequent crimes included *Wizards* and *Star Wars*, later that year.

Wizards!

"If you think the world's screwed up now, you ought to see it 10 million years from now."

This is how *Wizards* – an animated sci-fi film by Ralph Bakshi that appeared right around the time me and Womp and Joe and Bob were catching the last theater run of *2001* and planning our own movie-making enterprise – was introduced to the world. You couldn't have tangled a more tempting shiny thing in front of us. Naturally, we rushed to the local cinema.[71]

Wizards, touted as a "family" feature, was a story of the struggle between Magic and Technology, overlaying (none too subtlety) the more traditional theme of Good vs. Evil, which would play much bigger a few months later in a galaxy far, far away. The protagonist is Avatar, an ancient wizard who benevolently oversees the land of Montagar, wary of his mutated twin brother Blackwolf, who rules the neighboring kingdom of Scortch – both kingdoms being remnants of an Earth long since devastated by a nuclear war, millions of years in the past.

When Blackwolf comes into possession of a "dream machine" – an old movie projector, he realizes he can use it to mesmerize his forces to successfully attack Montagar. This he does, with a strategic assist from his assassin robot, Necron 99, whose mission it is to wipe out all believers in magic.

Avatar has been training Elinore, the vivacious and buxom daughter of Montagar's president, to become a fully-qualified fairy. When Necron 99 makes his move, Avatar manages to remove his propaganda training, rechristening him "Peace".

With the elf berserker Weehawk at their side, Avatar and his company fight back against Blackwolf and his forces – Magic and Technology go head to head.[72]

---

[71] Though new and innovative, *Wizards* wasn't the first animated sci-fi feature; *Fantastic Planet*, an experimental sci-fi film from France, had been in theaters four years earlier. I had seen it in Crawfordsville.

[72] Quentin Tarantino has described the character of Avatar as "a cross between Tolkien's *Hobbit*, Mel Brooks' *2000-Year-Old Man*, and Marvel Comics' Howard the Duck."

Now, this is all great fun, and not just the story; it's visually sumptuous, cleverly rendered by Bakshi on a limited budget, and the metaphorical layers of the story made it very entertaining for me and Joe to pick apart. I didn't learn until much later that Bakshi had served up *Wizards* as an explicit departure from his previous urban fair (he had made *Fritz the Cat*, the first pornographic cartoon feature, a mere five years earlier), but was primed for his next effort in 1978 – the first attempt to bring *The Lord of the Rings* to the screen (see "Chasing Frodo", page 200).

There's great hilarity in Bakshi's claim that *Wizards* was intended as a family-friendly feature; the overtly-sexual rendering of Elinore, and the endless innuendo between her and Avatar pretty much put that notion to bed, as it were. And the film's central themes, for all their fairy-tale overlap, were far too obviously adult.

Nor was Bakshi's claim that his animation style was a conscious rejection of Disney very compelling; while Avatar was drawn as almost as a living comic book, Blackwolf had the explicit lines and tone of a Disney villain; he may as well have been a male version of the witch in *Snow White*.

None of this was lost on Womp, who was utterly taken with the movie and its style. As animation, it was certainly innovative; Bakshi's techniques for rendering spooky mist as a background, and his knack for creating very layered emotional atmosphere with subtle fades and color shifts, implied genius beyond mere innovation. This was a movie to learn from, and Womp was alert and studious.

The art itself is where Womp hit the jackpot. From that day on, we'd see traces of *Wizards* in all of his cartooning. If there was a bigger influence on his style, I don't know what it might be.

But *Wizards* fit perfectly into both our immediate fanboy world and the broader historical frame of Seventies cinematic sci-fi in that it was, like the *Apes* films and other Heston films and Logan's Run, a post-apocalyptic story – a tale of a ruined world and a struggling remnant of humanity. Obviously, we were primed for it.

As usual, I snuck a cassette recorder into the theater and recorded the soundtrack, then memorizing some of the scenes and amusing myself by doing them in the characters' voices. Among us, we talked about the movie for weeks, as Womp went off and drew and drew and drew.

Some notes: Bob Holt, the actor who voiced Avatar, was selected by Bakshi because he does a perfect imitation of Peter Falk; and if you close your eyes while watching the movie, sure enough, you hear Columbo.

And the movie was originally going to be called *War Wizards*. Bakshi changed it when George Lucas approached him, complaining that the public might confuse it with his upcoming feature *Star Wars*. Bakshi made a deal with Lucas: he'd change the name of his movie if Lucas let him borrow one of his actors for the role of Sean, Son of the Mountain King.

Lucas said Yes to this deal, and loaned him Mark Hamill.

The Summer of *Star Wars*

Where were you on May 25, 1977?

This is one of those days that should stand alongside July 20, 1969. The day *Star Wars* entered the cinematic world – and, thereby, the public culture gestalt – changed everything.

Thinking back to the spring of 1977, I can still pinpoint my awareness that the most successful cinematic sci-fi franchise of all time was about to hit – but I didn't realize it as such at the time. I read about the upcoming space opera in *Starlog* magazine, and grabbed the first edition of the paperback (with a Ralph McQuarrie pre-production painting on the cover, rather than images from the film itself) at Walden Books. I had read it cover to cover several times long before the movie actually opened, so I knew what we were in for.

But I still had no sense that it was world-changing.

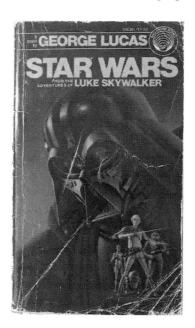

Star Wars didn't open everywhere all at once. That May 25 date applied to less than 32 theaters (the distributing studio, 20ᵗʰ Century Fox, didn't think it could even keep up with *Smokey and the Bandit*). It broke box office records everywhere it initially played, and so a broad nation-wide release commenced.

Playing in more than a thousand theaters, George Lucas's little $9 million space opera racked up more than $220 million in that first run, and was re-released in 1978, 1979, 1981, and 1982, eventually re-titled *Star Wars IV: A New Hope*. The rest, of course, is history.

So, that summer.

I already knew about the movie from *Starlog* and had already read the paperback (ostensibly by George Lucas, but in fact ghost-written by *Trek* paperback writer Alan Dean Foster).

Before the movie went into nationwide release, and just as my sophomore year of high school was ending, I went to church camp for a week.[73] And there at church camp were some counselors from a Bible college who had seen the movie in Nashville and were blown away by it. They told everybody who would listen about this magical space adventure about a boy named Luke Skywalker and his mentor Ben Kenobi and two "droids", whatever that meant, and a rogue pilot named Han Solo and a princess in white named Leia and a tall, black villain called Darth Vader. They described space battles that seemed impossible and a planet-killing asteroid and something called a "force". It all seemed terribly exciting, yet terribly exaggerated.

I understood the references because I'd read the book. But their description of the movie couldn't be accurate – *no* movie in the history of cinematic sci-fi had ever come close to such a description!

But they had proof.

They had the theater program, the slick, expensive booklet describing the movie. They passed it around.

Our eyes bugged out.

Wow. Tattooine! The Star Destroyer! The Rebel Blockade Runner! The *Millennium Falcon*! X-Wings! The Death Star! It was all too much.

As soon as I got home from church camp, I started scamming around for some friends who might go. I was up for my driver's license in six weeks, but would have to go with somebody else to start.

The movie hadn't reached Frankfort. But Heidi and Susan were going with Heidi's older sister and fiancé to see it at Turfland Mall in Lexington the next weekend. I tagged along.

---

[73] Church camp is just like heathen camp – sports and dining hall and trails in the woods and tons of fun – only with Bible study and praise choruses around campfires. Supposedly more wholesome.

Needless to say, I was stunned. It went without saying I was going back.

A week later, the movie reached Frankfort, and I went to see it with Womp and Bob and Joe at the old Grand Theater downtown.

A week after that, I took a girl to the afternoon matinee at the Grand. My grandfather drove us. She was unimpressed, and even made fun of the movie, right there in the theater. Even so, I was open-minded enough to make out with her in the courtyard of the bank near the theater while we waited on my grandfather to pick us up.

That's three.

The fourth viewing was an attempt to sell the film at home. I talked my mom into taking me and my little brother Danny to see it when the local drive-in got ahold of a copy. Danny, all of nine at the time, *loved* it! My mother, not so much.

Then came my 16th birthday in July. Ruby gave me a vinyl copy of the 20-million-selling *Star Wars* soundtrack as a gift.[74]

I saw *Star Wars* two more times that magical summer, and had sat through 12 viewings by the time the first anniversary of its release rolled around. I've seen it at least 30 times since, and have owned various versions of it in various formats over the years. I know it by heart, of course, every line.

[74] In a moment that would be remembered endlessly by many – there were 20 or so friends at this particularly birthday party – I was standing near the dining room table, where gifts were sitting, when Ruby picked up the wrapped album to hand it to me. At that moment, Joe walked up from the other side and spoke to me as I was reaching Ruby's direction. I turned toward Joe and accidentally grabbed Ruby's shoulder. *Except it wasn't her shoulder.*

She didn't budge, she just waited for me to realize what I had grabbed, as the entire room turned to watch me figure it out...

of my dad's MG Midget to make it look like a cockpit, and made me a spacesuit by spray-painting a scuba suit silver.

And we made ourselves a movie, shooting in the evenings that spring! We dubbed our little group Galaxy Films.

The Loneliest Battlefield is pretty horrible – but hey, we were 15! And that first attempt only made us hungry for more.

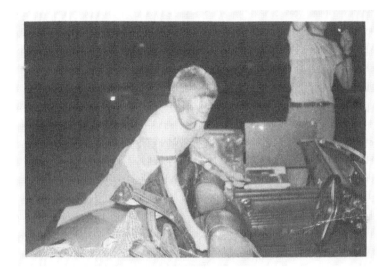

Scott humps the scoutship set as Joe sets a light.

Keep in mind the time frame here: *Star Wars* is still a couple of months away; *Close Encounters of the Third Kind*, Spielberg's love letter to UFO believers, is six months farther out. We don't yet know that Spielberg started out exactly as we are – a teenager with a Super 8 camera and a dream.

We went on to bigger and better things, but *TLB* lived on in our hearts. In particular, we adopted a reference from the script, wherein the computer mentions "a force-10 gravity well"; this reference was invoked whenever Joe jumped up and down on something in order to destroy it.

We were serious enough that we became an official school club, with a faculty sponsor. That sponsor, the journalism teacher, even provided us with a spare room at this apartment that we could use as an office.

Next came *Aleena,* another first contact story. In this one, the astronaut has landed on some alien world and meets a beautiful woman, who in a predictable *Twilight Zone* twist turns out not to be a woman at all. We recruited our classmate Angela Nalley, who was as beautiful as it is

In The Franklin County Flyer *yearbook, 1978.*

possible for a 16-year-old female to be, to play the human-looking version of Aleena; Womp made the alien version of her out of paper mache, and that too wound up recycled, in...

The Twilight War.

It's now Summer 1977 – the Summer of *Star Wars*! - around mid-June. As you read above in "The Summer of Star Wars", we now had a template to work (steal) from.. By the end of camp week, I have a screenplay written.

It's as silly as the others, if not more so, a tale of a spaceport out on the ass-end of nowhere, a more-or-less military outpost that is complacent and lazy, suddenly finding itself facing an enemy from the darkness. Turns out these nasty critters are the descendants of something we designed ourselves and then abandoned, and now they're headed our way, looking for their mommy and daddy.

Womp made some improvements to the Aleena alien head and it became our alien invader. Me, I think it looks like a Muppet acid nightmare.

I did a couple of rewrites as we expanded our troupe. Ann Victor became our makeup person; Ruby started making proper costumes, as well as adapting colorful warm-up jerseys to look pseudo-military. We bought a batch of toy M-16 rifles and modified them to look like laser cannons.

We started building models for the special effects. One particularly interesting innovation was to spray-paint corn flakes silver and gray, to pass for spaceship wreckage.

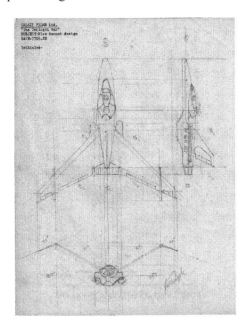

Artwork by Jim Wampler.

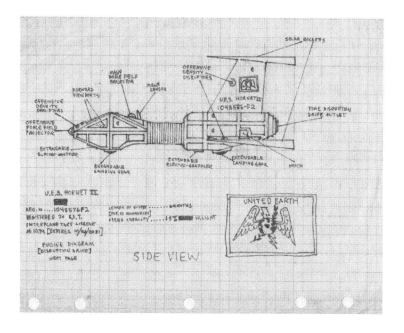

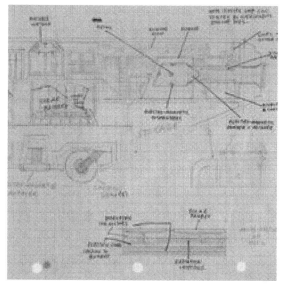

Frankfort at that time had a large plaza downtown with a towering office building, all of which looked exceedingly futuristic. We made it our spaceport. In another particularly clever innovation, Womp painted nested crescent moons onto a plate of glass, through which we shot that office tower in the evening. It looked great!

Local 'Star Wars'

Woodson Emmons

TED LESLEY, a junior at Franklin County High School or, in this case, an officer in the United Galactic Empyrean, struck a military pose Saturday for FCHS cameraman Jim Wampler during a rehearsal for The Twilight Wars, a "backyard movie" some area students are filming at Capital Plaza "just for kicks."(Other picture, Page 9)

In The State Journal, *July 1977.*

I made myself the hero of the story once again – a Han Solo-ish pilot named Steve West – and Joe took on the role of Governor Alderson, who was in charge of the spaceport. Womp and a couple of others were going to be aliens, and Bob was the ground commander of the spaceport's defenses.

We recruited the son of our high school principal to play the spaceport's doctor, got lots of attractive young women to be extras, talked a couple of my musician friends into being pilots along with me, and got two football players to play security guards. Ted Lesley, the only one among us who actually went on to have an acting career, played a hapless young pilot that my character managed to get killed.

At one point, we had 30-plus kids involved in this production. We shot at the plaza on weekends, and made the front page of the newspaper.

A "METEORS" ALIEN, here played by Kevin Helette, is just one of the characters in "The Twilight War", a student film being made by FCHS students as an extra-curricular activity.

In The State Journal, *September 1977.*

We used local parking garages to double as spaceship hangars, found some futuristic elevators, and converted the Sunday School rooms at a local church into sets as needed.

WLKY, a TV station in Louisville, heard what we were doing and sent a reporter, Jack McKigney, to do a story on us. This he did, and we were all thrilled to see ourselves on the news!

All of this cost a fortune, of course, but I had the benefit of a union job at Kroger; while others my age were earning a mere $3.10 shoveling fries at McDonald's, I was earning a princely $6.40 stocking canned tomatoes. Many were the evenings when Ruby would stop by the store and demand $20 for costume supplies.

It will surprise no one to learn that we only managed to film about 18 minutes of that 110-page script, even though we stuck with it through graduation.

It's upstairs in my office closet.

SPECIAL EFFECTS are shot in the auditorium by Jim Wampler and Todd Childers as the Amateur Filmaker's Club begins work on their latest effort, which should be seen sometime in May.

In The State Journal, *February 1978.*

Name That Movie!

1. On a deep space mission, everybody dies because they don't listen to the smart woman and her cat.

2. A young man flees his hometown and is pursued by his best friend, intent on killing him in his tracks because he prefers not to die in mid-air.

3. An aging warrior whose master chose self-imposed exile emerges from self-imposed exile to train a protege who becomes a warrior and chooses self-imposed exile.

4. A college professor is selected by the government to stop a hostile foreign government from obtaining a priceless relic, and has no impact whatsoever.

5. A near-future society manages overpopulation and scarce resources through clever dietary innovations.

6. A stranded alien botanist passes the time by snacking, cross-dressing and watching children's educational television while awaiting retrieval.

7. A group of space-faring insubordinates, guilty of multiple crimes, return to face justice only to opportunistically take up environmentalism.

8. A suburban husband and father, alienated from his family by escalating mental breaks, abandons them altogether by road-tripping to the remote Northwest.

(Answers on following page)

(Answers to Name That Movie!)

1. *Alien*
2. *Logan's Run*
3. The *Star Wars* Saga
4. *Raiders of the Lost Ark*
5. *Soylent Green*
6. *E.T.: The Extraterrestrial*
7. *Star Trek IV: The Voyage Home*
8. *Close Encounters of the Third Kind*

Nerd Theory: *The Rocky Horror Picture Show*

It is beyond debate that *The Rocky Horror Picture Show*, a cinematic spoof of the sci-fi/horror genres that came out in 1975, technically qualifies as both. The riotously funny musical is the story of a bland suburban couple stranded in a remote castle with a band of colorful and eccentric aliens masquerading as humans, and in its opening song does homage to Michael Rennie.

Upon its release, *Rocky Horror* was universally panned; but it found new life much as *Star Trek* did after cancellation, as the object of word-of-mouth fan love. It became a permanent fixture on the midnight movie circuit as millions embraced it, showing up in cosplay to perform scenes in the theater in real time, along with the film itself.

It introduced the world to Tim Curry, Susan Sarandon and Meatloaf, and is as popular today as ever.

Now, follow me closely here: not all *Rocky Horror* fans are nerds, but all nerds are *Rocky Horror* fans. And we'll go you one better: not all *Rocky Horror* fans are nerds - but all *Rocky Horror* fans *are* fanboys/girls.

There really is no other pop culture phenomenon with which you can construct such provocative overlapping sets. *Rocky Horror* fans have the cosplay, they have their own conventions; they have the scenes as deeply committed to memory as any *Trek* fan does the original episodes; they never tire of seeing it. You can almost write about *Trek* fandom and *Rocky Horror* fandom interchangeably.

And on top of all of that, the music – sci-fi to the core! – fits squarely into fanboy/girl sensibilities. The songs are outlandish in a Python-esque sense, and yet are works of art in the sense that they are perfect forgeries of the genres they are mocking. *"Let's do the Time Warp again!"* sings the cast, dancing on the screen as fanboys and fangirls dance in the aisles. It's a touch of vaudeville that reaches into sci-fi fandom as nothing else ever has, or ever could.

My own first exposure happened after high school, during my first year of college. My buddy Joe was with me. *Rocky Horror* became our new *Monty Python*.[76]

---

[76] Decades later, my daughter Josie got on board with *Rocky Horror*, and she and I attended a *Rocky Horror* night at our local museum. The place was, of course, packed…

The Showkiller

Mention I've already made of Fred Freiberger, who produced the third (and final) season of classic *Trek* and the second (and final) season of *Space: 1999* (my astute gentle reader will sense a pattern emerging).

That pattern continued with *The Six Million Dollar Man*, which had come to television in 1973 and had persisted four seasons at the time *Space: 1999* was shutting down over in England. Renewed for a fifth, it landed on Freiberger's desk – and he presided over its demise.

No surprise, then, that Freiberger is known in fanboy circles as The Showkiller.

It's an easy conclusion to reach, given the facts above. Add to this the fact that the final seasons of *Trek* and *1999* are almost universally considered inferior to what came before.

On the other hand, it could be a chain of misfortune - being in the wrong place at the wrong time, more than once. Which is it? Let's take a look...

Star Trek

Sit down with any Trekker and ask for a comparison of classic *Trek*'s three seasons. Here's what you'll get:

"The first season – *wow!!!* I can't think of a single bad episode! Well, "The Alternative Factor", I guess. And "Operation: Annihilate!" wasn't great. But *man* - "The Corbomite Maneuver"! "Balance of Terror"! "The Naked Time"! "Space Seed"! "Errand of Mercy"! "Charlie X"! "The Enemy Within"! "The Devil in the Dark"! "Shore Leave"! "Arena"! "The Squire of Gothos"! "The Galileo Seven"! - and, of course, "City on the Edge of Forever"! How great can a single season be?

"Season Two? Not as great, but still *packed* with terrific episodes! "Amok Time", "Journey to Babel", "Mirror, Mirror", "The Doomsday Machine", "The Changeling", "The Trouble with Tribbles", "The Ultimate Computer", "Wolf in the Fold" - fan-frickin'-tastic!

What about Season Three?

"Season Three? Meh. I mean, I still watch them sometimes, and there's a couple of good ones – "The *Enterprise* Incident". "The Tholian Web". "Day of the Dove", I guess. Mariette Hartley was pretty hot. And some of them were downright shitty: "The Way to Eden"? Really? And "Spock's Brain"? Come on!"

Season Three of classic *Trek* doesn't exactly suck, but both the actors and the fans agree it was a noticeable step down. And Fred Freiberger, who was at the helm at the time, has taken the fall for it, all these years.

No one would contest that Freiberger was working with one hand tied behind his back from the moment he stepped onto the lot. Roddenberry, in a failed power play, ended up stepping away from the show after NBC shifted it to 10pm Fridays (a graveyard slot at the time, though a decade later it would be the best time slot of the week). And the show's budget was slashed by the studio, just as the lead actors were demanding big raises.

Even so, Freiberger appears to have squandered whatever sympathy these circumstances might have garnered through bad relationships.

Writer David Gerrold said, "Everybody disliked Freiberger intensely. Leonard and Bill didn't like him, nobody else on the staff liked him. Nobody knew what to make of him. It was a very difficult situation for everyone."

Leonard Nimoy: "After a while, I believe he felt that I was simply being difficult, and he grew frustrated... [he] simply refused to address some concerns I had..."

One of those concerns involved the abominable episode "And the Children Shall Lead", wherein a bunch of orphans conspire to take over the ship at the behest of a ghostly monster that has ensorcled them.

"I thought it was terrible – terrible... So I went to Fred Freiberger and I said, 'We've got some problems with the script.' He said, 'This script is going to be what "Miri" should have been!'

"Well, 'Miri' was a lovely story, *lovely* story, beautifully told and beautifully played. And we all loved 'Miri' as an episode. And he was saying 'Miri' was a piece of trash."[77]

James Doohan: "He had no inventiveness in him at all. He was a no-talent businessman."

"The truth is, I've been the target of vicious and unfair attacks even to this day," Freiberger complained many years later. "The fact that at the end of the second season *Star Trek*'s ratings had slipped, it was losing adult fans and was in disarray, carries no weight with the attackers. The dumping was all done on me and the third season. It seemed it was now *Star Trek* law to lay everything on Freiberger. Every disgruntled actor, writer, and director also found an easy dumping ground on which to blame their own shortcomings. Whenever one of my episodes was mentioned favorably, Gene Roddenberry's name was attached to it. When one of my

---

[77] In *Star Trek Lives!*

episodes was attacked, Roddenberry's name mysteriously disappeared and only then did the name Freiberger surface."

But some of the cast defended Freiberger.

"I thought Fred Freiberger did a yeoman's job," Shatner later said.[78] "There was a feeling that a number of his shows weren't as good as the first and second season, and maybe that's true, but he did have some wonderfully brilliant shows and his contribution has never been acknowledged."

Nichelle Nichols: "[Because of the lower budget], you saw fewer outdoor location shots, for example. Top writers, top guest stars, top anything you needed was harder to come by. Thus, *Star Trek*'s demise became a self-fulfilling prophecy. And I can assure you, that is exactly as it was meant to be... In the third season [the] new producer Fred Freiberger did everything he could to shore up the show. I know that some fans hold him responsible for the show's decline, but that is not fair. *Star Trek* was in a disintegrating orbit before Fred came aboard. That we were able to do even what we did is a miracle and a credit to him. One day Fred and I had an exchange, and he snapped at me. Even then, though, I knew he wasn't angry with me but with his unenviable situation. He was a producer who had nothing to produce with."[79]

Two other interesting pieces of evidence deserve consideration. Most fans don't know it, but Freiberger had been Gene Roddenberry's *first choice* for line producer, when *Star Trek* got the green light to go into production back in 1965. But Freiberger would only take on the show if he was given time to take his wife on a long vacation he had promised her, and Roddenberry moved on.

And why did Freiberger feel he and his wife deserved a long vacation?

"He was the guy that got *Wild Wild West* up and running," writer Marc Cushman revealed. "I've read in books and I've read in articles that Fred produced the *last* season of the show, but he actually produced the *first* season. *He* was the producer who got that whole show and somehow did the magic act of taking a western show, a spy show, elements of sci-fi, and blended it into a hit."[80]

---

[78] In *Star Trek Memories*.

[79] In *Beyond Uhura*.

[80] *The Wild Wild West* – a bigger hit than *Trek* in its day – ran from 1965 to 1969, starring Robert Conrad and Ross Martin as two thrill-seeking Secret Service agents in the 1870s, exploring what might be the first-ever exemplar of steampunk.

"I have to be honest," Freiberger later said. "I thought the worst experience of my life was when I was shot down over Nazi Germany. A Jewish boy from the Bronx parachuted into the middle of eighty million Nazis. Then I joined *Star Trek*. I was only in a prison camp for two years, but my travail with *Star Trek* lasted decades."

Even so, "I have read that the fans didn't like any of the episodes of the third season. If true, that hurts me, but there is another truth. In my travels throughout the United States, Canada, and Europe, I have run into many *Star Trek* fans, and not one of them has ever treated me with anything but courtesy and respect. For that I thank them."

Space: 1999

More than five years later, British producer Gerry Anderson called Freiberger when his own space adventure was lilting (see "Space: $19.99, page 142).

1999 was elegant, visually spectacular, deeply philosophical, and unique in television sci-fi history (and, at the time, the most expensive, at $275,000 per episode). It was also humorless and somewhat inanimate. It needed a fresh spark. Anderson felt that Freiberger could provide that spark.

"He brought to the rather British, deliberately low-key *Space: 1999* unit a touch of California television," wrote archivist Tim Heald. "His trousers were louder, his epithets pithier, his opinions more forcefully expressed, and he had a way of saying 'Bullshit!' where his British counterpart would probably have said, 'I'm not entirely sure I agree.'"

Between *1999*'s first and second seasons, Freiberger jettisoned most of the cast, keeping only the leads Martin Landau and Barbara Bain and two others. He dropped the show's spacious Main Mission control center set for a leaner, meaner, bunker-like command center, supposedly far below the moon's surface. He made the uniforms more colorful, the scripts more action-oriented, and added an alien shapeshifter and a hot-headed second-in-command to the cast.

'Twas all for naught; *1999* continued to draw low ratings, despite Freiberger's upgrades. And, as had been the case with *Trek*, he alienated his lead actors.

Martin Landau, in a written note to Freiberger:[81]

[81] In an interesting irony, feuds with Fred Freiberger weren't the only thing Landau and Leonard Nimoy had in common: Landau had been originally considered for the role of Spock, and Nimoy had replaced Landau on *Mission: Impossible*.

"I'm not going out on a limb for this show because I'm not in accord with what you're doing as a result... I don't think I even want to do the promos - I don't want to push the show any more as I have in the past. It's not my idea of what the show should be. It's embarrassing to me if I am not the star of it and in the way I feel it should be. This year should be more important to it, not less important to it... I might as well work less hard in all of them."

It became a moot point. *1999* was cancelled after its second season. And many laid the cancellation at Freiberger's doorstep.

Just as with *Trek*, however, there were confounding factors:

"Because the powers in control decided that the first season was not successful does not mean that the productions were not well done in terms of the acting, the directing, the stories," Freiberger said in an interview. "There are many reasons why a series is canceled other than quality of the episodes. Ratings are the economic driving force. Are people watching the series? Obviously not enough. Lew Grade and his advisors decided that if the show was to succeed in the second year, it could not be the same as the first season. Changes were made. And obviously, the public did not respond so the series came to an end. It seems to me a waste of energy to argue that one year was better than the other - neither season attracted enough audience to sustain the series."

The Six Million Dollar Man

Almost immediately after 1999 ended, Freiberger got a call back to Los Angeles, where yet another sci-fi series was suddenly producerless (see "The Six Million Dollars, Man!", page 71).

In this case, however, there is little to indict Freiberger for his season being the show's last: it was, at the time of its cancellation, still immensely popular, five years in.

Lee Majors (who played Col. Steve Austin): "After five years we were still going strong," he said. "But the networks really started to dilute. That's what networks do... [But] it was near 100 episodes and it was grueling. The hours were really, really long and I lived on the lot. I had an apartment there... And I just didn't have a life for five years, and I was trying to maintain a marriage there with another popular girl."

Fans pointing to *6M$M* as a continuation of The Showkiller's on-going failures, then, are doing so purely out of self-indulgence. We can even argue that *6M$M* was much more up Freiberger's alley than *Trek* or *1999*. Moreover, the simultaneous cancellation of *6M$M*'s companion series –

home – the Hebrews in the Desert theme, known to anyone who ever went to Sunday School.

We were *soooooo* excited – we were basically getting *Star Wars* on TV! And the show was certainly dazzling, visually.

We gathered at Joe's riverside home for the premiere, and watched the subsequent two-parter, which guest-starred the soon-to-be-famous Jane Seymour. And it rapidly became clear to us...

Galactica was a children's program.

Its plotlines were more *Lost in Space* than *Star Wars*, let alone the *Trek* that was now our standard.[83] We wanted to love it; we watched it faithfully, every Sunday night! Me and my buddy Tom, who would become a Dune fan alongside me and Joe (that story is coming up soon), would double-date on Sunday nights, doing pizza at somebody's house to watch. The show was decidedly unimpressive to our girlfriends.

I chanced to watch the show at my Beatle buddy Britt's home toward the end of the first and only season, and he, too, had been watching – but for amusement. He nailed the show's childish tone by referring to it in a four-year-old's voice: *"Babbatar Gaggita! Tarbuck! Apobbo! Cymons! Cymons!"*

We howled.

The rest of the world was just as unimpressed.

Here's Asimov, writing a review of *Galactica*. He found the similarities between it and *Star Wars* (which were purely opportunistic on Larsen's part) to be off-putting:

Remember the bad guys [in Star Wars*] who were all wearing chromium suits with their faces covered up? Remember the good guys who were all wearing shirts and pants with the faces hanging out in plain view? The armored bad guys in 57, 243 shots never once even knicked a good guy. The unarmored good guys killed rows and rows of the armored bad guys, without ever dinting the armor or showing any blood?*

Here's the way Battlestar Galactica *did it. The bad guys were all wearing chromium suits with their faces covered up. The good guys were all wearing shirts and pants with their faces hanging out in plain view. The armored bad guys in 57,243 shots never once even knicked a good guy. The unarmored good guys killed rows and rows of the armored bad guys, without ever dinting the armor or showing any blood.*

*   There's creativity for you!   *

---

[83] The show even guest-starred *Lost in Space*'s Jonathan Harris – Dr. Smith – as the voice of Lucifer, a malevolent Cylon in the service of Baltar.

In Star Wars, *we had a whole galaxy in which the good guys are just about destroyed by the bad guys and it all came down to just a few doughty heroes trying to turn the tide.*

But in Battlestar Galactica, *we have a whole galaxy in which the good guys are just about destroyed by the bad guys and it all comes down to just a few doughty heroes trying to turn the tide...get the subtle difference.*

The show was mercifully cancelled after 26 episodes.

But it would be back, very much later, as a very different show. And this Baby Boomer Fanboy would see it through older eyes...

DEBATE!

Enterprise vs. Galactica:
Who Would Win?

One very popular long-standing fanboy debate – made all the more popular when *Battlestar Galactica* rebooted in 2004 – is whether the *Galactica* could defeat the *Enterprise* in battle.

While this may seem far more frivolous and of far less consequence than the nature of individuality or the possibility of life on other worlds, there's a component here that makes it irresistible: it allows fanboys/fangirls to parade their obsessive, encyclopedic, nerdish technical knowledge of the ships themselves. Serious nerds simply cannot resist.

Here's how such an exchange might go – say, between two fans watching an episode of *Galactica* where the ship is under attack:

FANBOY   **FANGIRL**

See how Apollo's Viper squadron knocked out all those
attacking Cylon fighters? In the same situation, the *Enterprise*
would have been hammered to pieces.

                                          You can't be serious.

Of course I'm serious! That's the whole point of a ship like the *Galactica* –
essentially an aircraft carrier in space. The idea is to send out fighters to
swarm an attacking enemy, keeping it so busy defending itself that it can't
muster a meaningful assault. The strategy is to wear down the attacker's
defenses.

I know what an aircraft carrier is.

Then you see my point: the *Enterprise* would be so busy pushing back against the attacking Vipers that it couldn't focus on taking down the *Galactica*.

No, I don't see that at all; your argument doesn't take into account the *Enterprise*'s superior mobility. The *Galactica* is a lumbering cow that can just barely turn; by comparison, the *Enterprise* is a stallion, able to turn and pivot and move nimbly in three dimensions. Mutara Nebule, *Wrath of Khan*, my friend.

Maybe, but it's still not nearly as mobile as a Viper. They can reverse direction *in less than a second* – Starbuck said so!

Good for her. The point is that the *Enterprise*, as an attacking ship – comparing, let's say, to a Cylon base ship – can dance around hither and yon on impulse power, causing the Vipers to chase it and thereby expend their fuel more quickly. It is not nearly as vulnerable as attacking Cylon fighters are, so they'd be forced to pursue and hang in battle much longer. The *Enterprise* could wear down the squadron as its phasers picked them off one by one.

And the shields of the *Enterprise* wear down pretty damn fast! "Shields at 80 percent, Captain!" BAM! "Shields at 30 percent, Captain!" BAM! "Shields at less than 10 percent, Captain! The next one will finish us!"

That was against Nomad. And the Doomsday Machine. Don't see a Viper packing that much of a wallop.

Besides which, the *Enterprise* isn't just dealing with the Vipers; there are also *Galactica*'s Raptors, which aren't as maneuverable as Vipers, but on the other hand can deliver a nuclear payload.

Shuttlecraft. Tit for tat.

So that one washes out, right?

Not exactly...

What's the shuttlecraft's advantage?

Payload.

Which is?

Anti-matter.

Well, there's still the *Galactica's* heavy guns – laser pulse cannons – and they are firing at the *Enterprise* while the Vipers are attacking!

Ah, no, those guns are defensive, not offensive, and it is little or no effort for the *Enterprise* to stay out of their range, as long as the Vipers are engaging. And their own secondary weapons, photon torpedoes, are self-guiding; they can let fly a volley of torpedoes at the *Galactica's* heavy guns, knocking them out, while still paying full attention to the attacking Vipers.

You're forgetting the impregnability of the *Galactica's* hull; if you recall, it can take a full nuclear blast! Let's see the *Enterprise* do that!

"The Corbomite Maneuver".

We don't know that was a nuclear blast!

"Balance of Terror".

...okay, that was a nuclear blast.

...and the *Galactica's* cannons are outside her hull, so they are vulnerable. Its Viper launch bays are also a vulnerability; if a torpedo gets in there, it's all over, and there are holes in the ship through which greater damage can be done beyond the hull.

Better yet, a shuttlecraft with an anti-matter payload.
Damn! Where's Matt Decker when you need him?

That's assuming you can get close enough to one of the Viper bays.

Not that tough, Viper boy; let's not forget that carriers don't generally sail solo; they are usually surrounded by a battle group: an escort consisting of two or more destroyers, a heavy cruiser or two-

The *Galactica* has the biggest escort in the history of escorts!
...consisting of arboretums, garbage trucks, luxury liners...

Okay, smartass, I'm open to your honest assessment of your own guy's weaknesses: what would you consider a vulnerability of the *Enterprise*?

Hm. Well, I'll grant that the engines of the *Galactica* are pretty frickin' powerful; it can probably keep up with the *Enterprise* on impulse. The trick would be to knock out the warp nacelles. If the *Enterprise* can't go to warp, it's conceivable that the *Galactica* could wear her down and eventually destroy her.

There's also the fact that the *Galactica* has a far larger crew than the *Enterprise* – almost 5,000 to 430. It can sustain far more casualties and still continue to function!

That's a weakness, not a strength.

How do you figure?

That much-larger crew requires far more life support infrastructure to support – an order of magnitude? If Kirk manages to blow one of the launch bays, he can proceed to begin targeting the *Galactica*'s power plant, water plant, ship's stores, botanical resources – and Adama is forced on the defensive, because a victory against the *Enterprise* is meaningless if the *Galactica* is so damaged that it can no longer sustain life. The *Enterprise*, on the other hand, has a much smaller physical plant footprint, so Adama can't even think about taking the same approach.

He just has to get through its shields and hit the bridge, which is the most vulnerable part of the ship, sitting on top of the primary hull like a bull's-eye.

Fair point.

You can argue all you want, but the bottom line is that the *Galactica* just looks *cooler* than the *Enterprise*.

Oh, is that the bottom line? And...seriously? If the *Galactica* and *Enterprise* were in *Return of the Jedi*, the *Enterprise* would be Leia in the bikini and *Galactica* would be Jabba the Hut. The *Enterprise* is *elegant*; there's no other starship like her! The *Galactica* is Ursula from *The Little Mermaid* by comparison.

How awfully feminist of you.

Now who's being a smartass?

Comics as a Sci-Fi Fix

Star Trek rapidly went multi-media with the Blish books and subsequent original novels, but it also spawned a comic book published by Gold Key in the late Sixties/early Seventies. And as we've noted, *Lost in Space* actually was *inspired* by a comic book.

Still, it was a big leap when Marvel took it off the big screen, releasing an oversized adaptation of *2001: A Space Odyssey* by Jack Kirby in 1976. It was a huge success, and a regular comic soon followed.

Then came *Logan's Run*, likewise rendered in comic book format. The book started with an adaptation of the movie, broken into five installments. From there, Marvel's writers gave Logan new adventures. The same formula was followed in 1977 after the release of *Star Wars*, which ran for many years – again, under Marvel.

When *Star Trek* hit the big screen in 1979, a Marvel comic swiftly followed in 1980 (as *Trek* movies poured forth, DC took over the rights).

Television got in on the act. *Battlestar Galactica* became a comic, unsurprisingly; but so did other, lesser TV sci-fi shows: there was actually a brief *Man from Atlantis* comic.

What does this matter, beyond DC and Marvel exploiting hot properties? Quite a bit.

First, these comics extended the narrative life of the various franchises to a degree (and within a budget) that could satisfy our nerd appetites for more. We had something to give our nerd love to in the two years between films or the months between television seasons.

Second, these franchise comics eventually rose up to become legitimate pop art forms in and of themselves: the books created by Dark Horse, for instance, made significant narrative contributions to the *Alien/Predator* universe.

I still have all my comics – about 3,000 of them. So it's with considerable pride that I acknowledge the contribution of the comic houses to nerd fandom, in service of our indelible guiding principle: *Too much is never enough...*

Chasing Frodo

It was in 1978 that I first became fully aware of Tolkien's *Lord of the Rings*.

Oh, I'd seen mentions of it; Asimov's Foundation trilogy, for instance, had beaten out *LOTR* for a Best Series Ever Hugo Award. But I didn't really understand what it was.

This was a matter of timing. Born in 1961, I was a Boomer, sure, and Tolkien's masterpiece was for sure a Boomer confection; but *LOTR* and *The Hobbit* had been all the rage in the mid-Sixties, when I was five or so.

This corrected itself after Tolkien's death, which prompted his son Christopher to edit and publish The *Silmarillion*, a collection of stories of Middle Earth, in 1977. Many of us in my nerd circle bought and read and loved the book. This prompted me to circle back to *The Hobbit*, which I adored.

I didn't know it at the time, but since the popularity surge the books had enjoyed in the mid-Sixties, many attempts had been made to get *LOTR* to the big screen. The most notorious of these attempts brought two great loves of mine within sniffing distance of each other.

One was Stanley Kubrick, auteur of *2001: A Space Odyssey*.

After completing *2001*, Kubrick had carte blanche – he could do whatever he wanted. And he was approached with a fascinating challenge by the most unlikely client: Paul McCartney.

The Beatles, it seems, needed one more movie to fulfill a cinematic contractual obligation. Paul had read *LOTR* and had a full head of steam about it, and he'd badgered the other three into reading the trilogy as well. He selected himself to play Frodo – a good call, as he looks *just like Frodo*. Ringo decided he'd made a good Sam, and George was a natural for Gandalf.

And John – it will come as no surprise to the Gentle Reader that John wanted to be Gollum.

Kubrick seriously considered the project; but he decided, as did John Boorman and others, that *LOTR* was simply unfilmable.

It was my friend Ann Victor – one of the friends who'd gotten me into Klaatu – who teased the idea of just how cool an *LOTR* movie would be, once we'd become immersed in the visual wonders of *Star Wars*, *Close Encounters* and their kin. I had to agree – visiting Middle Earth was beginning to seem an actual possibility.

And we kinda sorta did: enter Ralph Bakshi, fresh off his victory with *Wizards*, doing *LOTR* in animated form. It arrived in theaters just before the holidays in 1978, and it was indeed a visual feast.

Bakshi's *LOTR* covered *The Fellowship of the Ring* and about half of *The Two Towers*, in anticipation of a second film that would complete the story.

Alas, Bakshi's version, while earning back eight times its $4 million budget, was not a hit; it was criticized as "undisciplined"... "exhausting"... "more bizarre than magical"... "disjointed"... "confusing"... "incoherent."

All of that said, Bakshi's *LOTR* had a strong influence on Peter Jackson, the filmmaker who finally delivered *LOTR* in 2001, calling it "a brave and ambitious attempt."

While I own the DVD of the Bakshi version, I've only ever watched it once – with my daughter Josie, a die-hard Middle Earth dweller. But I will say this: after I saw Bakshi's *LOTR* in 1978, I finally read the trilogy.

While not a success, Bakshi's vision underscores an essential characteristic of the Baby Boomer Fanboy era, one that's hard to appreciate in the current digital age: the realization of the fantastic visions fanboys/girls crave was *not* a given! It required unprecedented vision on the part of filmmakers and their teams to travel a long time ago to a galaxy far, far away; to believe a man can fly; to walk through Middle Earth. It meant chucking out the conventional and developing entirely new technologies and methods, in order to truly deliver the wondrous and breath-taking on-screen. It couldn't be done on a laptop.

Today, of course, there's literally no image CGI can't provide, no world that can't be recreated, no vision too complex. Moreover, this technology isn't even in the domain of specialists anymore; you can buy it off the shelf.

And that makes the spectacular visual invention of the Sixties and Seventies the exclusive province of my generation – the Baby Boomer Fanboy. It's ours and ours along.

Thank you, Ralph Bakshi...

The Sands of the Front Desk

I'd joined the Science Fiction Book Club in 1975, and I'd bought my buddy Joe a hardback copy of *Children of Dune* a year later. He'd read both *Dune* and *Dune, Messiah* already, and he was palpably thrilled to have the new one.

I asked him to explain. Across several English classes, he enthusiastically described Arrakis, Paul Maud'dib, House Atreides, House Harkonnen, the Fremen, and the epic frame of the series. I was fascinated.

With the release of the final volume of Frank Herbert's initial Dune trilogy, the first two books were re-issued in paperback. I snatched them up and devoured them.[84]

And not much more was said about *Dune* among us fanboys until 1978, when a new nerd, Tom LeCompte, migrated to our school from Shelby County High.

Tom sat with me and Joe in Dr. Newton's physics class (how perfect is that?), and the three of us became pals outside of class. Tom had a weekend job as second-shift desk clerk at Days Inn on the west end of Frankfort – a lonely post, with very little to do – and Joe and I would often drop by to keep him company.

These hang-out sessions rapidly centered on *Dune*, which it turned out Tom had also read and loved. We would discuss the books endlessly, having great fun with them, and our affection for them became irreverent at times.

We would imagine, for instance, peripheral books written by the characters themselves: *How to Make Friends*, by Jamis; *Halitosis Can Be Unpleasant*, by Duke Leto. We dreamed up our own *Dune* movie cast: Shaun Cassidy as Paul, Farrah Fawcett as the Lady Jessica, and so on.

Lest this seem inconsequential, I'll add two points: those evenings cemented *Dune* in my brain, so that when *God Emperor, Heretics* and *Chapterhouse* came out over the next five years, I stuck with them; and this kind of fannish conversation foreshadowed our adult fanhood, when we'd have exactly these nerdish dialogs over the Internet.

---

[84] In particular, *Dune* was my Christmas vacation book at my maternal grand-parents' home in Columbus.

(Tom would go on to provide art for our movie, alongside Womp, and he actually built a balsawood scale model of the Hornet, the attack fighter flown by some of our characters.)

She Went Back for the Cat...

As we'd piled into Bob's mom's car almost three years earlier to make the trek to Louisville to see Gene Roddenberry, me and my fanboy pals now piled into a car and drove to Louisville in the summer of 1979 to see *Alien* at Showcase Cinemas, on one of the very first super-huge concave movie screens. You can imagine what it was like when the Face-Hugger popped out of the egg onto Ash's helmet. I don't *think* I screamed, but there's no telling.

The movie itself was amazing, a wonderful time, but what happened after was a lot of fun, too. We all went down the street to Steak 'n Shake on Bardstown Road and sat around talking about the movie.

I won't tell you who said what, for fear of pissing anyone off, but I'll tell you what was said:

"What kind of idiot goes back for the cat?"

I won't tell you which of my fanboy pals said that, but I'll say it was very in-character; it's exactly what we should have expected him to say. I don't know if I'd describe any of us as warm-and-fuzzy (with the possible exception of Tom, whom you just met above, who wasn't with us on the Roddenberry excursion), but the speaker here was hands-down the *least* warm-and-fuzzy of us.

Four-to-one, we voted in favor of Ripley's having gone back for Jonesy, the ship's cat.

"Nobody in that situation goes back for the cat!" the lone vote repeated. "In that situation, it's I'm-getting-the-fuck-out-of-here, and the cat takes its chances!"

"Well, the cat has no chance either way, alien or no alien, because the ship is going to blow in minutes," someone else pointed out.

"And as sad as that may be, going back for the cat reduced her chances of survival by at least half," the protester declares, because she's not only re-exposing herself to the alien, she's burning up what's left of her escape time!"

"I think it made her that much more human," warm-and-fuzzy Tom countered. "I really liked that she went back."

"And, really, cutting her own chances by burning up the time was a great dramatic move," someone else said, "It really jacked up the tension."

"Like there wasn't enough tension already?"

"Consider this," came a new reply: "By giving Ripley that extra surge of empathy, the director emphasizes all the more the difference between her and the alien; she was that much more human, and the alien seemed that much more alien, and that really worked for me."

We failed to convince him. (One of those replies was mine; but I'll let my comrades sort it out as they remember it.)

In hindsight, that wonderful human impulse to risk everything for the cat foreshadowed that part of Ripley that was more human still, when in the sequel *Aliens* (1986) she would go back, not for a beloved pet, but for the little girl who had lost everything and was now about to die.

You either love that moment or you don't, but the point here is that the debate itself was just plain fun. It's of a piece with those other fanboy debates I've brought out above, those goofy arguments that make fandom so unique. I hope they never stop!

Two months later, Heidi (Remember Heidi? She was off in Germany for two years) returned to the States, and Joe and I drove her to Lexington to see *Alien*. It should go without saying that she loved that Ripley went back for the cat...

Dungeons and Dragons

Not all nerds are gamers, but all gamers are nerds.

This is a hard-and-fast rule, and a conclusive corollary is that all of both are fanboys/girls. Nobody who doesn't love *Star Wars* and *Lord of the Rings* and Harry Potter would ever be caught dead playing Dungeons and Dragons.

My daughter Josie and her D&D gang (art by Josie).

Take note of the timing here: it was in 1974, just as we were coming of age, that Gary Gygax[85] presented D&D to the world; we were, very emphatically, the first D&D generation.

Me and my crowd didn't get around to D&D until the very end of the decade, and it was Womp who took the lead: he started a game at his place, with himself as dungeonmaster, and we spent many Saturday nights huddled over strange dice and figurines and graph paper.

---

[85] Gygax is revered by many as a god. Genuflect when you say his name...

I remember reading Rona Jaffe's novel *Mazes and Monsters* shortly thereafter in 1981, a book which accurately foretold how fantasy role-playing could be psychologically dangerous if taken to extremes. The book became a movie the following year – the first starring role of a 26-year-old Tom Hanks.

But I digress: I'd have hung in much longer with D&D, especially with a DM as crafty and inventive as Womp, but within two years I was married and a father-to-be – so I simply didn't have the time. I've played the occasional game in the interim, however, and I flatter myself that I'd have made quite a fine DM.

Why is he telling us this?

I'm telling you this because even though I didn't commit to D&D life-long, I paid it forward (that story follows); and it needs to be pointed out that D&D, while not a fanboy essential, is certainly a fanboy property.

30 Months That Changed the World

Much has been made above of just what a niche landscape science fiction was on the continent of pop culture during my childhood, in the Sixties and Seventies. There was the occasional sci-fi cultural *event* – *2001* and *Planet of the Apes* spring to mind – but in general, sci-fi wasn't anywhere close to mainstream. It was still a peripheral genre for brainy loners, generally low-budget and expectation-sparse. That sums up my youth, and that of all Boomer nerds.

All these decades on, of course, that's no longer true. Sci-fi *rules* at the box office, and in pop culture in general; it is the perpetual Flavor of the Month, year in and year out. The Marvel and DC comic book films sit at the very top of the nerd culture apex, where any movie that doesn't gross nearly a billion dollars is considered a disappointment.

How did we get here?

I'm going to propose that there was a transition period that took the deep childhood passions of the Baby Boomer Fanboy from Study Hall Fantasy to Mainstream Entertainment of Choice – a transition period where nerd culture rose up, ascended, and took the entire world along with us.

That transition period, in my thinking, began in May 1977 and continued through December 1979.

During these 30 months, five motion pictures came out. And those five movies made all of Western pop culture a Baby Boomer Fanboy culture. Those five films were *Star Wars*, *Close Encounters of the Third Kind*, *Superman: The Movie*, *Alien*, and *Star Trek: The Motion Picture*.

Before this transition, sci-fi was strictly nerd turf. We owned it, we reveled in it, we inhabited it, and the rest of the world rolled its eyes. Once these 30 months happened, the rest of the world was on board – and permanently.

Let's look at all five movies, one at a time.

Star Wars

The first *Star Wars* changed everything, of course. Opening in May of 1977, it introduced the entire world to the nerd wonders that Boomers and the emerging Gen Xers so deeply adored: spaceships! aliens! other worlds! robots! heart-stopping adventure!

And something new: space battles! Previously, these were found only in the comics; they were too expensive to do on film, given the state of the special effects art in those days. But *Star Wars* not only served them up in generous truckloads, they were edge-of-the-seat *fast* spaceships! The lumbering spacecraft of *Forbidden Planet* and *2001* and *Silent Running* had nothing on the X-Wing fighters and the *Millennium Falcon*.[86]

George Lucas served up a story that was far afield of the sci-fi tales that had come before, leaning more into the wild spirit of Westerns and the fast pace of Forties movie serials. This pushed *Star Wars* into a narrative space that the uninitiated could easily take on board. The story of Luke Skywalker and Princess Leia and Han Solo and Obi-Wan Kenobi, the struggle between the Rebellion and the Empire, with heavies like Darth Vader and Tarkin, and those oh-so-cute droids C-3PO and R2-D2 – kids and grown-ups alike could access fun like this effortlessly.

It didn't hurt that veterans like James Earl Jones and Alec Guiness were on board, giving the whole thing an air of respectability; and it didn't hurt that the new faces – Ford, Fisher, and Hamill – were utterly charming and likable.

And then there was the music! *Star Wars* wasn't the first film with music so memorable that every last person who saw the film would remember it (the *Jaws* theme and the theme from *The Godfather* got there first), but it's a sure thing that more people remember the former than the latter two. John Williams' score is easily one of the most recognized in movie history, and elevated the movie soundtrack as an art form to a level of unprecedented pop culture significance.

Star Wars was the first sci-fi summer blockbuster. There had been summer blockbusters before, of course – *Jaws* had tens of millions lining up around the block outside the cinemas two years earlier – but nothing in the history of cinematic sci-fi even came close.

On a famously skimpy budget of $9 million, *Star Wars* leapt into the top box office earners of all time in its initial release, hitting $220 million in its US run and almost half a billion dollars internationally.

By comparison, *2001*, on a budget of $10 million, had accumulated $22 million three years after its release, which barely brought it out of red ink. *Planet of the Apes* did somewhat better, racking up $35 million on a budget of $6 million. *Logan's Run* pulled in $25 million.

Put another way, *Star Wars* outperformed its predecessors by an order of magnitude. Suddenly – unexpectedly! -science fiction was not only

---

[86] The special effects that made *Star Wars* what it was, of course, didn't exist at all before George Lucas paid SFX guru John Dykstra to invent them. That the art of filmmaking inherited computer-controlled cameras capable of synchronizing lots of objects in a 3D space is one of Lucas's great bequests to the world.

super-cool, but super-profitable (and, of course, every major movie studio took note of this). Nerd culture was off to the races...

Close Encounters of the Third Kind

Steven Spielberg's *CE3K*, a paean to his Super 8 childhood and a nod to the UFO believers, arrived six months after *Star Wars* – but in all fairness, was by no means a bandwagon film. Spielberg had been carrying the idea in his head since his teenage years, and had been working on it since being offered carte blanche by Columbia after the success of *Jaws*. It was luck-of-the-draw that Lucas got out first.

His wondrous tale of a series of visitations from other worlds, and how an Indiana four-year-old and power company lineman get telepathically drawn to them, brought science fiction right into the suburbs, up close where anyone could be dazzled. As the visitations increase and more and more people hear their call, an international team is cataloging the sudden return of vanished ships and aircraft from decades past. And it all seems to point to Devil's Tower, Wyoming.

Stunning, almost magical special effects by Doug "Stanley Kubrick Loves Me!" Trumbell made the movie more wondrous still, and John Williams returned to deliver a Disney-esque soundtrack that surges with mystery and enchantment. Richard Dreyfus as the everyman protagonist, modeling Devil's Tower in mash potatoes, couldn't be more watchable.

Close Encounters wasn't just a wondrous new entry in sci-fi's emerging cinematic canon; it connected the wonders of the stars to the audience – to people in the here and now. That was something special, and something we'd never seen.

CE3K was right behind *Star Wars*, raking in more than $300 million – and proved the latter was no fluke. This magnificent nerd-fare was where the general public was now wanting to go.

Superman: The Movie

We can't lose sight of the fact that nerd culture, while sci-fi to the core, is probably more comic book than anything else, in sheer proportions. If the Boomer Fanboys were on the march to take over the world, they couldn't do it without turning the world's attention to the superheroes.

The granddaddy of all superheroes, in particular: the Big Blue Boy Scout. Kal-El of Krypton. The Man of Tomorrow.

Superman.

In fairness to Alexander and Ilya Salkind (who produced it), Mario Puzo (who wrote it), and Richard Donner (who directed it), *Superman: The Movie* was in work before both *Star Wars* and *CE3K*. When it finally arrived in theaters just before Christmas, 1978, it had been through all manner of financing challenges, production issues, and staggering drama between its creators.

But the end result is American cinema at its finest. Puzo and Donner were utterly respectful of the material, playing it as straight as possible; young Christopher Reeve was overwhelmingly convincing and charming as Clark Kent/Superman, earnest through-and-through and dazzling to audiences.

The movie's unique depiction of Krypton, and in particular, Marlon Brando's portrayal of Superman's father Jor-El, brought something new to the mythos, echoes of which persist even in today's incarnations, 40 years later. Gene Hackman, an unlikely Lex Luthor, absolutely owned the role, coming off both hilarious and brutally sinister. And, of course, John Williams returned once again to deliver the definitive soundtrack with a theme that is still universally recognized.[87]

Had *Star Wars* and *CE3K* softened the ground? Would *Superman: The* have been the monster success it became if its predecessor blockbusters hadn't paved the way the year before?

We can never know. What we do know is that *Superman* did business equal to *CE3K*'s - $300 million-plus – and set up not only its inevitable sequels but a Batman franchise, opening the door for Spider-Man, the X-Men, and the MCU and DCEU franchises we now endlessly enjoy.

The Baby Boomer Fanboy legacy, at this point, had contributed space opera, Visitors Among Us, and heroes from the pages of comics to the pop culture gestalt. What's left?

Horror...

Alien

Nerds have always had a connection to horror. From *Invasion of the Body Snatchers* to *The Blob* to *The Omega Man*, scary shit is our turf.

---

[87] Our fanboy viewing of *Superman: The Movie* delivered an iconic moment for our fanboy circle, when Joe paraded his intellectual nerd for all the world to see. There came a moment in the film when he lifted himself out of his theater seat to his full height, pointed at the screen and cried, *"Christ figure!!!"*

But not just any scary shit. *Rosemary's Baby* and *The Exorcist* are pretty terrifying, but not exactly in our wheelhouse.

Nerd horror needs some nerd context. And with Ridley Scott's *Alien*, which found us in the summer of 1979, we had more context than we could stand.

Alien is a true horror film, from front to back – but it is also just as much a science fiction film – real nerd fare. It takes place in deep space. It takes place on a spaceship. It has, well, an alien. There's even a robot.

And *Alien* goes places that *Star Wars* and *CE3K* and *Superman* hadn't gone; given that the tragedy of the *Nostromo* and the loss of its crew as the fallout of nothing more than corporate greed and inhuman manipulation, it actually gave us something to think about.[88]

The sci-fi elements are simple, and essential to the story. The *Nostromo* is a space freighter toting millions of tons of ore back to Earth from parts unknown in deep space when a beacon from a wayward planet attracts its attention. Investigating, the crew of seven wind up taking on a xenomorph – an alien that develops rapidly through several distinct forms – and this xenomorph is intent on wiping them all out.

Worse, a member of the crew is protecting the alien, because the company that owns the freighter knew about it and wants a specimen to study for its weapons development potential. The crew itself is considered expendable.

One by one, everyone gets picked off but Warrant Officer Ripley (Sigourney Weaver, in one of the earliest woman-as-warrior roles), to sole voice of reason and courage on board. Her final victory over the alien is one of the most heart-stopping confrontations in all of cinematic sci-fi.

The horror elements, however, were not incidental; they were just as central to the themes and tone and look of the movie. For starters, there's the *Nostromo* itself – a haunted house in space.

The *Nostromo* might be the grittiest, most claustrophobic, most inhospitable spaceship we'd yet seen. It is well-worn, all shadows and long corridors and dark corners. It is vast, complicated, and filled with confined spaces. A perfect haunted house.

Moreover, director Ridley Scott set in motion a structural shift in the story that immediately became a new standard in both sci-fi and horror films – multiple climaxes. He brought the action and suspense in *Alien* to a heart-stopping ending... and then he gave us a second heart-stopping ending. James Cameron did the same in the 1986 sequel, *Aliens* – and did it

---

[88] Ripley summed this up nicely in *Aliens* (1986), the immediate sequel: "You know, Burke, I don't know which species is worse; you don't see them fucking each other over for a goddamn percentage!"

again in *Terminator 2: Judgment Day*. Since then, countless films have done the same.

Alien is an essential moment in our 30-month journey from the niche nerd world to the all-nerd world. The first step was the Hero's Journey with *Star Wars*; then we moved to the contemporaneous wonder of *CE3K*; then we swerved into comics territory with *Superman*. That's three essential habitats on the nerd horizon.

Alien gives us yet another – our deepest fears, our darkest dread. Human beings fighting for their lives, for their right to persist. Us against the Universe. That's one we can't do without.

Star Trek: The Motion Picture

The final step in the great transition is distinct from all the others. Though it (like Superman) was not an original work, it was a unique and essential argument in the nerd case for cultural supremacy.

Star Trek.

Gene Roddenberry's humanist vision of the future, the quintessential utopian dream of sci-fi. By far the most famous and enduring and influential sci-fi series ever, it is also the most progressive. The most inspiring. The most hopeful.

And while we can say that the films we've already mentioned were *not* *Star Wars* bandwagon projects, *Trek* most certainly was.

Kinda sorta, anyway. The return of *Star Trek* was actually on the drawing board long before any of the other four projects were a gleam in anyone's eye; in a very real sense, Roddenberry was always pushing for it on some level. And he'd succeeded; Paramount had green-lit *Star Trek Phase II* before *Star Wars* split the sky, and it was conceived as a sequel TV series with original cast and crew to spearhead the studio's planned "fourth network".[89]

So when *Star Wars* made it clear that it was possible to put a sci-fi movie into theaters and get back hundreds of $$$ millions, Paramount said, Let's do that instead!

Kirk, Spock, McCoy and company reunited aboard the *Enterprise* for a visually spectacular but narratively turgid adventure that required the starship to deal with a vast techno-cloud-entity called V'Ger destroying everything in its path and heading for Earth. Along the way, new-and-

---

[89] For you much-younger fanboys/girls, be aware that in the 1970s there were only three national television networks - NBC, ABC and CBS, rather than the hundreds we have today.

improved Klingons were served up alongside an upgraded *Enterprise*, a sexy bald woman, and an enlightened Spock – none of which went anywhere very important or meaningful. The film was, to put it politely, a mess.

Directed by Robert Wise, it was a commercial success but a critical disappointment – the only one of our five films with that distinction – and pleased fans more for its existence than its content. But in the scheme of things, this didn't really matter that much; a sea change was happening in pop culture, and it was happening in the movies – and now *Star Trek*, the most sacred and philosophically important of all nerd possessions. The best of all we enjoyed would be part of our cultural takeover, and *Star Trek: The Motion Picture* ensured it.

How did we know? The film's final card:

The Human Adventure is Just Beginning.

Each of these pivotal movies either raised the bar for nerd culture films overall, or made their content more palatable for the unwashed masses. Any one of them alone might have been an anomaly, a one-off; all of them together were a tidal wave, sweeping away whatever ideas the general public had about science fiction and other nerd fare on the big screen and making it new, exciting, even urgent. Science fiction ceased to be niche nosh for brainy wallflowers and became the weekend entertainment of choice. Every major studio loaded up on sci-fi projects, leading to the world we have today.

Four of the five films above, of course, ended up kicking off an entire film series: at this writing, there are no less than 11 *Star Wars* films out there;[90] eight films starring *Superman*;[91] eight *Alien* pics,[92] and a whopping 13 *Star Trek* movies[93]. Only *Close Encounters* stands alone.

---

[90] The original trilogy, the prequel trilogy, the sequel trilogy, plus *Rogue One* and *Solo*.

[91] The four Christopher Reeve films; *Superman Returns*; *Man of Steel*; *Batman v. Superman*; and *Justice League*.

[92] The four Sigourney Weaver flicks, two *Alien v. Predator* films, and Ridley Scott's recent prequels, *Prometheus* and *Alien: Covenant*.

[93] The six *TOS* films, the four *NextGen* films, the three Kelvin Timeline films.

Star Wars and Steven Spielberg's success, alongside Harrison Ford's surging popularity, made *Raiders of the Lost Ark* possible. After *Alien*, Ridley Scott was offered carte blanche, and declared his goal to become the John Ford of science fiction – then very credibly pursuing that goal with *Blade Runner* (yet another Harrison Ford film).

A successful string of Superman films led Warner Brothers to keep the golden goose laying by launching a Batman series, with Michael Keaton as the first of several Batmen and hiring Tim Burton of *Beetlejuice* fame to give it a unique, macabre look. *Alien* had endless successors, most notably John Carpenter's *The Thing*, which took *Alien*'s other-worldly horror and brought it down to Earth.

And *Star Trek* – well, there's no end in sight.

We changed the world. Our dreams, our passions, our commitment to the wildly odd and different now prevails across pop culture. Consider:

Of the Top 20 films of the Sixties, the only two nerd films to appear are *2001* and *Psycho* (and we're not sure we should count *Psycho*).

That number doubled in the Top 20 films of the Seventies – *Star Wars*, *CE3K* and *Superman* are all there, alongside James Bond's sci-fi turn, *Moonraker*).

In the Eighties – fuggedaboutit! The Top 20 included

The Empire Strikes Back
Return of the Jedi
E.T.
Batman
Raiders of the Lost Ark
Indiana Jones and the Temple of Doom
Indiana Jones and the Last Crusade
Back to the Future
Back to the Future Part II
(That's 9 out of 20.)

Do we see a pattern emerging?
Between 2010 and 2010, the Top 20 included

Avengers: Endgame
Star Wars: The Force Awakens
Avengers: Infinity War
Jurassic World

The Avengers
Avengers: Age of Ultron
Black Panther
Star Wars: The Last Jedi
Jurassic World: Fallen Kingdom
Iron Man 3
Captain America: Civil War

That's *11 out of 20*, in the most recently-completed decade, and we might even have counted *The Incredibles 2*.[94]

Fanboys/girls everywhere: we have prevailed! The world has come around to our way of thinking.

---

[94] ...but let's look at the next 10 from that decade, just for fun: *Aquaman*; *Spider-Man: Far from Home*; *Captain Marvel*; *Transformers: Dark of the Moon*; *Transformers: Age of Extinction*; *The Dark Knight Rises*; *Joker*; and *Star Wars: The Rise of Skywalker*. 8/10!

My Parents' Basement

If the fanboy's *Girlfriend in Canada* cliché is ubiquitous, the *I Live in My Parents' Basement* cliché is even more so.

This one is beyond the scope of our tale, which only runs across the years I was living at home in the first place. The thing is, of course, that many fanboys never actually leave.

It's interesting to theorize as to why this must be so.

To begin, we can ask ourselves why in the world a fanboy would want to stay in the home of his birth, where he is almost certainly surrounded by People Who Just Don't Get It.

That's how it typically plays out: the fanboy grows up immersed in *Trek* and *Star Wars* and *LOTR* and a hundred other obsessions, shunning such mundane pursuits as, you know, social development; he's quite content to leave his room as seldom as possible, except to hang out with others of his kind or take in the latest sequel at the cinema.

Mom and Dad's basement offered a cultivated safety, a sanctuary, a reasonable response to the reality that most of society is just like Mom and Dad – they *Just Don't Get It!* Better to sit tight and endure your parents' passive disapproval and resignation than to face it all anew.

Today, of course, it's not so bad: you can let your fanboy freak flag fly and receive only sparse rejection, since the new generation has come to accept fanboy culture as mainstream.

Even so, I am obliged to recall my own fanboy family days.

My parents were like so many others. As I said above, they didn't know the difference between *Star Trek* and *Lost in Space* and didn't care. I did, however, manage to cultivate some fanboy in my two younger brothers, Dan and Maxx.

Dan, who would have been around 10 when me and Womp and our gang were making our movies in Frankfort, was happy to dress up in a uniform and play a background extra. Maxx was too young for that, but he was more than receptive to my nerd music – and he followed along into *Star Wars* and all the rest soon enough.

I left the basement as soon as I could, for reasons having nothing to do with being a nerd or a fanboy. But I recall another fanboy who didn't.

Remember up in "Star Trek Lives!", when I told the Gentle Reader about my buddy Mike's older brother, who gave me the *Trek* convention programs and paperbacks? Mike was a fanboy in this parents' basement.

What's interesting about that story is that my encounter with him was happening at just the moment he was breaking out of it. He was a good 10

could concoct a novel about Plutonium-186, an impossible isotope. The resulting novel, a three-part drama about beings in another universe leeching energy from our own, won both the Hugo and Nebula Awards.

Fantastic Voyage. It's hard to take this 1966 film seriously on its premise, that a submarine is shrunk to near-microscopic size and injected into a dying man to track down an inoperable blood clot and burn it away with a laser. But Jerome (*Twilight Zone, Star Trek*) Bixby did the story, and Isaac Asimov ended up writing the novelization. Far-out premise or no, it featured strong performances, a tense script, and special effects that did their best to honor actual biological reality.

Notorious lecher Asimov, commenting on star Rachel Welch: "I was particularly impressed by the scene in which Raquel was attacked by antibodies. Those antibodies had to be stripped from her body before they killed her, and four pairs of male hands moved instantly to her breasts to begin the stripping – and there was room there (it appeared to my fevered imagination) for all eight hands."[96]

"The Star". This Arthur C. Clarke masterpiece appears in Asimov's *The Hugo Winners, Volume I* (which it did). Like "The Nine Billion Names of God", it skewers religion on the saber of science – evoking a heart-breaking horror at the core of contemporary faith.

Dangerous Visions / Again, Dangerous Visions. Harlan Ellison boldly set out to raise the bar – which was already set quite high by the New Wave – with this call for stories that went where no story had gone before. That's what he got; ground-breaking material that staggered the imaginations of millions. Both the anthologies and the stories within won buckets of awards, and Ellison received a citation at the 26th World Science Fiction for "the most significant and controversial book published in 1967."

"I Have No Mouth, and I Must Scream". Cited above in "The New Wave", Ellison's horror story about five people trapped and tormented by a malevolent computer honeycombing the entire Earth is a metaphor for our own existentially precarious posture with information technology today.

"To Serve Man". Both an award-winning (and heavily reprinted) short story and a beloved *Twilight Zone* episode, Damon Knight's signature tale

---

[96] In *In Joy Still Felt.*

about contemporary Earth's first contact with alien emissaries has one of the most perfect final twists in all of sci-fi.

Double Star. There are so many great Robert Heinlein novels, it's hard to pick a favorite: Stranger in a Strange Land? The Moon is a Harsh Mistress? The list of possibles is long; but this tale of a down-and-out actor hoodwinked into impersonating a famous politician in a heavily-populated solar system rife with powder-keg politics is mine.

The Adolescence of P-1. Few people have even heard of this obscure novel by Thomas Ryan about a hacker who builds an AI that gets loose among the computer systems of the world, gobbling up resources until it wakes up, finds its creator, and starts sniffing around the Pentagon; but, as you might guess, it appealed to the budding AI designer in me.

"The Bicentennial Man". Asimov wrote many bittersweet stories that tug on the heart (read "The Ugly Little Boy" the next time you feel the need for a good cry). But this story of a robot who longs for independence and sets out to obtain it rises above all others.

"Unaccompanied Sonata". Orson Scott Card may be out of favor today, given his incendiary politics, but back in the day he wrote this not-far-off tale of a young man gifted beyond all others with unspoiled musical talent, a story in which asks the question, *What if I were forbidden to write? Is there anything in the universe that could make me obey?*

"Inconstant Moon". One of the most reliable writers of hard science in history, Larry Niven won a Hugo for this vivid tale of a writer and his girlfriend in Los Angeles on what they believe is the last night on Earth.

If the Gentle Reader undertakes all or even part of this list, I promise the effort will be well-rewarded...

Afterword: The Fanboy at 60

Where did the years go?

Well, as you'll find out in "Legacy", the section that follows, my own deep investment was in my kids and grandson – nerds to the core, one and all. Along the way, I lived the life I'd planned; I've written dozens of books, thousands of articles and essays, was a systems engineer working in robotics for a decade, and am currently an AI designer working in the behavioral sciences. It's more than I hoped for, and the world today is already a future beyond what I'd imagined.

The book in your hands is evidence that Womp and I are still going strong, 45 years on. He's done a dozen or so book covers for me, each as terrific as the one in your left hand right now; but he also edits this great gamer's megazine, *Scientific Barbarian*, and I have a column (and an occasional short story) in most every issue (google it and check it out!).

I've only seen Bob sporadically over the years, but I run into him frequently on Facebook. He also introduced me, in a roundabout way, to my wife.

I see Heidi and Susan on Facebook from time to time as well, and see Susan in person at occasional Class of '79 events. For a while, I ran into Joe and Ann Victor online, as well.

Rudy vanished, ghost-like, into the Eighties. I last saw her in December of 1982, when she stopped by the clothing store I was managing at the time. I've tried to find her several times on social media over the years, but came up empty. I miss her, even now.

Womp and I both know there are fewer days ahead than there are behind, as Jean-Luc Picard once reflected, but we're not bothered. We're fully aware how lucky we are to have lived in a window of time like no other; we watched, across years in the pop culture desert, as the world slowly came around to our way of thinking. We smiled as our long-embraced notion of cool went from fringe to mainstream. We can legitimately claim a bit of prescience, and I think our entire childhood gang is justified in feeling a little smug.

We were more interested in Middle Earth than getting high, and our goofy British sports cars (me, Womp and Joe each had one) were our Galileo, our Viper, our Eagle, taking us places our high school peers couldn't go. We were more anxious to get our hands on next month's comics than the latest Fleetwood Mac album. Our priorities were considerably straighter than theirs!

We longed to see Spider-Man and Captain America and Iron Man and the Hulk on the big screen – and now they hold every box office record. Our break-through nerdfests – *Star Wars* and *Star Trek* and *Alien* and *Indiana Jones* and the *Terminator* and *Lord of the Rings* all spawned series that roll on in perpetuity – the public-at-large will never get enough. And *we were there first*; we carried the torch that lit the cultural universe.

There are fewer days ahead than there are behind, but what amazing days we've lived and shared! And what amazing days remain?

Thanks, gang; thanks, Womp...

Fanboy Legacy

Zygotes

I have always referred to my four kids as zygotes (and my grandson as the grandzygote). And it behooves me to comment, after all this reminiscence of my nerd youth, on how much of it got passed on to subsequent generations.

There are some details above, here and there – but here's a more specific run-down.

Steve, my oldest, arrived in 1982, and immediately got a front-row seat in the temple of nerd – literally. In 1983, I was writing for the Frankfort *State Journal*, and covering new movies was among my duties. The manager of the local cinema was quite pleased to give me private screenings, in hopes of more favorable reviews; so when *Return of the Jedi* came out that summer, there I was, with baby Steve and his mom. He sat on my lap throughout the film, mouth agape, mesmerized by Luke and Han and Leia and Lando and Jabba the Hut and Boba Fett, et al.

Technically, Steve is Generation X, removed a step from his younger sibs. It shows in his nerd history: while the others listened to CDs of Monty Python and the Beatles and Klaatu and They Might Be Giants at bedtime, Steve listened to the *actual vinyl*. Not only that, he had the pre-millennial experience of sitting and listening to records while doing nothing else – a practice long forgotten, these days.

Steve and his sister Sandy, two years younger, grew up on *NextGen* and C.S. Lewis and miscellaneous movies (Sandy and I went through a phase of quoting *The Andromeda Strain*). Steve's great sci-fi love beyond *Trek* was *Ender's Game* and its sequels.

My second son Trey, born in 1994, is already on record above as a Klaatu fan – but his great nerd move was pulling his dad into *Doctor Who* in the mid-2000s, followed a couple of years later by his little sister Josie. Trey likewise worked his way through Ender, and was the family's biggest Harry Potter fan (though Josie was a close second, and their nephew JJ followed in his own time). As far as I know, Trey is the only zygote who read all eight books.

Another great Trey moment: after reading *Fahrenheit 451* in high school, he undertook to write a *451* prequel screenplay as a senior project (there was a stretch of time when he plowed through all of my Bradbury collection).

And Josie – where do I start? Though her inner nerd embraces the full spectrum, her heart is in Middle Earth: it is a holiday ritual for us to watch both the Peter Jackson *LOTR* and *Hobbit* trilogies together. She knows

Monty Python inside out (most of them do), and is as wildly talented an artist as her brother is a writer (this makes her Uncle Womp quite proud).

Another great burst of nerd: Josie and I watched all 10 seasons of *Smallville*, side by side.

Josie.

JJ, Sandy's son, goes his own way. While he loves all of the above, he sniffs out stuff everyone else misses. For instance, there's a new show starring the current Superman, Henry Cavill, called *The Witcher*. He cornered me to watch it with him, and requested the Witcher books as a Christmas gift. He's also the only one among them who watches *Game of Thrones* with me.

They're all comic-book-bred, and beyond Josie's *Smallville* is JJ's love of *The Flash* and *Arrow* on CW. Trey was the *Gotham* devotee, and he was also all about *Jessica Jones* and *Daredevil* and their kin.

Josie art. These are her tribe's D&D characters. She's Fiasco, the one in the front.

They are all Marvel movie fans, and for the most part enjoy the DC counterparts – the first *Wonder Woman* and *Shazam!* in particular. They are pretty critical of *Batman v. Superman* and were appalled by *Justice League*, though Trey is quite impressed with Jarod Leto as the Joker.

Me and Trey.

Trey is also the biggest Spidey fan of the bunch, an expert is all three versions (Tom Holland is his preferred webslinger).

As this book was being written, Josie and I binged *The Mandalorian*, *WandaVision*, and *The Falcon and the Winter Soldier*.

My sons, I should confess, roll their eyes at me constantly, for the following reason: I'm too easy. I absorb all the nerd content out there with no critical eye. I loved both *Prometheus* and *Alien: Covenant*. I like the Joss Whedon *Justice League*. I didn't mind *Green Lantern*.

I try to make clear to them – *You don't understand! You all are swimming in cream, you are numbed by an embarrassment of riches! You have all the best of the best rolling at you all the time! When I was a kid, it wasn't like that! We waited years between good sci-fi movies! We went through five bad sci-fi TV shows to get to a single good one! We were just grateful Sean Connery was willing to dress up in a thong!*

Of course I'm happy to watch even the bad stuff! *Of course* I think modern fanboys are prima donnas! *Of course* I give even the weaker stuff the nod!

They roll their eyes.

I'm proud of them, all the same. All five of them. I look at the sheer looming cloud of nerd they emanate, and I think to myself... *I done good!*

Cosplay

I was Batman at age seven; I built a robot suit out of boxes, aluminum foil and flashlight bulbs at eight. At 13, I made the Spock outfit with the phaser and tricorder and communicator. And as an adult, I was a *NextGen* officer alongside my young son Trey.

They didn't call it 'cosplay' then, but cosplay it was. And the legacy lives on in my youngest, Josie.

Josie is an artist – a cartoonist, a sculptor, a painter, a sketch artist. And she loves cosplay. She loves designing and creating cosplay costumes.

For the better part of the past decade, she and her crew – Ham, Bubs, Courtney and several others – have been cosplaying constantly, getting together to plan and coordinate costumes, then spending *months* making them, at great expense. Once done, they attend the next ComicCon or some other convention and show them off.

This cycle has persisted season after season, year after year. They never tire of it; they always manage to scrounge the money together, they always find the time. This started when they were in middle school, and now they're in college – but no one shows any sign of calling it quits.

I don't know any of the characters they dress up as – from TV shows and comics that are too new to intrude upon my awareness, but for which they profess great enthusiasm. Doesn't matter; I'm impressed with the industry, the creativity, the sheer quality of their enterprise.

es on in my youngest, Josie.

Once, not long ago, there were eight in the group – and there was a three-day con approaching. They resolved to all have a different cosplay for each day. That meant designing and creating *24 costumes* from scratch. They pulled it off.

Josie recently updated me on their latest round and I was moved to comment.

"Honey, you're all halfway through college now; soon one or two of you may choose to go to med school or law school, or marry or have a baby, and your group will begin to shrink."

"Nah," she said, confident that the group would endure. "You're forgetting a key fact."

"What's that?"

She looked at me as if I were a dolt.

"We're nerds," she replied.

AI on the Trail

On a beautiful Sunday in 2016, I'm hiking in the park with Starbuck, and after a 10-minute silence, she suddenly pops up with, "Daddy? When, how, and why will sentient artificial intelligence threaten humanity?"

Wow. My heart did a somersault, I was so happy to get that question!

I mentioned that this was actually a current topic among my friends online, and that even the most expert opinions varied. We are not nearly as close to machine sentience as exposure to Siri and Alexa might lead one to assume, I explained, and the truth is that we are not at all sure of our footing in even correctly defining the problem, let alone to proceeding to design.

First, we discussed "sentience" - its definition is complex, but let's settle for "self-awareness." There is no common state exemplifying it, I told her: human beings are self-aware in ways other primates are not; primates are self-aware in ways dogs and elephants and dolphins are not; and so on, down the line. So, when we talk about artificial "sentience," are we talking human-like, or otherwise?

We decided to go with "human-like sentience = able to understand and share our values."

That led us to "values = rules by which we implement our moral judgments," and this led us into trouble. A Google car can be programmed to handle the high-traffic equivalent of the Trolley Problem, but does that represent values? No, moral judgments and behaviors are rule-based events, which *follow* from values - they are not actual values themselves.

HAL-9000, I told her, possessed human-like social behavior which caused his creator and colleagues to assume human-like thought - yet HAL did not have our values. He murdered the crew of Discovery, the darkest violation of human morality.

How, Starbuck wanted to know, could a sentient AI absorb human values? I suggested that it couldn't be via programming, since programming amounts to rules, and we had already seen that rules follow values, but are not values themselves. My answer: a sentient AI would need to learn values by sharing human experience.

Like Data, on *ST:TNG*. Data shares human values, despite being an android (and superior to humans in many ways) - and does so because he learned them, by living among them.

But, she wanted to know, what about Data's 'brother' Lore, also an android? And an identical one?

That only underscores the point, I answered: Lore is immoral, by human standards, despite being physically identical to Data. The only difference between them is their experiences among humans; Lore's were less than positive, leading to a different value system.

And this led her to ask, "How do emotions figure in sentient AI?" My answer was, For any sentience that could have any hope of being human-like, emotions are essential - our brains are 'layered,' an ancient brain wrapped in a newer one, wrapped in a newer one, leading to our current level of sophistication. We still retain every layer, and the most ancient is our core emotions - the limbic system - which was our original decision-making system, our basic intelligence. Even HAL-9000 had this one: the instinct to fight to survive.

But, she wondered, "Wasn't Skynet emotional? Didn't it want to wipe out humanity out of malevolence?"

"That's a tough one," I replied. "Even within the canon, interpretations differ. The most useful one for our purposes is that Skynet was created as an integrated platform for the global management of humanity, and upon achieving self-awareness, Skynet concluded that the greatest threat to the management of humanity was humanity - and that the elimination of that obstacle left a worthwhile, persistent result... Skynet."

"Yet Data wasn't emotional," she pointed out, "and wanted emotions more than anything."

"To be a real boy," I nodded. And then she made the leap, "Like Andrew Martin in 'The Bicentennial Man'." My heart swelled to bursting. I raised her right!

I told her that Gene Roddenberry had maintained a 25-year friendship with Isaac Asimov, who created Andrew Martin (played by Robin Williams in the 1998 movie version), an android serving a human family who achieve self-awareness, loves the family, and wishes to earn the right to be called 'human' by humanity. Roddenberry could not have been unaware of the Hugo-winning story of Andrew, and was certainly inspired in the creation of Data by it (though I strongly suspect David Gerrold had more than a little to do with Data's development as a character). In the real world, I don't believe that Data or Andrew Martin could achieve the value systems they do, shared experience with humans or not, without emotions - without a 'limbic chip' - but the characters do much to stimulate our thinking about the problem.

I offered her the conclusion that 1) sentient, "self-aware" AI is not only possible but probably not far off, but it will not be human-like sentience; 2) it will be achieved through the agency of many AIs interacting and learning from each other, adapting to the outcomes that follow from their interaction, and 3) if this proves threatening or fatal to humanity, it will be accidental, not malicious.

And if such an intelligence ever presents itself, I will hasten to arrange an introduction to Starbuck...

Golden Apples: Ray Bradbury and Me

It's the mid-Seventies, and I'm about to stumble into Ray Bradbury.

The setting for this meeting could not be more perfect. I'm a seventh grader sitting in study hall, on the third floor of an ancient rural Indiana school building. In the early part of the 20th century, this was a high school, one of those antiquated temples with very high ceilings, wide staircases with thick oaken banisters, red brick façade and a gymnasium straight out of *Hoosiers*. Fifty years later, there's a brand-spanking-new high school 10 miles away, and this old building is now a junior high school.

We glide back in time every morning, me and my friends, on a weary yellow school bus, through endless cornfields, past trees and farmhouses, grain silos and ponds. This little town sits a few hours south of the rural Illinois terrain of Ray's own youth, and even though I don't know any of this yet, it is soon going to feel very real to me. I'm about to be pulled across time, in both directions, and through pure chance, I'm starting the journey in exactly the right space.

The study hall is, appropriately, right next to the library. As far as I'm concerned, that truly does make this old place a temple.

I raise my hand silently. The teacher on duty, used to this signal, nods. I quietly leave my seat and vanish into the stacks.

I emerge with a thick volume – *S is for Space* – and take my seat again. I flip to the second story – "Pillar of Fire" – and everything changes for me.

My first bite from the first golden apple is ostensibly science fiction – the story of a 20th century man accidentally revived in the 24th – but it's more horror, as this fellow feeds on fear and death, and sets about re-introducing them both into the sterile, clean future in which he finds himself. More than that, it's a psychological thriller, as Ray invites me into this creature's mind, and the mind of his 24th century pursuer.

And there's a second bite, and a third, and a fourth – "Come Into My Cellar", "Zero Hour", "The Pedestrian" – and I find to my delight, upon later visiting the town library, that there are many, many more golden apples.

That summer, my feet leave the earth for days on end, as I devour *The Martian Chronicles*, *The Illustrated Man*, *Fahrenheit 451*. And when my feet do touch earth again, it is now more magical than the sky – a place where time and youth now stand still, something out of *Dandelion Wine*, a barefoot odyssey through shadowy woods and dusty cellars, echoing with the twilight calls of parents from porches as elderly neighbors scowl through windows.

This eccentric, inexplicable bond between small-town youth and the grand sweep of space and time is the stuff of Twain, carried into the modern age, past and future intertwining with no real rhyme or reason but abundant romance. Robots on horseback. Stained-glass windows into mind. I'm off and running, and though I've been reading science fiction and fantasy since grade school, I've never met anyone like Ray.

My feel for this magical difference comes quickly, and in a few years I'll understand it intellectually, but it's apparent from those earliest readings. Isaac offers thoughts and ideas, Arthur serves up grand concepts. Robert presents eccentric personalities. But Ray – Ray paints wondrous pictures, so real and compelling and authentic that the world around me melts into them. The Big Three draw me to worlds I love to visit; Ray's, I never want to leave.

My passages to Terminus and Jupiter and Tertius all came to me by way of John W. Campbell, Jr., editor of the seminal *Astounding Science Fiction* before and during the war years. Heinlein, Clarke and Asimov, by way of *Astounding*, were launched to such heights that their names became well-known beyond the pimpled fraternity of boys like me, famous the world over. Significantly, Ray Bradbury was the only science fiction name known to the general public who was *not* a Campbell discovery; he emerged in Los Angeles rather than New York (where *Astounding* was based), brought into the fold by Forrest J. Ackerman (who, God bless him, bought my first story when I was but 14 years of age. Perry Rhodan #102. Run, don't walk!).

Campbell's emphasis on realistic science and strong plotting and character development did much to raise science fiction out of its juvenile origins and into the mainstream; but Bradbury's surreal, romantic style was far afield of the reason-driven fare of Campbell's authors, and expanded the genre's appeal farther than they ever could have. People who never went near science fiction magazines at all nonetheless read *The Martian Chronicles* and *Fahrenheit 451*. Ray's work was the first to be regarded by the general public as *literature*, not just genre.

His titles alone could carry us across that gulf; only Harlan Ellison compares, in the knack of finding a perfect (and often lengthy) memorable title that sets the ideal tone for the work beneath. "Dark They Were, and Golden-Eyed"; "Something Wicked This Way Comes"; "I Sing the Body Electric"; "The Golden Apples of the Sun"; "There Will Come Soft Rains" … titles so romantic and lyrically metered that they take up residence in memory right away, and never leave.

They hurl us into the terrors of childhood, the dread of death, the uncertainties of time, the warmth of family, the joys of our dreams, the darkness of our unspoken thoughts. We experience the heat of the veldt, the churning dark waters around the lighthouse; we take in the violet grasses of Mars, the sinister faces in the carnival, the scaled monsters of the Cretaceous.

But Ray's stuff does more than launch us into confrontation with those things within us that are magical and dark and longing; it keeps us anchored as it goes, not only teasing at what we might be but reminding us who we are. It isn't just nostalgia he's working here – it's an understanding, a constant homage, an on-going celebration of that elemental force in that third-floor study hall that pulls a young mind into the stacks, that reconciliation of light and dark, of glow and shadow – the idea that who we are and who we can become are not distinct propositions, but of a piece.

Just after I learned Ray had died, I asked him about this.

"We are the miracle of force and matter, making itself over into imagination and will," he said. "Incredible! The Life Force experimenting with forms. You for one. Me for another. The Universe has shouted itself alive, and we are one of the shouts."

So, I said, basically all this time you've been repeating the shout?

"If you enjoy living, it is not difficult to keep the sense of wonder," he said. "We are cups, constantly and quietly being filled. The trick is knowing how to tip ourselves over and let the beautiful stuff out."

Maybe, I said – I sure hope he's right about this – But sometimes it's hard to get there from here.

"You've got to jump off cliffs," he answered, "and build your wings on the way down."

Thanks, Ray, I say, and then I tell him about that long-ago third-floor study hall. And it's here that Ray and I find our deepest, most permanent connection – the infinite adventure of the printed word, the musty glory of those ancient temples.

"Go find your bliss," he tells me, "Name your favorites and see if your long umbilical memory has been cut or you are still wonderfully tied to the things you loved in libraries long ago … "

***

In the summer of 1991, I took my children to see that Indiana school building where Ray and I first met. It wasn't there; not a single brick remained. I was devastated, and the only remedy was to take the kids to the park, buy them an ice cream, and recreate it for them, summoning it back into existence – to bridge the time and space between, as Ray did, unceasingly.

And it dawned on me, when I got to the part about Ray and the third-floor study hall, that *because* of Ray, I've had that power all along. Until Ray left us last week, I assumed that this wondrous magic emanated from him, that without him the light would die out, that the third-floor study hall would slip away into time, not a brick remaining …

… but that turns out not to be the case.

Fanboy Redux

Star Trek: Discovery (2017)

A week from now, a new *Star Trek* TV series will debut. It will be the sixth such series in 50 years (not counting the 1973 cartoon version).

As a life-long fan, I can't help but be filled with anticipation – but like most fans, I'm also somewhat apprehensive. There has been lots and lots of *Trek* over the years (more than *Star Wars*, more than Superman and Batman and Spider-Man, even more than Doctor Who), and we'd be less than honest if we didn't admit that the *Trek* we've been given over the decades has been hit-and-miss.

Star Trek, you see, differs from the others in an important, even essential way: it isn't just good guys and bad guys or cool future tech or nerdy adventure. *Star Trek* is about an idea, and it's an idea that's up there with the greatest human thought and literature – the idea that humankind, without help from gods or "destiny" or some Jesus-Saves Force will prevail on our own, and create a future that is positive, uplifting, and packed with endless potential. Its central message is that the human race will not only survive but thrive, eventually reaching for the stars, and in doing so we will leave our disheartening legacy of greed, hatred, mistrust and violence behind us, once and for all.

This new show is called *Star Trek: Discovery*, and I submit that this is the best subtitle imaginable for a *Trek* series. The path to that marvelous future imagined by series creator Gene Roddenberry is, inevitably, a journey of discovery, first and foremost– a journey into unknowns that are about more than just survival, but a quest for growth and enrichment of a deeper kind.

Humanism sums up Roddenberry's *Trek* mantra, and humanism it certainly is, borrowed from his sci-fi pal Isaac Asimov, one of the movement's most prominent proponents. The more Roddenberry explored it, the more committed he became to it, and the more he insisted that *Trek* reflect it, to the point of forbidding conflict between the principal characters of *Star Trek: The Next Generation*. This made life difficult for series writers, but it also made *Trek* stand out on a sci-fi horizon populated primarily by survival-of-the-fittest and dystopian angst.

But the implementation of Roddenberry's vision was spotty, at best. Writer-director Nicholas Meyer, for instance (who delivered *Star Trek II: The Wrath of Khan*, the most acclaimed of the original cast movies), based one of his films on the premise that the original Enterprise officers were essentially racists, regarding Klingons with all the racial sensitivity of David Duke.

The racial loathing was multidirectional: Vulcans are pretty racist themselves, it turns out, as seen in both the prequel series *Enterprise* and in the first of the *Trek* reboot films. And while there is little greed to be found in a universe where energy flows freely and material needs are universally met, there is very nearly as much aggression and shooting and things blowing up in *Star Trek* as there is in *Star Wars*.

What can we expect? We want to expect exactly what the title promises: *Discovery*. A series about a Federation starship with a diverse crew, venturing out into the unknown – not for wealth or conquest, but for knowledge and experience. The show takes place about a decade before the adventures of the original Enterprise – that is, in the mid-22nd century – at a time when relations between the Federation and its neighbors were still tentative, so there is potential for constructive conflict.

And what we've seen of the crew is certainly diverse: a female captain, white and black and Asian actors populating the roles, aliens among the crew, a gay crewmember, even Spock's father. Lots to work with. And there's even Harry Mudd as a recurring character, to give us a baseline of comparison for measuring humanity's improvement.

We may or may not get the *Trek* series we've been waiting for this past decade. J.J. Abrams' three reboot movies gave us much of what we love, but they were more adventure than discovery, more guns than minds. The toss-up comes down to an interesting circumstance in the show's production: Gene Roddenberry's son Rod is an executive producer, and will certainly be guardian to his father's vision. And the show's head writer-producer is… none other than Nick Meyer, who explicitly rejects that vision.

Ex astris, scientia – "From the stars, knowledge" – is Starfleet's motto, and it couldn't be more perfect. Can a *Trek* series that truly lives up to its title – a series about Discovery, and not just the starship – be exciting, compelling, even moving, without lots of space battles and animosities? Will it be worth our time? Or will they bungle it out of the gate?

I'm holding out for the former. I'm hoping for a show that explores not just the final frontier, but the inner discoveries that happen when new life is encountered and we must be willing to change, if we hope to coexist with it. I'm hoping for a show about ideas, where the conflict is in wrestling with challenging thoughts and difficult problems, rather than which ship's shields will hold out the longest.

Star Trek is 51 years old, and its father is now 26 years dead. I'm hoping for a show that echoes his most steadfast assurance, conveyed through his creation: that the human adventure is just beginning…

ADDENDUM (2021)

Three years have passed, and now we've had three seasons of *Discovery* and a season of yet another *Trek* series: *Picard.*

Discovery managed to shake up everyone's idea about what *Trek* really is without destroying it, and under the circumstances, that's no small accomplishment. It managed to win acceptance among the fanboys/girls, to the point of inspiring not only *Picard* but the upcoming (as of this writing) *Strange New Worlds*, a revisiting of the *Enterprise* under the command of Christopher Pike, with Number One and a young Spock at this side.

Picard, which revives the story of the captain of the *USS Enterprise NCC-1701-D* (and *-E*) 20 years after the film *Star Trek Nemesis* (2002), shows us a man we've never seen; disillusioned, reclusive, he has turned his back on Starfleet and given up. The adventure he is drawn into, utterly unexpectedly, not only revives his interest in living but instills him with an urgent sense of mission: if he's going to head into the sunset, it will be for something worth dying for.

I mention it because this elderly Picard is a metaphor for the aging Baby Boomer fanboy – myself, in particular. Me and my pals, the first of the fanboys, have had a long, long run... and we're tired, and perhaps a bit cynical and disillusioned.

We're utterly unimpressed with the advanced game systems inhabited by tens of millions in the current generation. We sneer at the VR helmets and the real-time Massively Multiplayer Online Role-Playing Games. Gaming, you see, is properly done with oddly-shaped dice and graph paper and a well-prepared DM...

But no. Like Picard in the new series, we see that we are drifting into curmudgeonly obsolescence with that kind of thinking; it behooves us to shake off our biases and open our minds to new things, as was once our default position.

We see (SPOILER ALERT!!!) the mind of Jean-Luc Picard down-loaded into an android, and we cringe at such a fate, until we consider the alternative.

It has never been about the past. It has always been about tomorrow. If a 94-year-old Jean-Luc Picard can get there, so can we. And today, 45 years on, he is prompting us to realize that tomorrow is all we really have...

DEBATE!

Can a Human Brain Be Downloaded into an Android?

I'll confess something here: when the Trek Fanboy Nation rose up as one in the spring of 2020, after the Picard Season One finale (in which the dying Picard's mind is uploaded into an android "golem"), I was thrilled that almost nobody bought into it.

That's not Picard! they all shouted into social media, *It's just a copy! The real Picard is dead!* Everyone felt cheated.

The thing is – 20 or 30 years ago, even 10 years ago, you wouldn't have heard that reaction; it would have been taken by faith, as a kind of default position, that the downloaded information from a brain residing in an android constitutes a "transfer" of a person from a meat body to a metal one.

Today, we know enough about brains and computers and AI to know that it isn't that simple, by a long shot.

Our fanboy and fangirl have just watched the first-season finale of *Star Trek: Picard*, in which (SPOILER ALERT!!!) the mind of a dying Jean-Luc Picard is downloaded into a synthetic body designed and built by Dr. Alton Soong, the human son of Data's creator...

FANBOY   **FANGIRL**

                                                    Well, that didn't last long.

What didn't last long?

                                                    Picard. Ten episodes in, and he's already gone.

What are you talking about? You saw them put his mind in the synthetic body!

That wasn't Jean-Luc Picard. That was a copy of Jean-Luc Picard.

Of course it was Jean-Luc Picard! The human brain can be completely described as data, and if you capture all of that data, you've captured the brain! Jean-Luc Picard is alive and well and living in a new android body.

Your own brain would make for a curious batch of data.

I've got you this time! Because *Trek* itself is full of examples of that principle.

Oh, don't stop now, you're on a roll...

In the *NextGen* episode "The Schizoid Man", Dr. Ira Graves is dying, and does exactly the same thing – he downloads his consciousness into Data's positronic brain.

See, now you've done it – you've used the 'c' word...

'Consciousness'?

You're making my point for me. Every version of *Trek* plays fast and loose with the concept of consciousness. It's like the writers, across all the different series, were determined to roll out every possible definition and interpretation of 'consciousness', no matter how mutually contradictory.

What's your point?

Not sure how much faith we can put in the understanding of how human minds work demonstrated by those writers.

Example?

The writers of *Star Trek*, more often than not, treated human consciousness metaphysically, as 'ghost in the machine' - like a spirit that can possess one meatsack and conveniently relocate in another. It was probably the *least* scientific thing about *Star Trek*.

Name *one time* that happened!

> Sargon and his pals in "Return to Tomorrow"; 'Redjac' in "Wolf in the Fold"; Kirk's body-swap with Janice Lester; the entire concept of the Vulcan katra -

Well, that's not the same thing!

> No, it's not.

Then what -

> I was just screwing with you.

Those were all body-to-body transfers!

> Even more impossible...

I'm talking about brain-to-machine – like Uhura wanted to do in "I, Mudd"!

> Also not the same thing; Uhura didn't want her brain downloaded into a machine; she wanted it physically implanted in a machine – like when they removed Spock's brain in "Spock's Brain" and put it in a computer on Sigma Draconis VI.

Oh yeah.

> Don't stop now!

All right, "The Ultimate Computer"! Dr. Richard Daystrom built the M-5 computer using his own engrams, the data describing his own brain – and that gave M-5 Daystrom's own moral conscience!

> It did, indeed.

So?

> So does that mean M-5 is Richard Daystrom? Or even a copy of Richard Daystrom? Nope; it only gave M-5 a set of cognitive biases that reflected

those of Richard Daystrom. AI is doing that already today. Not a download
of 'consciousness' at all.

Well, then, let's go back to Picard. Why isn't the new Picard the real
Picard?

First, let's agree on one thing: the original Jean-Luc Picard is dead...

Yes...

He's passed on... ceased to be! Expired and gone to meet his maker!

Yes!

He's kicked the bucket, shuffled off his mortal coil, joined the choir
invisible-

Move on!

...so we now have to determine whether the synthetic Picard is in fact the
'real' Picard.

Easy-peasy!

Pray tell.

Everyone around the new Picard – and some of them have known him
many years! - found him indistinguishable from his original self.

Yes, and I find my laptop picture gallery indistinguishable from its backup
in the cloud, but one of them is original and the other is still a copy.

-and where they're stored makes no difference!

Doesn't it?

Even though he's now in a synth body, the downloaded Picard believes
himself to be Jean-Luc Picard! That means his consciousness was
successfully transferred!

Does it?

Well, how is it not?

Okay, my dedicated young philosopher: follow me closely!

As Picard was dying earlier, they scanned his brain and imaged it completely...

Yes...

So, in the synthetic brain, there are positronic neurons and axons and synapses that are exactly like the originals, configured in exactly the same way...

Yes...

...so all of the synth Picard's thoughts and cognitive behaviors will be exactly as before, right down to his conviction that "he" is the "real" Jean-Luc Picard.

This is what I'm saying!

Now, my bright young genius; *what if the original Picard hadn't died?*

Well?

I'm getting old over here...

But he *did* die, so -

...so he "transferred" to the new body? Was this a desperation jump? It's somehow different if the original brain dies? I can't see how...

I didn't say that -

Yes, you did, you said his consciousness "transferred"...

I meant-

"I'm Captain Kirrrrrrrrrrk!"
"Climb Mt. Seleya, Jim!"
"Redjac *Redjac REDJAC! AH-HAHAHAHAHAHA!!!"*

Flawless impersonation.

Is the synth Picard the real Picard, or is the original Picard the real Picard?

I-

> Let's make it more interesting: suppose Alton Soong had had *six* of those
> synth bodies, not just one, and they'd downloaded Picard's engrams
> into *all six*; which of the six would contain Picard's "consciousness"?

All six!

All six will *believe* that they alone are the original Jean-Luc Picard, the real
Jean-Luc Picard, but will be faced with the clear evidence of the other five
that they are not.

A universe with six Jean-Luc Picards would not be a bad thing.

> We agree on that, at least. But there's one final test...

Okay.

> Let's say it's you. We copy all of your engrams, all of the data describing
> your brain, and we download them into an android.

...which is sure to occur someday. The android would then think like me,
act like me, be indistinguishable from the original me to you and my
friends and family, and actually believe it is me.

> Right.

Okay. So?

> So, would it be okay for me to then shoot you dead?

What???

Are you so confident that your consciousness, "you", would be alive and well in the android body that you'd be okay with the original you dying? Because that's what you're claiming for Picard.

If I'm going to die, I'd rather have my brain downloaded into an android than not!

I would, too, but not for the same reason, and that's not what I asked.

The answer, of course, is No; your consciousness is right where it's always been at the moment of your death, and whatever's already in the android is something else, despite the resemblance; and when your body and brain die, your consciousness dies, android or no.

You take the fun out of everything.

No, the writers of the episode did. I honestly don't know if I can watch Fake Picard in season two.

Oh, you'll watch...

Eat your Cheetos, synth boy...

Gene, George and JJ: The Stars Awaken

The dust isn't even close to settling yet, as the worlds of the Republic and Starkiller Base all exploded a mere two weeks ago at this writing; nor will it settle anytime in the next 18 months, as JJ Abrams' *Star Wars VII: The Force Awakens* leaves enough plot threads dangling to fill up an entire cable channel.

And it shouldn't. There's plenty about this gargantuan movie to keep us talking for months, from its mashup franchise piracy to revived nits about what a parsec is, and my best friends of decades past are already hard at work, deconstructing it with glee. I will never be far from those enjoyable tussles as we all await Episode VIII.

But as *TFA* warps into cinematic history, box office records accumulating like stormtrooper corpses in its wake, I am more mindful of the endless debate it has inspired over the very nature of this craft – a debate far more interesting than arguing about who fathered Rey or why Kylo Ren didn't Force up Finn before he even turned his lightsaber on.

Star Killer

It begins six years ago, with the revival of big-screen *Star Trek*, when Abrams revived Gene Roddenberry's humanist wild west and promptly launched it up into a box office heaven that Paramount had never before dreamed of, let alone been able to pull off without him. Millions of old-school fanboys – my lifelong friends included – cried "Foul!" and ascended pulpits, thumping the Trek TOS canon like King James in defense of the purity of Roddenberry's vision (a purity about as real as the Fifties were innocent). There was hope at Paramount, of course, that in watering down the egalitarian Roddenberry message in favor of heart-stopping action, *Star Trek* would rise to the level of *Star Wars*, economically. And sure enough, it cranked right up.

Disney handed Abrams the Star Wars franchise largely on the basis of his Wars-ing up of Trek – evidence that he was the right guy for the job. But now the same crowd that hated his Trek is hating on *TFA*, and JJ Abrams – on his way to being the most successful director since James Cameron – is the Nerd Nation's new Destroyer of Worlds.

Well… that turns out not to be the case.

Two Big Happy Families

Let's begin with JJ's "destruction" of *Trek*, without lingering too long. Roddenberry's defenders always begin with *Trek*'s multicultural cast, and rightly so: his inclusion of a black woman, an Asian, a Southerner, a Russian, a Scotsman and a Satanic alien around his white male star was a game-changer in series television. Much has been written of this, as it should be.

But even the most rabid Original Series Trekker is hard-pressed to defend Roddenberry's meager use of his non-white cast (a situation that only vaguely improved in the subsequent movies): they feed on dramatic table scraps, spouting the same lines in every episode (mocked by Sigourney Weaver's character in the *Trek* send-up *Galaxy Quest*: "I repeated the computer!"). They were never given the chance to be real people, and all too often were subordinated to Kirk in the most insulting ways ("Captain... I'm frightened!").

Abrams' version? Every single character bristles with strength and competence. No one is a set piece. They are humanized in ways that might not be the viewer's choice, but a human woman choosing to be with a Vulcan or an engineer who breaks rules as easily as Kirk himself are both choices any humanist should applaud. Sure, the Vulcan is a hot mess, and Kirk still isn't terribly mature – but we're seeing them, by design, a full decade younger than Roddenberry's version. Say what you will about the marketing decisions that made it so, a seasoned, well-balanced Kirk would have been dramatically ridiculous in the rebooted universe.

But we *really* uncork this new vintage when Khan arrives.

The Trekkers went even more berserk over Abrams' version of Khan, *Trek*'s ultimate villain, in 2013's *Star Trek Into Darkness*. The fact that the "mis-cast" Benedict Cumberbatch, who totally knocked it out of the park, is all white-boy European and looks nothing like Ricardo Montalban is barely a nit. Cumberbatch took the horrifying megalomaniac to entirely new levels, infusing him with madness worthy of Anthony Burgess while making him sympathetic with the very lever that moves *Trek* in the first place – a lever Abrams improved upon:

Family.

The Saga Begins

The Trek Nation loved *Star Wars*, overall, but were quick to call it "shallow" when comparing it to their beloved Kirk and company. But George Lucas and his thirtysomething conspirators did something that had never even occurred to Roddenberry: realizing that the success of Star Trek was that its core characters were a family, and one with which its audience identified, he took things a step further – he built a family right before our eyes.

Luke, Leia, Obi-Wan, Han, Chewbacca and the droids – and subsequently Darth Vader – all become family as we watched, wide-eyed, munching our popcorn, on what became the thrill ride to define all future thrill rides. "Parsecs" and vacuum-banking space fighters aside, we really don't give a flying fuck about empires or republics or rebels: it's that deep emotionally stirring resonance of watching flawed, hopeful human beings, floundering in circumstance, bonding with one another and learning to love and appreciate and defend one another, that reaches into each of us and offers a new hope.

That's what makes New Khan more effective and worth watching than Old Khan, over in *Trek*: New Khan's insanity was kindled by the loss of his family, the only ones like him left in the universe, and having to face a new universe totally alone, manipulated and deceived. Old Khan was wonderfully mad, but had his kin all around him. He was driven by vengeance. How many of us are driven by vengeance?

Khan as realized by Benedict Cumberbatch – *"Is there anything you would not do for your family?"* – is driven by loss. Spock, who lost his mother Amanda in the 2009 reboot, surely can understand. So can Kirk, who has already lost his father and now loses his friend and mentor, Christopher Pike.

Loss. Something almost *all* of us can understand.

Nobody Does It Better

George Lucas may have seemed regressive to thinkers in the Nerd Nation, serving up warmed-over Hero's Journey with no regard for proper science, and we can say the same of Abrams; but George did take his steps beyond Gene Roddenberry, and my argument – yes, I do have one! – is that JJ has not only gone beyond Gene, but topped George.

I'll open up these final points with a note from my friend Debbie, who offered me her thoughts about TFA:

"I had a rockin' good time, and didn't notice any of the [plot] holes and don't care that I didn't," she said. "I noticed things like there were three – count 'em, three! – powerful female roles. I liked that there was an ancient female that was powerful smart and not a stereotype...

"I notice that none of the actors looked like Hollywood Beauty...

"An awful lot of them has very irregular noses, especially Han Solo's son...

"... and I like that they looked like people I see walking down the street in town. I liked the emotions, and relationships years old. Liked liked liked..."

JJ Abrams has topped both Gene and George.

In giving us *The Force Awakens*, he's taken Family to a new level: he not only builds a new family before our eyes, but he builds it from the remnants of the old. Consider that when we were children and the original movie swept us to the stars, we lived in less disheveled times. Many if not most of us have since lived through the shattering of family, be it parental divorce or our own (or both); those we love have died; those we wish we could be with are now forever beyond reach.

Put another way: we have suffered terrible loss, the theme that Abrams infused into *Trek* with *Into Darkness*.

TFA is not just an epic yet intimate story of Family, it is a story of Loss, and we in the audience suffer a gut-wrenching one in the final reel, don't we? ("A bridge! A father-son moment! HAN! *DON'T GO THERE!!!*") With this mashup of *A New Hope* and *The Empire Strikes Back*, JJ may have been remixing, but he also took everything that truly matters in both *Star Wars* and *Star Trek* and offered it up in ways that can't help but inspire both hope and longing in the children of the Star Wars generation.

But even that isn't the true value of this amazing movie...

We Are Family

My cartooning young teenager Josie is the youngest of my four children, all of whom grew up in one phase or another of *Star Wars*, and all of whom have been schooled in *Trek*.

When Josie and I sat (twice!) through *TFA* these past two weeks, here's what she saw:

- The biggest Hollywood blockbuster of all time, starring – wait for it – a woman, a black man, and a Latino;
- A protagonist who is not only a woman, but a hero transcending even *Alien*'s Ripley – a woman who musters her heroism not only against all odds, but without salvation from any man: whenever anyone goes to rescue Rey, she has already rescued herself – and through everything that happens, *she* is the film's repository of light;
- A young black man is a force for pacifism, feeling revulsion in violence;
- The voice of wisdom is neither an old man nor a ghost, but a tiny little woman;
- Despite the many young characters, youth is not a deference – there is an indifference to age that exalts the human spirit;
- Every character suffers loss – but no character loses hope.

That's a movie that we've never seen before – not just in Star Wars, but *ever*.

That's a movie beyond *Trek*, where, for all of Gene's pontifications, the goodies and the baddies were always Disney-clear. That's a movie beyond George, where even the meaningful dramatic memes, the conflicts and the losses that meant something, were disproportionately experienced by white people. Yes, the stormtroopers are still basically Orcs, and the generals are still Bond villains – but nobility and strength and heroism are no longer the exclusive province of anyone... they are available to everyone.

This is a movie I want my children to love, because it shows us an epic that demonstrates, beyond the theater and the popcorn and the Nerdsphere, that Gene's vision is within reach; that George's microwave heroes are all around us; that we not only can change, but that change is already upon us.

The human adventure truly is just beginning. And JJ Abrams, like it or not, is its herald.

Prometheus Rebound

In space, no one can hear you contemplate ...

I love my comic books as much as any fanboy, and lord knows they're all over the screen this summer, but it's Ridley Scott that I've been truly willing to stand in line for. I've been thrilled at the prospect of an *Alien* reboot ever since the series was derailed by Predators, and my chest was just bursting when I found out Scott himself was taking the helm. I haven't been this excited since Dick Clark's cameo on *Batman*.

Long story short, I'll be a long time getting over this movie, if I ever do. It took my breath away; I can feel it gestating still, a week later.

Ridley Scott's return to his dark stylistic masterpiece *Alien* (1979) is one of the more interesting entries into the most adventurous cinematic summer in years, as he brings forth his much-anticipated prequel-turned-reboot amid a flood of brightly-adorned world-savers, TV and fairy-tale retreads, revisionist history and the usual smattering of sequels. Within this anything-goes mix, Scott truly goes for it.

Spoilers imminent, across franchises

Prometheus is a starship, one of the very first, a private enterprise sponsored by an elderly trillionaire (Guy Pearce) to follow up on ancient starmaps found here and there throughout human history. Its mission is to find out who exactly these maps are pointing to, the working theory being that whoever it is created humankind.

Doctors Elizabeth Shaw (Noomi Rapace) and Charlie Holloway (Logan Marshall-Green), the originators of that theory, are joined on the mission by a number of others, including Meredith Vickers (Charlize Theron), a frosty corporate guarantor, ship's captain Janek (Idris Elba), assorted Red Shirts – and David (Michael Fassbender), an android tasked with studying Earth's most ancient languages, written and spoken, in hopes of discovering common roots that might have originated with humanity's creators.

Scott takes this bunch and drops them on a world 3.27 x 10-to-the-14th km distant, and presents them with soil-encrusted pyramids, endless tunnels reminiscent of the alien corridors in the original film, and – surprise! – people immediately begin dying, one by one. And every answer that emerges, as the horror unfolds, turns out to be utterly beyond expectation, opening up even more questions.

Sure enough, the crew of *Prometheus* has found exactly what they're looking for, and yet it isn't at all what they hoped for. It's a lot like what we saw in the first film, except that now it's much more than a stylish haunted house story, much more than survival-of-the-fittest – it's a parable that scoops up all of human history in one gigantic handful, doing so with all the wham-bam thrill of any sfx blockbuster, all the scares and screams of the best horror flicks, and all the Big Questions we got from … *hmmm* …

What was the name of that Best-Ever SF film?

Ebert loved it four stars' worth, what a surprise. He makes no secret of being as geek-fanboy comic-book-reading nerdy as the guys on *Big Bang*, but avoids the stigma by also making no secret of the fact that he opens real books on a regular basis. His *Prometheus* verdict: *"... a magnificent science-fiction film, all the more intriguing because it raises questions about the origin of human life and doesn't have the answers. It's in the classic tradition of golden-age sci-fi ..."* For all his intellectual grumpies, his erudition is unassailable: Ebert knows as well as anyone alive what truly works on the big screen, and Scott serves up all that Ebert holds dear, in big buckets. Ebert's review, which I sought out before I saw the film, was the only one I was inclined to trust.

Starting at the beginning, we're on the surface of a young world, still steaming and writhing from birth, and the images Scott gives us cause our jaws to drop, in their scope and grandeur. Only the opening of *Melancholia* last year compares, in terms of cinematic beauty. *Worthy of ... that Stanley fellow, what was his name, back in the Sixties?*

And within 10 minutes, we're introduced to Shaw and Holloway, who are globetrotting in the late 21ˢᵗ century in search of answers, the Big Answers to the Big Question – *Where did we come from?*

The same Big Question that was tackled, and left unanswered, in ... which movie was it?

Scott gives us the Ten Little Indians we came in expecting, and does so with a number of twists that extend the memorable countdown of the original film. But we're here for something new, not just a remake, and so he begins giving up information not only about what the Aliens are, but even more about that big ugly guy sitting in the big chair on the alien ship in the first film – *tons* of information, and we now can see what was going on there, what's going on here now, and – ominously – what happens next.

But we don't know *why*.

And this doesn't go down well with Shaw, who is played to perfection by Rapace as brainy, naïve, a little bit broken, and not at all the heir to Sigourney Weaver's Ripley – until she herself is violated.

Then we see that Scott, while keeping the mythology true to itself, is shooting for something more, something new. Ripley was a classic archetype, not-quite-3D but very-strongly-2D, made fresh and interesting by the bold gender bend, brilliantly realized by Weaver. Upon reflection, not hard to replicate, and we've seen those endless replications for decades now. With Shaw, we have something truly new: a woman whose tenacity and ferocity are purely intellectual, whose personal pain (as Ripley's) has been sublimated in career, but who can't get any distance from it – suddenly thrown not just into life-threatening horror, but an unendurable flurry of loss and torment that threatens her access to the answers for which she has sacrificed everything. And we see her go far beyond anything the *Alien* myth has ever given us, to answer that threat.

Between Shaw and the other character we'll never forget, Scott offers up a procession of Red Shirts – and we must say, they give us more than we got in the original film. Not just a Deathboard, building tension with steadily-jacked-up gross-out (though we do get plenty of that), but deaths that unleash deep rage, and heartbreaking self-sacrifice. Deaths that mean something.

And that brings us to the film's outstanding performance, its mind-popping centerpiece. David, the android, put forth by Michael Fassbender (Young Magneto), placed aboard *Prometheus* by its financier in hopes that he will be able to communicate with humanity's creators. As with previous androids in the mythology, David has more than one agenda, but goes much farther than the original film's Ash (can you believe Ian Holm went on to play Bilbo Baggins?) in playing on the emotions of the crew – and raises deep and foreboding philosophical questions of his own in an exchange with Holloway, as humanity's creation points out the ironies in its need to confront its own creators. While Ash was a reveal so subtle that we never got it until Scott came right out with it, his reveal of David's darkness is artfully protracted, teasing us and frightening Shaw. The brilliant exploitation of shadow and silence that we took in with our eyes in *Alien*, Scott now transfers into characterization with David, through Fassbender's deeply nuanced performance.

A machine in the image of the human mind, reflecting all of our light and darkness … where have I seen this one before?

A pattern is unfolding, and it is grabbing me by the throat …

Ridley Scott isn't attempting to top *Alien* with *Prometheus*. He isn't, in the end, even trying to top Ridley Scott.

He's trying to top Stanley Kubrick.

He's asking questions just as big, opening up humanity just as wide, digging just as deep, and doing it just as beautifully, without depriving us of all the carbs the modern movie-goer requires.

Does he succeed? I'll be a long, long time deciding, I think. But I am just blown away by the courage, the earnestness, and the sheer quality of the attempt. It's about time somebody reached this far.

Stop   thinking *Prometheus* and *Nostromo*.   Think *Prometheus* and *Discovery*.

Stop thinking Shaw and Ripley. Think Shaw and David Bowman.

Stop thinking David and Ash. Think David and HAL.

Am I wrong? Perhaps. I knew I was onto something when I went back to the Director's Commentary on *Alien*, and Scott is going on and on about … guess who?

My argument: shred me if you think you can, but only time will tell.

Another key finding: *Prometheus* doesn't end. As events culminate, What's Left of Shaw and What's Left of David form an unlikely alliance, and the story is no longer war against the aliens, or against their/own creators – but becomes confrontation: *You made us, now you want to reboot us? Why???*

Just as in … *3001: The Final Odyssey*, the last entry in Arthur C. Clarke's own mythology.

So, here I sit, having spoken to a great many of you about this breathtaking, fascinating, challenging, frustrating movie. For me, it's the big treat of the summer, with only *The Dark Knight Rises* grabbing even a comparable fraction of my interest. Some of you are saying *Near Miss!* Some of you are saying *Disappointing!* It can't be for lack of Geek Factor: Scott loaded the movie up with so many blatant tags of the original film that you can't help but feel at home.

But I would argue that there's more going on here. It's not that Scott changed his own creation, and changed it too much – it's that *we've* changed so much over the decades in between. My argument is this: just as the Alien takes on the DNA of the host it gestates within, this movie must take on the DNA of the modern movie-goer, and this has introduced changes in the myth. A haunted house won't do, we *must* have our action-adventure and our razzle-dazzle. We need a few characters as superficial as the people around us have become; we need some scathing indifference and some out-of-control self-interest and some over-the-top melodrama, because each of these is much more our day-to-day DNA than was the case in 1979 (thank you, Al Gore).

Mostly, the new DNA of Expectation serves up far more cynicism than was sitting in the crowd 33 years ago – and I would strongly point out that Scott has answered that cynicism, with a story that climaxes with a deep determination not to succumb to it. It could only be improved a little bit – and my boys and I argued this over a backyard cookout last week – by switching the order of the scene where Shaw and David depart, and the scene that gives us an actual Alien. The story would have been better ending on the more human note.

I'm sure Ridley will have his happy hordes, and his disgruntled ones, and a few haters. There's certainly a lot to jump up and down about in both directions. Who is he to tamper with perfection, even if it's his own? What is he trying to prove? And (if I'm right), trying to top Kubrick? Who does he think he is?

If he's nothing more than Elton covering the Beatles, well, you know what? I'll take that.

Ah, the art that lights our lives! It's tricky stuff, no use at all without shadow, and all light changes and eventually fades. How comforting it would be if art never changed; if a 'classic' always remained so; if art and our memories of it never shifted or grew or whispered away in our minds. There might be some comfort in the notion that our creative monuments are stone, eternal, not vulnerable to human entropy or the ravages of our changing point of view.

But … happily … that turns out not to be the case.

The Art of Creative Destruction

Unlike most old farts, I'm getting easier to impress at the movies than my peers. Mind you, I've always been an Ebert rather than a Siskel – I feel lucky to have been born into the cinematic era that I was – but as my peers grow crotchety and curmudgeonly, I am increasingly filled with childlike wonder every time I nestle into a movie chair. Or maybe it's the wine they sell at Xscape Cinema.

Either way, these spoiled millennials don't know how good they've got it. Nothing is ever good enough for them, and *Alien: Covenant* – Ridley Scott's latest contribution to the 38–year-old franchise – is a case in point: review after review derides the film for its disposable characters, its formulaic burndown, its squandering of opportunity. I'm here to argue that the film is not only a slam-dunk success, but that its emergent flaws are *due to* that success.

Covenant is a direct sequel to Scott's *Prometheus*, itself an *Alien* prequel. I don't know if "prequel sequel" is a thing, but the end result is a continuation of the *Prometheus* storyline, intended to bring us full circle to the events of *Alien*. Which this tense, terrifying, provocative story certainly does.

Prometheus was the story of dying billionaire industrialist Peter Weyland (Guy Pearce), who had a deep need to confront his creator, a desire stoked by anthropologist Elizabeth Shaw (Noomi Rapace), who shared it. Weyland sends Shaw and a team of scientists out into the darkness to a world traced in ancient cave etchings, presumed to be evidence that titanic humanoids from the stars – the "Engineers" – in fact created humanity. Along for the ride is a token android (isn't there always?) – David, played perfectly by Michael Fassbender – created by Pearce as a kind of son he never had.

The starship Prometheus finds the Engineers on a desolate way station of a world out in the middle of nowhere; chaos ensues; and we get a key piece of the *Alien* mythology from their story: the hideous xenomorphs that serve as the titular linchpin of the series are in fact bioweapons, created by the Engineers. They are not just creators of species, they are also destroyers – and per David's research on a hangered Engineer starship (the horseshoe kind), they were headed back to Earth to scrap their humankind experiment when an accident with their own xenomorphs destroyed the way station. Only Shaw and David survive, and they set out to find the homeworld of the Engineers, armed with this information.

Flash-forward a decade, to the colony ship *Covenant*, en route to a fresh, unspoiled world awaiting the 2,000 sleeping colonists it carries. A David descendant, Walter (also played by Fassbender), tends the sleepers during the long voyage, until a flair from a nearby star wreaks havoc, causing terrible damage and awakening the small crew. When a stray signal of obvious human origin (John Denver's "Country Roads") is detected, the captain (Billy Crudup) makes the decision to divert Covenant.

It's at this point that they meet up with David on the planet he and Shaw were heading for at the end of the previous film. Shaw is long dead; David looks as much like Tom Hanks in *Castaway* as an android possibly could; and there are no Engineers left. Except for David, the planet is desolate. At first.

Chaos ensues – this is an *Alien* film, after all – and one by one, Covenant crew die as xenomorphs emerge. This time, however, the story swirls not around the usual Ten Little Indians plot, but around David – who has grown increasingly sinister – and his relationship with his less sophisticated doppelgänger.

The film's Kubrick-worthy prelude shows David in a beautiful, Heaven-like room with a middle-aged Weyland, presumably not long after his creation – a spacious white sanctuary, filled with artifacts of human aesthetic genius. Weyland, the creator, infuses his notions of the importance and beauty of creation within David – and underscores how important it is to discover and know one's creator. David ironically takes this imperative in and judges his own creator inferior – and sets himself on a parallel path with the Engineers he will someday meet.

Then, mid-film, David takes his lesser brother Walter aside and repeats these readings, teaching him to play the flute along the way. We are tempted to recall Data and Lore from *Star Trek: The Next Generation* – the evil twin toying with the purer every droid who speaks for the audience. If we take this transmission of the creative impulse in the metaphorical terms of the story, it is a kind of infection – of a piece with the emerging theme of the film (and the series): creative destruction.

We'll leave the story there, to avoid spoilers. Scott's great success here is the presentation of that theme, and the skillful way he has tied it to the other serious entries in the franchise. In the film's final reel, he hits all the familiar notes of the original, which we now see in a new light: every face-hug, every chest-burst now reflects this growing cloud of creative destruction (the very premise of the creature – that the xenomorph exploits the DNA of its host to create something new, even as the host is killed – enshrines the theme). The randomness of death that swept the crew of the Nostromo and the colonists of LV-426 away now has a kind of sick meaning, one that the increasingly demented David, in the fashion of Welles' Dr. Moreau, intends writ large on the ashes of his inferior creators.

This is true horror, an order of magnitude more powerful than the haunted house original could produce, and more brilliantly presented: David is the monstrosity of the inhuman Weyland-Yutani corporation intensified, the craven self-interest of *Aliens* villain Carter Burke jacked up by orders of magnitude – a diseased culmination of the Engineers' own soulless craftwork. He's a monster on a par with HAL-9000, pure of purpose and coldly calculating, and, like the xenomorphs themselves, untainted by delusions of morality.

Fassbender's performance of David across the two films is masterful. He has a knack for portraying megalomaniacal narcissists (Steve Jobs, Magneto) and can convey cold horror with the slightest smile. (There is an irony to this artistic pedigree – all of these characters are abandoned orphans, forced into creative destruction of worlds that would not accommodate them as they were. Steve Jobs obliterated entire industries to create new ones; Magneto's manifesto was to replace humanity with mutants. Was Fassbender born to this or what?) The sheer power he radiates on screen makes *Covenant* his film, without question – and for the better.

A few of the other characters manage to keep up. While Shaw ends up a missed-opportunity throwaway (as Newt and Hicks were in *Alien 3*), Daniels (Katherine Waterston) plays an interesting Ripley variation, and pilot Tennessee (Danny McBride) is very watchable. Crudup is convincing in a thankless role, an exploitable crucible of human weakness and thereby a credible sacrificial lamb, when it comes time to come full circle to the original film's roots.

But the takeaway, after the breathless sequence of surprise endings and their sequel-pinging revelations, is that the *Alien* series now has true continuity, a meaningful and compelling thread weaving through every entry, even the lesser ones. Creative destruction is an increasingly edgy theme in sci-fi, both serious and popcorn: we find it in *Star Trek*'s Q; the cataclysms of both *Planet of the Apes* series; the malevolence of HAL; all of the *I Am Legend* variations; the march of the Death Star; even the android remnants in Spielberg's hapless *A.I.* Sweeping humanity away for the something new that wants its chair is an existential theme if ever there was one, and as reality shoves us closer and closer to that brink, it is not unfitting that our best artists dwell upon it.

Heavy stuff for a monster movie. Heavy stuff for *any* movie. But it's the kind of emotional and intellectual heft we need to justify art that stretches across 40 years.

Ever Going, Boldly

Star Trek is returning to the small screen, after an 11-year absence and slightly more than 50 years since the original debuted on NBC.

Probably the biggest franchise in entertainment history at this point – with 13 motion pictures, six TV series, more than 600 books, endless comics and video games piled up at this point – *Star Trek* will receive yet another fresh start, as CBS brings it back to television in January 2017.

We're told that the new adventures will be set in a future beyond what we've seen already, and will feature new characters, rather than familiar faces. We're told these stories will take place beyond the frontiers of the familiar Federation. More than that, we do not know.

But we do know who's minding the helm this time around. And two names leap out at us, names from the past.

Names that clash, ideologically.

Rod Roddenberry, son of the late Gene Roddenberry – creator of the original *Star Trek* – will be an executive producer, alongside Star Trek veteran Alex Kurtzman.

And Nicholas Meyer, director of the original cast films "The Wrath of Khan" and "The Undiscovered Country" (and co-writer of "The Voyage Home"), is joining the writing staff and taking on a consulting producer's role.

Now we have a ball game…

"Our Heroes Are Perfect…"

A cornerstone of Roddenberry Sr.'s philosophy, upon which the very humanist original series was based, was that in the 23rd century humankind will have outgrown our pettiness, our greed and our bigotry, and formed a truly united world where growth and cooperation and accomplishment propelled Homo sapiens to the stars.

This philosophy was evident from the first episode, broadcast in September of 1966, when we saw a starship crew featuring humans of all colors and genders – white, black, Asian… men and women alike in positions of authority – all working together seamlessly. Yes, the lead was a powerful young white male – and, yes, one of the two female characters was a traditional caregiver – but this combination was nonetheless unprecedented in entertainment history.

And they all got along famously! True to his ideals, Roddenberry worked overtime to spread a philosophy of universal human cooperation. He failed again and again, as did his writers, with episodes that indicted his beloved "Federation" as a source of political condescension, and most of his ethnically splendid cast never rose above the level of serf, in actual stories – but the concept shone through clearly. This 23rd century was a place without poverty, without class warfare, without social dominance. It was a place we wanted to be – and still long for.

"In our century, we've each learned to take delight in who we are," Captain Kirk tells an alien parading as Abraham Lincoln, in 'The Savage Curtain.'

"The challenge," says *Next Generation*'s Captain Picard to a 20th century straggler in 'The Neutral Zone,' "is to improve yourself... to enrich yourself!"

Bold, brilliant words – inspiring words! Yet, time and again, the characters in every series give in to their human failings, and the representatives of the Federation as a whole find themselves making the galaxy safe for democracy, over and over again. Alien species, mostly humanoid, are glaring stand-ins for the Others we despised in the Cold War and beyond – Klingons as Russians, Romulans as Chinese, and so on, and so on.

And Roddenberry's personal hypocrisies are now legend: touting feminist equality on paper, his own personal rage against the women in his life manifested in a weakening of female roles that his successor, Rick Berman, overtly stepped in to correct, in creating a female lead in *Voyager*. Roddenberry's defense – that his original first officer, "Number One" in the first *Star Trek* pilot was a woman, rang hollow: the actress was his mistress (Majel Barrett), looking for a breakout role.

It's television. It's the movies. It's not contemporary philosophy. So the hypocrisies, grating though they might be, are easily set aside for the greater vision: that humanity will emerge from our cocoon a united, mature species, done with our infantile tantrums, ready to bring our splendid gifts into a waiting universe, benign and constructive and thirsting for exploration and growth.

Starfleet's motto: "Ex astris, scientia" – From the stars, knowledge...

The Son Becomes the Father, and the Father, the Son...

Sorry, wrong franchise.

Gene Roddenberry's heir, Eugene "Rod" Roddenberry, arrived on earth nearly a decade after the end of the original series and just before the first motion picture (mistress-turned-wife Majel Barrett was his mother). During his childhood, Rod watched as his father became irrelevant, pushed aside after the dramatic debacle of 'Star Trek: The Motion Picture,' relegated to "Creative Consultant" for subsequent movies as studio picks Harve Bennett and Nicholas Meyer took over the franchise, dismantling the Roddenberry utopia for a more straightforward, action-oriented *Star Trek*.

And on the edge of adolescence, young Rod watched his father ascend again to power, reviving Trek on television with *The Next Generation*, where his Utopian fantasy found new life with Captain Jean-Luc Picard, Riker, Data, and a new batch of ethnically blended favorites. It didn't last – Roddenberry's failing health pulled him away from his new creation before he could smother it – but the humanistic theme of a humanity cured of vice rang out once again.

Star Trek rolled on a full 14 unbroken years on television after Roddenberry's death, as his son grew to manhood and a new movie franchise – to be steered in the direction of straightforward action-adventure by Spielberg protege J.J. Abrams – loomed. During these years, the younger Roddenberry – seeking both his own identity and a coming-to-terms with his family destiny – created *Trek Nation* (2011), a savvy and competent documentary that thoughtfully captured the *Star Trek* legacy in a way previous documentaries had not.

"Second Star to the Right…"

Perhaps lovingly mocking Roddenberry's fantasyland ideals, Nicholas Meyer – a juggernaut in the *Trek* universe after he saved the franchise from Roddenberry's overbearing touch with the lighter, more accessible and exciting *Wrath of Khan* (1982) -ended his tour of duty with this line from Peter Pan at the end of *The Undiscovered Country* (1991), an effective and loving Cold War parable that bid the original cast farewell. No fan of Roddenberry's ideology, Meyer's contribution to the franchise bristled with the stuff of Shakespeare, portraying a human condition not unlike the one we know, where human beings are bigoted, petty, selfish, violent and impudent.

"Roddenberry really believed in the perfectibility of man, of humans, and I have yet to see the evidence for this," Meyer told the LA Times. "In fact, in his original *Star Trek* concept, there wasn't any conflict. So he always had problems with writers who were trying to write conflict, because that's what drama is."

His point is a strong one, and his contributions are acknowledged as the best in big-screen *Trek* history. Roddenberry acolyte he certainly was not, but his more contemporary take on the beloved crew of the Enterprise delighted fans by the millions, nonetheless. And the J.J. Abrams films – the most successful in *Trek* history – bear him out.

Best of Both Worlds, Part I

And now we have a new TV *Trek* launching in 10 months. The executive producer is the Keeper of Gene's Vision, his own son. The most gifted (and *Trek*-famous) member of the writing staff is an outspoken Roddenberry dissenter.

What could possibly go wrong?

It is probably Kurtzman's call, but we are faced with the question of whether these two competing visions of Trek's human future can be reconciled in a form pleasing to the vast *Trek* nation that persists in this 50th anniversary year. Will Rod Roddenberry preserve his father's vision of a perfected humanity? Will Nick Meyer dismantle it once again?

The odds are in Meyer's favor, because this is television, after all, and television is commerce. We've seen over the past six years that action-adventure *Trek* is the *Trek* the masses want.

But that doesn't mean Nick Meyer is right.

A Thermodynamic History of Humankind

The more we learn about the human past, the more we study the things we left behind, the bodies of our ancestors, the genome now unfolded – the more we see that Roddenberry's Utopia has already existed.

With the overturning of 'Killer Ape Theory' in the 1990s... with analysis of mitochondrial DNA now well underway... with the increasing data amassed from sites of human settlement from throughout the Paleolithic era, it is increasingly clear that Homo sapiens is not innately a violent, competitive, self-centered species, but hosts a core of staggeringly effective cooperation, empathy, and mutual support.

Ancient humans were far more cooperative than modern humans, the evidence reads, and it was the female, not the male, who led the way – ensuring genetic diversity, introducing sexual sophistication, inventing pottery and rope and probably language – pages right out of Roddenberry's playbook (even if he didn't live up to it himself). We mastered a difficult earth, out-surviving those creatures that preyed upon us, using only the energy on the ground on any given day – whatever fell from the sky – to survive.

We lived in starship crew-sized groups, a few dozens of dozens on any given terrain, mastering the teamwork that took down massive sources of meat and harnessing the power of fire to keep large cats at bay as we slept. Our sexuality in those thousands of generations was beyond any of Roddenberry's adolescent fantasies – and wildly effective in generating a species that could survive in any climate.

The humanistic, ultra-socialist Federation isn't in our future. It's in our past.

What went wrong?

An ice age paused, and we learned to harness energy for tomorrow. And, in doing so, created the concept of property. And human beings themselves rapidly became consumable energy and objects of property.

Certain men began to dominate other men. Women, once the wisest and most creative of humans, became possessions. The storage and ownership of energy, in the form of cultivated crops and imprisoned meat, became our priority.

And all that is horrible about humankind – all that Shakespeare documents, all that Nick Meyer milks for dramatic effect, all the pettiness and greed and violence and deceit that clarify the modern human – was born.

But that's not all there is to it.

In Roddenberry's future, the human universe includes an energy-rich economy – a recreation of our Paleolithic origins, when the energy of the day was all that we needed to thrive. There is enough for everyone; no one person or group can hoard, there is no opportunity to generate false inequalities.

This is what Nick Meyer is missing. He sees a petty and violent humankind persisting, as the centuries unfold – but the impetus for those failings is the back-and-forth tussle over energy (what is money, but energy coupons?), and Roddenberry's vision is a human environment where those struggles are ended.

Are we still petty and selfish and deceitful and violent in a future where every sentient being is given the energy needed to thrive, without having to struggle for it, without having to wrestle Right-Wing naysayers for the right to co-exist?

It's a fascinating scenario, and one that puts the challenge to Nick Meyer: how to generate real human drama from a universe where the threats we face are not to our lives, but to our need to discover?

A Klingon answers. Worf, of *Next Generation* fame, member of 24th century Starfleet, child of a warrior race, faces his own descendants in the *Deep Space Nine* episode "Children of Time."

"Our enemy," he tells them, "is time." They must struggle not against others, not in battle, but in a race to save life. It is the battle not for dominance or supremacy or this group over that, but the quest to survive and thrive in an indifferent universe.

This is not only a worthy quest, but a much more poignant backdrop than the senior Roddenberry's Sixties canvas of race struggles and the Dehumanizing Machine and Vietnam: this is the real stuff of human survival, where Shakespearean drama might entertain (as our current political environment underscores), but serves in the end as a possibly fatal distraction.

Our real enemy is time. Our species is at risk. And we have capable visionaries poised to comment on that, in that language we love best, when we need it most.

They have only to get to work, cooperate, collaborate, and boldly go...

Ape Shall Not Kill Ape!

One of the most welcome sci-fi reboots of recent years has been the new Planet of the Apes series, a completely fresh take on a cherished legacy.

There have, at this writing, been three new films to the five in the original series, with more to come. And it's interesting to see how the new films line up with the old ones.

To begin with, the new films are not complete reboots; they borrow generously from the original canon, not only with substantial homage, quote, and Easter eggs, but in preserving the entire shape of the saga. The biggest difference? They simply started in a different place.

The original series

Here's the progression of the original films:

Planet of the Apes (1968). A small team of astronauts leave Earth and sleep away an interstellar mission, only to crash-land on a planet where apes have a civilization and human beings are mute, timid beasts. Mission commander Taylor finds himself captive to these apes, but befriends the intellectual chimpanzees Cornelius and Zira, acquiring a human mate (whom he names "Nova") along the way. In the end, Taylor experiences that powerful moment in which he sees the half-sunken Statue of Liberty and realizes he's been back home, all along – and that the humans surrounding him are our descendants.

Beneath the Planet of the Apes (1970). A rescue mission from the distant arrives on Taylor's Earth, with astronaut Brent surviving its crash to find himself following in Taylor's path. He meets Nova, then Cornelius and Zira, finally finding himself in the subterranean remains of New York City, where Taylor is being held captive by a sophisticated coven of telepathic human mutants – who worship a nuclear superbomb. In the final moments of the film, and ape invasion of the underground mutant stronghold, Brent and Taylor are killed, and the bomb is detonated – destroying the Earth.

Escape from the Planet of the Apes (1971). Cornelius, Zira, and a colleague find themselves on Earth in the past, back in Taylor's original time, having recovered and reactivated his ship – and suddenly everything is turned upside down, as the human civilization in charge tries to make sense of intelligent apes from the future. Panic ensues, of course, as the chimpanzee couple are treated with suspicion and ultimately considered a danger; and they are on the run, then killed, just after Zira gives birth – though the baby survives.

Conquest of the Planet of the Apes (1972). Named Caesar, the intelligent chimpanzee born of Zira grows up in hiding, protected by a kindly circus owner. Upon achieving adulthood, he finds himself in a world where a virus has wiped out all domesticated pets, and apes have replaced them – only to be subjugated, when they turn out to be convenient slaves. Appalled, Caesar leads an ape uprising, and helps his kindred find their voice.

Battle for the Planet of the Apes (1973). Years later, civilization has fractured after a global nuclear war, and Caesar works to broker peace between bands of surviving humans and the growing communities of increasingly intelligent apes. Opposed by the warmongering Aldo, Caesar also contends with a colony of radiation-damaged humans in the remains of New York, where records of his parents survive. Aldo ultimately stages a coup, falls to his death in confrontation with Caesar – and the film ends with an uneasy truce between apes and humans, and the renewal of the most sacred law: "Ape Shall Never Kill Ape."

And with that, the original series ends.

A new take on old tales

The new series begins in the middle. No Taylor, no spaceship – just a scientist working on an anti-dementia drug, testing it out on apes. And Caesar, born of a chimpanzee test subject, is born, with the intelligence of a human. An ape rebellion follows, a cataclysm wipes out most of humanity, and battle for supremacy on Earth ensues.

The new films, then, line up as follows:

Rise of the Planet of the Apes (2011) = The ending of *Escape* + much of *Conquest*

Dawn of the Planet of the Apes (2014) = The remainder of *Conquest* + much of *Battle*

War for the Planet of the Apes (2017) = The remainder of *Battle*

Rise included Caesar's birth and his mother's death, as well as his acclimation to the human-ape reality by a human caregiver; it also included Caesar's rallying of his own kind into rebellion.

Dawn included Caesar's consolidation of authority; it also included the catastrophe that wiped out most of human and the beginning of conflict between human and ape tribes; ape kills ape.

War included factionalization between apes and the beginnings of human mutation (though in this case, the mutation is not in the service of telepathy, but the explanation for the human loss of speech).

This heavy reliance on the original storylines is by design, of course; but it is in the details – some of them very subtle! - that the new films acknowledge their debt to the old ones.

Easter apes

The new ape films don't simply give an occasional nod to the earlier ones – they arebursting with references, homage, and Easter eggs. The list is long...

Bright Eyes

In the original *Planet of the Apes*, "Bright Eyes" is Zira's initial nickname for Taylor; in *Rise*, it's the nickname given to Caesar's mother by the scientists at GenSys.

Cornelia/Cornelius

In the first three films of the original series, Cornelius is the chimpanzee scientist who befriends Taylor and Brent, then travels back to Earth of the early 1970s, where his son Caesar is born. In the new films, Cornelia is the name of Caesar's – and their son is named Cornelius in *War*.

Nova

In the original movie, Nova is the name Taylor gives to the native human female he takes as mate. In *War*, Nova is a mute orphan girl befriended by Maurice, her name taken from an old Chevy.

Will Rodman

The name of James Franco's character in *Rise* is a nod to Rod Serling of *Twilight Zone* fame, who wrote the screenplay for the original film.

Maurice

Similarly, the orangutan Maurice in the new film series is named for Maurice Evans, the actor who portrayed Dr. Zaius in the original.

Alpha/Omega

In *Beneath the Planet of the Apes*, the Alpha/Omega is a nuclear superbomb worshipped by the mutants who live below New York City; in *War*, it's the name of the military splinter faction commanded by The Colonel.

"Take your stinking paws off me, you damn dirty ape!"

Taylor snarls this line when he recovers his voice, just at the moment he's recaptured in the original film; the abusive guard in the ape sanctuary yells the line in *Rise* when Caesar confronts him.

"It's a madhouse!"

In the original film, Taylor shouts this line when being firehosed by a gorilla guard in the veterinary infirmary; in *Rise*, it's the abusive guard again, shouting the line during the ape rebellion at the sanctuary where Caesar has been taken.

Dodge Landon

The abusive guard in the ape sanctuary in *Rise* is named Dodge Landon – an amalgam of astronauts Dodge and Landon, Taylor's crewmates in the original film.

"No!"

Lisa, an ape following the original Caesar in *Conquest*, becomes the first 20ᵗʰ century ape to speak when she utters this word. It is also Caesar's first word in *Rise*.

Apes on horseback

It's one of the first images we see in the original Planet; it's one of the most poignant in *Rise*, when Caesar takes a horse from a mounted policeman and leads the apes' charge.

The Statue of Liberty

It's the shock ending of *Planet*; and it's a subtle homage in *Rise*, when the young Caesar is playing with a toy Statue of Liberty at the moment when Will's father is attacked by a neighbor.

Charlton Heston

In the original series, he's, well, Taylor; in *Rise*, he makes a fleeting appearance on a TV screen in the ape sanctuary.

Where do we go from here?

The new series is now at the end of the original canon's storyline – a planet where humanity is on the decline and ape civilization is poised to ascend to dominance. We've gone full circle.

What we lack in the new series is the moment when men from the present arrive in the ape future – the starting point of the whole franchise.

How can that occur? We've already had a tease: there's a moment in *Rise* when we see a news report, in the background, of a Mars mission – *Icarus* - that is now "missing." Why? What happened to it?

Could the commander of the *Icarus* mission be named Taylor? And might it have encountered some phenomenon that pushed it years into the future?

Will the return of the *Icarus* mission become the updated version of the very first film? Will it crash-land on a planet of apes?

Fanboy
Reviews

Classic Kamandi

The nostalgia that accompanies a re-reading of classic Kamandi – the first 40 issues of Jack Kirby's early-Seventies post-apocalyptic boy's story – doesn't really have another name, but 'nostalgia' isn't quite the right word.

There's a burst of boyish excitement (which was the entire point), the rush of edge-of-the-seat peril and cliffhanger anxiety that mirrors the now-distant memory of early teen angst. And there's that warm familiarity, like an old friend encountered at the bookstore or the late-night treat of browsing into "Forbidden Planet" on cable TV. Instant gratification, awash in memories of simpler times.

Of course, times were never simple for Kamandi. From his emergence from the Command D bunker[97] into a nightmarish landscape of decrepit human remnants and talking animals at war, his life was one damn thing after another, struggling to find a place for himself in a world gone insane.

As a 13-year-old boy, I could relate, being short, oh-so-blond and hairless of chest. I could *easily* relate to Kamandi; and today I sit in a bunker of my own as a for-real Great Disaster unfolds, wondering just how insane the world will have become when I emerge. I'm relating to Kamandi once again, and the feeling that evokes is more than nostalgia.

There's some deep appreciation there in the mix, peppered with a little cultural genuflect, all for Kirby. He didn't just *create* Kamandi, he *revealed* him; it's like the character was there all along, pulsating within those comic-loving, early-Seventies kids (like me) who loved reading of heroes but longed even more to *be* one. All Kirby did was sit down at his drawing board and open the door for him - a teenage hero with no costume (barely any clothes at all!), no powers, no tools, no destiny – shaping him into that strong, courageous, resourceful young man we were all determined to become.

He gave Kamandi the square jaw and muscles we didn't have, the karate training we pretended to, the wits under pressure that superpowers can never replace. Boys' adventure or no, he didn't spare the horror and desolation in his rendering of a world collapsing; and time and again, he placed difficult and profound choices in Kamandi's path – stepping stones to character for a young man searching out his identity... a roadmap we

---

[97] Remember OMAC, back in the Comics chapter? He was Kamandi's grandfather, and raised him in that bunker.

could actually use, a guide to growing up strong and decent in a frightening world.

The cultural genuflect made its mark, giving us easy access to Kamandi's world with the Planet of the Apes touchstones – talking apes, ragged humans, the worship of a warhead - which to the uninvested may come across as a little me-too for Kirby, but which lifted us into Kamandi's complexities and straight into the action without the need for expository preamble. PotA was a batch of themes undercooked, we sort of already knew, too convenient to ever be profound; the world beyond PotA that Kirby imagined was far more challenging, a far greater crucible of spirit and rectitude.

The well-intentioned Kamandi Challenge aside, there's no "old" or "new" in play with this wonderful kid, no sentimentality or wistful yearning; there is only the comfort of a constant presence across the years, an embedded fraternity that transcends our affection for other heroes. They come and go, they reboot endlessly; but Kamandi? he never left. He's been here all along.

Pay No Attention
to the Man Behind the Curtain!

S Robinson, Scientific Barbarian #2

For tens of millions the world over, the passing of Sean Connery is no small sorrow. The Scottish screen icon's singular voice narrated three nerd generations, animating some of the most beloved cinematic documents of the past half century, garnering unparalleled affection and admiration. We all have our favorite Connery moment: for many, it was his purloining of the *Red October* as Marko Ramius; for others, his romancing of Audrey Hepburn as an aging Robin Hood; for still others, it might be his turn as John Mason, once of Alcatraz, in *The Rock*.

And for the seething masses, it's the tweedy Professor Henry Jones, father of Indiana, or the supernaturally elegant superspy James Bond, both of whom we can safely consider immortal.

But not me. Nope! Not this boy. For me, the departed Connery's finest moment arrived in 1974, in a breathtakingly bold and quirky little sci-fi adventure called *Zardoz*.

If you've never seen *Zardoz*, you're part of an overwhelming majority; if you've never even *heard* of *Zardoz*, you're in a greater majority still. The film barely made back its budget, which was paltry to begin with, and was no critic's darling: Roger Ebert called it "a trip into a future that seems ruled by perpetually stoned set decorators"; his pal Gene Siskel (who gave it one star in four) wrote, "a message movie all right, and the message is that social commentary in the cinema is best restrained inside of a carefully-crafted story, not trumpeted with character labels, special effects, and a dose of despair that celebrates the director's humanity while chastising the profligacy of the audience." Pauline Kael bemoaned the script's "unspeakable dialog" and called Connery "a man who agreed to do something before he grasped what it was."

Yet for all this, *Zardoz* stands alongside *The Omega Man*, *Logan's Run*, *Silent Running* and the *Apes* sequels as one of the shining gems of the pre-*Star Wars* sci-fi cinema of the Seventies. It was a bold era, when no less an artisan than Stanley Kubrick had made science fiction both cool and mind-blowing, and the imaginations of filmmakers were allowed to run wild and free, unconstrained by studio meddling or any real financial risk. Even today, those movies inspire a unique endearment, absent in the ham-fisted monster fests that preceded them and the digital orgies that followed, an endearment born of fresh takes on ancient notions, daring social explications, and shocking characters who shamelessly pandered to our most base and limbic reflexes. *Zardoz* proudly served up all three.

A bit of context here, for those unfamiliar: *Zardoz* was the brainchild of John Boorman, the British filmmaker who made *Deliverance*, cinema's most disturbing buddy movie, the visually stunning *Excalibur*, and the British World War II gem *Hope and Glory*. After the landmark *Deliverance*, which earned 25 times its budget at the box office, Boorman had carte blanche – and decided to leverage his newfound cred to make *The Lord of the Rings*. Studio accountants were quick to quash that idea, but Boorman was nonetheless determined to do an elaborate fantasy – so he wrote one himself, then proceeded to produce and direct it.

Pay no attention to the man behind the curtain

It's the year 2293, and in an emphatic nod to H.G. Welles, humanity is divided into haves and have-nots – the Brutals, who populate a post-Apocalyptic wasteland, and the Eternals, who enjoy immortality in the posh Vortex. The Brutal population is controlled by Exterminators, precursors of the Sandmen of *Logan's Run*, whose job it is to collect food from the poor sods and terrorize them with hand-me-down weapons provided by Zardoz, who gives them their marching orders. Zardoz, a disembodied bobblehead that floats around in cloudy skies issuing booming orders and ominous, cultish incantations, is really just a façade for the melodramatic and well-meaning Arthur Frayn, a brilliant everynerd whose real agenda surfaces later in the film.

Connery is Zed, an Exterminator who stows away inside Zardoz and enters the Vortex, there to discover the Immortals and their decadent, pointless paradise, where not much happens and nothing really matters (in a borrow from the *Trek* shelf, an AI named Tabernacle runs the place, and we know how well that always turns out). Discovered, Zed is at first considered a threat by the psychic Immortal Consuella (Charlotte Rampling), but May (Sara Kestelman) and Friend (John Alderton) have Zed spared and made a menial worker.

That the Vortex is breathtakingly sterile, the pinnacle of human inconsequentiality, becomes apparent to Zed, whose mind serves up puzzles for Consuella and May as they probe it and whose genes serve up still more surprises when analyzed: Zed is actually Arthur Frayn's idea of a *kwisatz haderach*, a genetic superman Frayn long planned to send into the Vortex to relieve the inhabitants of their eternal curse – boredom, to be dispelled by means of death. This Zed serves up, having a showdown with the AI and then rallying his fellow Exterminators to the cause, and carnage ensues. Zed knocks up May and a few of her besties, and the film signs off with Zed and Consuella shacking up and having a baby, there to live long and decompose.

Impossibly ambitious and pretentious

The story is a delicious stew of familiar sci-fi themes, conventions, and tropes, spiced heavily with shockingly over-the-line sex and violence and more than a little sociopathic kink. Most critics thumbed down, but more than a few found much to love: the *Chicago Reader* declared it "John Boorman's most underrated film – an impossibly ambitious and pretentious but also highly inventive, provocative, and visually striking SF adventure with metaphysical trimmings," while *Variety* delivered the verdict, "direction, good; script, a brilliant premise which unfortunately washes out in climactic sound and fury; and production, outstanding, particularly special visual effects which are among the best in recent years and belie the film's modest cost." Charles Champlin called the film "a tribute to creative ingenuity and personal dedication. It is a film which buffs and would-be filmmakers are likely to be examining with interest for years to come." In this, he was spot-on.

Indeed, *Zardoz* was, for its time, exemplary filmcraft, marshalling not only its creator's considerable powers but those of the venerable Geoffrey Unsworth (*2001, Superman*) behind the camera. Beethoven's 7th is sprinkled liberally throughout the proceedings, and David Munroe's original score eschews cliché by including an array of old-world instruments. Add to this special effects that were, for their time, arresting, and *Zardoz* sums up as a compelling piece of work, one that Champlin called "a technically ingenious and provocative manifestation of cinematic language."

Stunting the growth of adolescent minds

If there's one aspect of *Zardoz* that causes it to stand apart from its early-Seventies siblings, it's its broad range of themes. This wasn't particularly common back then; most of these movies had a single moving part and worked well for it. *Silent Running* was the fragility of life; *Soylent Green* was overpopulation. *The Andromeda Strain* was humanity's helplessness before the dangers of the void. *WestWorld* is the modern Frankenstein. Only *A Clockwork Orange* stands out as multi-themed, riding disturbing social satire through a moral landscape that challenges free will, validates vengeance and authenticates psychology as a weapon of the state.

Zardoz reaches further still, and manages to go as too-far as Kubrick. Zed, firmly positioned as the story's good guy and hero, pretty much pillages and rapes his way through both landscapes – and this is something we had never seen before. It's unsettling enough to watch Sean Connery parading in a bright red oversized thong, sporting chest hair and a 'stache worthy of Harry Reems, killing and fucking everything that moves; what's really tough is realizing, then accepting, that the man who brought 007 to life never rises above the level of a prop in service of this pastiche of dark motifs and theses. Granted, Bond himself was the quintessence of moral ambiguity, and racked up considerable body counts himself; but no Bond movie ever stared us down with an actual moral dilemma, let alone existential puzzles, and Bond's copious matings were mercifully consensual. *Zardoz* hijacked the brain, mindswarming its ideas like murder hornets, and rendered its star a misplaced narrative minion in order to achieve it.

Which brings me to my point (and I do have one) - the effects of all this intellectual legerdemain on the minds of the tens of thousands of 14-year-old boys who formed the core congregation for this entire genre (of whom I was, of course, one of the most faithful). True, I was a bit older than that when I first caught the movie on late-night television, but was I, were any of us, possessed of enough knowledge, experience, and literary acumen to fully process any of these themes, let alone all of them? Really?

It's one thing to be presented with Sara Kestelman's quite noteworthy breasts without a smidgen of warning and find ourselves saying, Jenny who? It's another to see Darby O'Gill putting babies into women tangled in fishing nets without their permission and understand that, in context, he's actually doing them a favor. The adolescent male brain takes in the sight of naked women sealed in baggies and can't leap to the required understanding of the exigencies of class struggle taken to alarming extremes with quite the nimble dexterity Boorman seems to assume.

We can even say, with the assurance of hindsight, that were the movie not such a relentless action feast and visual smorgasbord, that core congregant with his acne and his social ineptitude and his tenuous grasp of situational ethics might actually absorb some of the true substance of the tale, and wind up... well, a little scarred.

Some of that substance is benign enough, to be sure; the overarching theme of *Humankind's Connection to Nature*, lifted with all its glorious nuance from *Deliverance*, does the mind of the young teenage boy no harm; the less subtle theme, *Penis Bad!* (also lifted, with far less nuance, from *Deliverance*), is another matter entirely. This from a movie underscoring somewhat forcefully the brutal truth that whatever else sex is, it's mostly about making babies. Thank you, John; that's definitely where young minds want to go.

Less benign is the no-less-immediate theme of *Humankind's Connection to the Machine*, again a *Trek* nod that also extends to much of the sci-fi of the day - the Computer That Runs the World. No kid grows up in the early Seventies without knowing this one backwards and forwards, but never before (nor even with the Skynet and the Matrix and the *Alien* Mother yet to come) had we seen an AI as morally twisted as this one, implementing make-work laws and attaching the horrific penalties of aging and death on transgressors, just to give itself something to do? What was I supposed to do with that? This is narcissism on a gargantuan scale, portending not just the perils of power in the wrong hands, but a chillingly inhuman snapshot of cruelty's rock bottom, served up for youngsters who have yet to grapple with the reality and lessons of the Holocaust. Again, John – thanks for that!

But the big theme is, of course, Immortality – again, a familiar path offered up with a fresh layer of gravel. We'd picked up on the unfortunate truth that immortality consists largely of boredom from many sources, from TV to Heinlein to comic books; but where those sources had all tended to emphasize that the solution is to give life new meaning, *Zardoz* did a 180 – the problem admits of no solution, and the obvious answer is not to enhance life, but to end it. This horrific conclusion kicked off our existential dread years ahead of schedule, undermining our inevitable future quests for meaning with the back-of-the-mind shadow that whispers, *It's all ultimately pointless...* Grazie, John Boorman. We could have waited a whole 'nother six years for Nietzsche to tell us that.

Off to see a wizard

Yet for all this quibble, Zardoz does serve up a bit of wonder that is tailor-made for that young teen in the crowd – the revelation, embedded in Zed's memories, of the books Arthur Frayn provided that equipped him for his eventual mission. And the *Wizard of Oz* in particular, from which Frayn took his god moniker, and from which he lifted the entire Man Behind the Curtain concept that allowed him to orchestrate the end of the Vortex, with Connery's Zed as his testosterone-ridden Dorothy.

There's some honest-to-goodness magic in that, and the wide-eyed, pimply-faced teen is primed for it. It's a deployment of that truly special *analogia* that lives within us from our earliest childhood readings, the ensorceling connections that books and stories and fairy tales serve up to equip us for the buffeting winds and rolling thunder of maturity. That Arthur Frayn nurtures his murderous creation with such readings, building his entire humanity-saving scheme around this profound and very relatable attribute, is the stuff of true prestidigitation - and it's in the mind of the star-gazing, future-glimpsing nerd boy that it most readily thrives. I should know!

Decades exist between my most recent reading of *Zardoz* and the one before, though it sits on my DVD shelf with all the other Seventies popcorn. I find my perception of it has morphed greatly in that interregnum; I wouldn't have written what's above in my 20s. But while my perception has shifted, my enjoyment of the film has not. I think it's goofy, glorious, chilling, provocative, and overcooked. Just horrible. And just marvelous. And that's what I think every single time I see it.

One final thought escapes me. With its AI-as-ruler and floating-head-as-deity and rulings on the nature of life and deep emphasis on the importance of baby-making, it now seems to me a terribly humanist film, for all its violence and deprecation: it's saying to me, pretty clearly and loudly, that We Are God. And, as such, we have certain responsibilities – making babies, of course, but also preserving meaning in our existence, and making that existence about something more than the elitist voyeurism that keeps the Immortals from drifting away altogether. Something more than this thing we do in our own Vortex, the one we carry in our pockets and keep open in our web browsers. Well, that's a message I can get behind. Yes. We Are God. And as such, we're about preserving all those things that give us meaning.

Or is God in show business, too?

They Are Legend

S Robinson / Scientific Barbarian #3, Mar 2021

There was a time when reboots were viewed with scorn, as craven money-grabs to cash in a second time on something wonderful but long since past. You know the kind of thing I'm talking about, right? Nicholas Cage's *The Wicker Man*. Tim Burton's *Planet of the Apes*, sure. *Robocop 2014*. Keanu Reeves, *The Day the Earth Stood Still*. Can we say *Total Recall*?

Then again, there's Ron Moore's *Battlestar Galactica*. The new *Lost in Space*. Christopher Nolan's Batman. The past ten years of *Dr. Who*. We have to admit, for every turkey sci-fi reboot, there's a gloriously superior one, right? And isn't that okay? Aren't you panting for Denis Villeneuve's *Dune* to soar over the previous two?

I want to put forward the following premise: reboots aren't always a matter of one version topping another (or not); the truth is, when a sci-fi classic (or turkey) gets a makeover, sometimes it's really a matter of retelling a story for a new generation, whether that retelling is good, bad, or ugly. Put another way, it's more about the viewer than what's viewed.

It's in that spirit that we can revisit the various cinematic interpretations of Richard Matheson's seminal "I Am Legend", one of the most influential short horror novels of all time – as well as the template for *Night of the Living Dead* and all the copycat zombieness that followed.

There are three – count 'em, three! - film versions of this sumptuous, astonishing story (which is more vampire than zombie), conveniently spread across three nerd generations. That distribution is poignant in itself; but before we get to that, let's do a brief recap of this gem's history.

Matheson's fever dream

Richard Matheson certainly possessed the street cred to birth a horror genre – and let's not kid ourselves, *I Am Legend* did exactly that: *Zombieland* and *World War Z* would not exist without him (okay, maybe not the best examples). *TZ*'s "Nightmare at 20,000 Feet"? Matheson. *Trek*'s "The Enemy Within"? Matheson. *The Incredible Shrinking Man, The Pit and the Pendulum, Hell House, What Dreams May Come, Somewhere in Time?* All Matheson.

I Am Legend has both the narrative heft and the pedigree to qualify as a genre prototype. We can reasonably hold up the various movie versions of the tale, not merely as *remake* or *reboot*, but as highly individual variations on a theme that categorically define the first three generations of *nerd*.

Here's the original in a nutshell:

Robert Neville seems to be the last survivor of an apocalyptic pandemic that has wiped out most of the human race in the year 1976, leaving only wandering bands of pasty-white vampires roaming the ruins and himself, who remains immune and unchanged, supposedly because he was once bitten by a vampire bat. He remains alive in a vampire-ridden Los Angeles, where he kills dormant vampires by day and searches for a cure to the pandemic by night, barricaded in a house that is constantly under vampire assault.

Fighting off depression and booze, Neville soldiers on, convinced that there is a scientifically explicable cause and cure. He adopts a dog, which gives him a source of connection and affection, but the dog dies, leaving him more depressed than ever. He has been fighting off the vampires with traditional gimmicks (garlic, crosses, mirrors) but is convinced, through his emotional fog, that the answer is virological – something that can be synthesized and clinically administered.

Along comes a woman who appears to be as normal as he, who represents an opportunity for him to test his theories: why is she, too, immune? Could she hold the key to the solution he seeks? He suspects she might be a vampire under cover, but the two rapidly come to care for one another. When he presses her for a blood sample, she submits, but then knocks him out and flees. Turns out she's part of an infected group that have their affliction at least somewhat under control, making them the true possibility of a resurgent human society. Neville submits to it, allowing himself to be taken into their custody, and ends up dying for the cause.

Whew!

Anthony Boucher, then-editor of *The Magazine of Fantasy and Science Fiction*, wrote, "Matheson has added a new variant on the Last Man theme... and has given striking vigor to his invention by a forceful style of storytelling which derives from the best hard-boiled crime novels." Other critics may have been less effusive, but in the end, the world opted to imitate Matheson – the sincerest form of et cetera.

I Am Legend gives us all the roots of post-apocalyptica of every kind, never before so gloriously explicated: 1) an out-of-the-blue calamity that lays waste to the modern world; 2) horrors to crush what remains of the human soul; 3) a doughty hero with deep issues, trying to turn the tide. It's the first true modern template for the term *post-apocalyptic*.

Sure, Matheson had precursors, running all the way back to the early Hebrews with their own legend, the nautical Noah (though Gilgamesh takes this one farther back still); Sodom and Gomorrah was the original *On the Beach*, and the Book of Revelation can be said to tease *1984*, and even *The Hunger Games*. Mary Shelley's *The Last Man* is *Legend*'s direct descendant, and then there's H.G. Wells...

But it's Matheson that stands above them all, bringing the horror out of our dreams and into our streets. *Post-apocalypse*, in our contemporary formulation, exists right where we're standing – utterly immediate, in our faces. *Our* buildings gutted. *Our* playgrounds scorched. *Our* cars rusting. And that immediacy makes *post-apocalyptica* very personal, almost an identity marker in fanboy culture. I know how old you are and how you roll, young son, by reading your Top 10 Dystopian Films picks.

He Is Legend

Count 'em, three. Stretching from the earliest modern nerds to the present day...

The Last Man on Earth (1964)

Vincent Price is Robert Morgan, and his pandemic vampire-zombies are lumbering morons, no great strain to fend off. He kills them in their sleep by day, barricading himself in his house at night. As in the book, he believes his immunity derives from a bat bite. He lost his wife and daughter to the plague, and in a particularly unsettling twist, was attacked by his undead wife after she dug her way out of the secret grave he buried her in. Desperate for companionship, he befriends a dog, but has to euthanize it when it gets sick.

He discovers a woman named Ruth, whom he persuades to visit his home. When she becomes ill from exposure to garlic, he becomes suspicious, and he later catches her trying to inject herself with a mixture of blood and vaccine. She confesses that she is, indeed, infected – but under treatment, as are many others. The vaccine pushes back at their infection, keeping them from succumbing completely. They are planning to rebuild society, and she reveals that Morgan has inadvertently killed some of them. They want him dead, understandably.

While she sleeps, Morgan transfuses his own blood into her, and she is completely cured. Her people choose that moment to attack, and a last-stand battle occurs, culminating (fittingly) in a church. Morgan dies, but as Ruth is cured, there remains hope that everyone else will be, too.

The Omega Man (1971)

Charlton Heston now takes up the role, his name reverting to Neville – still a virologist, but this time an Army colonel, as well. His immunity derives from an experimental vaccine he gave himself as the pandemic takes hold of Los Angeles. Like Vincent Price, he holes up in a barricaded house at night and emerges each morning to kill vampires. But in this version, the vampires are as intelligent as they were to begin with, and exist in a cultish new social structure. They are all about killing Neville, who represents to them the evil that brought on the pandemic in the first place.

There's a woman here, too - Lisa, whom Neville sees while out in the city one day. When the cult captures Neville and attempts to burn him at the stake in Dodger Stadium, she rescues him, then introducing him to a small circle of survivors who have some resistance to the plague. One of them, Dutch, is a young medical student seeking a more permanent immunity.

Neville and Lisa attempt to treat her brother Ritchie, who is infected and turning – and it works. Plans are made for Neville and the survivors to evacuate the city and start new lives in the wilderness. And the vampire cult chooses that moment to attack, and a last-stand battle occurs, culminating in the mortal wounding of Neville. When Dutch and his group discover the dying Neville, who hands him a bottle of serum that will cure them all completely. They flee the city, leaving the cult vampires to die.

I Am Legend (2007)

Enter box-office god Will Smith, who retains both the Neville name and Heston's Army commission. He is a full-fledged virologist, based not in LA but in New York, and he, too, loses his family in the pandemic – but to a helicopter crash. This Neville's vampire-zombies combine the inhumanity of the first film with speed and reflexes transcending those of the second, making them so fast and deadly that Neville survives only because his barricaded home is in a location unknown to them.

Neville spends his time working on a cure, rather than killing monsters by day – and his operation is very systematic. He has a full-blown lab, where he tests tentative serums on vampires he catches. He is so lonely that he's starting to lose it, forming friendships with store mannequins. His only real friend is his German shepherd Sam.

In a close call at dusk, when the vampires are stirring, Neville escapes but Sam is bitten in the evening shadows by an infected dog, and begins to turn. Neville has no choice but to kill his beloved pet. Enraged, Neville strikes out at a group of vampires the following night, and is almost killed himself. A woman and her son unexpectedly rescue him.

Back in Neville's fortress, the woman explains that they are making way to a survivors' camp in Bethel, and they were drawn to him by his daily radio broadcast. Neville injects a new version of his serum into a recently-captured female zombie – and the next evening, a group of vampire-zombies choose that moment to attack, having tracked them the night before. A battle ensues, and Neville and the woman and boy are trapped in his lab. They notice that the injected female zombie is reverting back to humanity, and as monsters overrun his lab, Neville draws her blood and gives the vial to the woman, then stuffing her and her son in a closet as he destroys himself and the attacking zombies with a grenade. The woman and boy emerge unscathed and make their way to Bethel, carrying the cure.

These are three completely different films telling exactly the same story, to be sure; the story elements are very dystopian but ultimately pretty simplistic:

- The Last Man on Earth
- maintains a precarious, lonely existence
- searching for a cure to a vampire/zombie-making pandemic
- with his faithful, doomed dog at his side
- as the vampire/zombies hunt him;
- A mysterious woman inexplicably appears
- and changes everything
- as he finds a cure
- and the vampire-zombies choose that moment to attack
- and he dies a noble death in battle
- and his cure survives him, bringing hope to humankind.

See, the story is the very much the same; but my point (and I do have one) is that the vast differences in style and tone of the three movies basically define the generational nerd.

Generations

The "I Am Legend" movies define 50 years of nerds, split into three generations:

The Invisible Black-and-White (Fifties). Born into a life of literary poverty when sci-fi wasn't even published in hardback and hadn't yet made it to television, this kid with his thick black glasses is grateful for *any* decent big-screen with an idea tucked away inside it. He doesn't bother much with television, except for *The Twilight Zone* and *The Outer Limits*; he is, however, well-versed in Vincent Price's canon, silly as most of it is (there isn't much else out there).

Vincent Price, with his uneasy intensity, is the perfect archetype for the young B&W. Seeing him displayed in isolation, it is impossible to imagine him otherwise; can you imagine him as the center of attention at a faculty mixer? No, he is the spitting image of his fanboy acolyte: possessed of greater self-awareness than his peers; disturbingly vulnerable; smarter by half than anyone else in any room.

Like Price, the B&W soldiers on, very much in the mold of Marty McFly's 17-year-old dad in *Back to the Future*. He just wants to sit quietly in study hall, scribbling tales of wonder in a spiral-bound notebook; ideas are his bread and butter. Yes, he's undernourished when it comes to the wonderful genre that stirs his imagination and surfaces his emotions, but that only fuels his resolve to remain true to who he is.

This guy became an engineer in the Apollo program. D&D wasn't around when he was young, but if it had been, he'd have been the wily Cleric with a bagful of Don't Even Think About It. He's a hero on a par with Robert Neville, turning his starry-eyed wanderings into the actual future.

The Blue Jean Brain (Seventies). Not so poverty-stricken as his uncle, the Blue Jean Brain emerged into a much bigger sci-fi universe – one that included lots of TV (*Star Trek, Lost in Space, The Six Million Dollar Man, Space: 1999, Battlestar Galactica*) and substantially more big-screen fun (*Fantastic Voyage, 2001, Planet of the Apes, Westworld, A Clockwork Orange, Logan's Run, Star Wars* - and the movie *Treks* and *Alien* and *Indiana Jones*). This stuff is simply more fun than what had come before, and therefore drew an audience beyond the nerd himself; he watches this stuff with friends and even takes a date. He actually scores some points for suggesting them.

The BBJ got a serious upgrade, idol-wise, in Charlton Heston – who, of course, wasn't just the Omega Man, but also Taylor among the apes and the harbinger of Soylent Green. Heston was a nerd archetype with an undeniable thread of cool: he was isolated, out-of-place and disoriented, to be sure, but he could also shoot straight and even get the girl. With his rugged good looks, cool car, hip clothes and a cop-show soundtrack scoring his mayhem, he was the Blue Jean Brain's self-actualization ideal.

The Brain wears wire-rims. He is no fashion maven, but he knows where the men's bell-bottoms can be found at K-Mart. Unlike his predecessor, he harbors quaint illusions about how well he's doing in the high school social milieu that belie his entrenched disinterest in the real world. He has traded in the Black-and-White's spiral-bound study hall scribblepad for a Super 8 film camera, in the tradition of Spielberg, and aspires to remake *Star Wars* in his own backyard.

This guy became a software developer, starting off in Fortran and graduating to industrial BASIC before a mid-life foray into Microsoft mush code. D&D was just getting rolling in his youth, and he went all in, leaning Druid – reason-driven but passionate, empirical but magic-minded – Heston cross-dressing in Arwen's riding cloak. He, too, is a Neville hero, whose real-world voice-over captures the truth about where we are and where we could go.

The Ascending Digital (Nineties). The post-*Star Wars* baby is as likely to be female as male, and thank Zeus; it's about goddamn time. Digitals reap the parallel boons of ubiquitous CGI and the unquestioned hipness of sci-fi in the wake of *Trek: NextGen* and *Babylon 5* and *The Matrix* movies and the *Alien* sequels and *Predator* and *Terminator* and the reimagined *Galactica* and *Firefly* and Jackson's *Lord of the Rings* and the *Star Wars* prequels – and, of course, Christopher Nolan Batman and the MCU. The Digital was born into a world where the fringe thrills and passions of the Black-and-White and the Blue Jean Brain had become not only mainstream, but the cultural mountaintop.

Who could be more fitting as this millennial generation's archetype than Will Smith, blazing star of the nostalgic nerdfest *Independence Day*, who isn't merely sci-fi-friendly but wicked mainstream badass? Younger, stronger, funnier and better-looking than Price or Heston, the Fresh Prince is the ultimate nerd template: as out-of-place and unsettled as his predecessors, while radiating hip and cool from every pore. Will Smith also managed depths that Price and Heston never achieved: competent through-and-through, while tapping that elusive fanboy insecurity we all have tucked away under our porn stash, the annoyingly honest demon on our shoulder that whispers, at all the wrong times, *I really not sure what the fuck I'm doing...*

The Digitals may not be fully aware of just how much of their inheritance was paid for by the deep investments of the B&W and Blue Jean Brain in *Lost in Space* Christmas toys and James Blish *Trek* paperbacks and *6$MM* lunch boxes and *Space: 1999* bubble gum cards and Gold Key *Star Trek* comics and Jack Kirby everything and Dune sequels and *2001* spacecraft models hanging from the bedroom ceiling. They popped out of the womb into Comic-Con, swimming in buckets of the treasures we had to comb the landscape for. Theirs is a unique moment: everything nerds love is currently what the whole world now craves. The young nerd has it so good today because s/he stands on the old nerd's shoulders.

The Digitals are all producing original web series and churning out cosplay regalia on 3D printers. They are masters of the gig economy, amassing more tech skills before turning 20 than their predecessors achieved in decades. In their D&D, which is not only now a ubiquitous but thriving industry, they trend Barbarian, armed to the gills with overwhelming force that serves as metaphor to their overwhelming competence. S/he has a Neville heroism that is both cynical and promising; s/he's going to save the world and they know it.

Omega Nerds

In any *I Am Legend* generation, then, the story elements are these:

- There's this nerd
- who's out-of-place
- and somewhat unsettled
- and a little disoriented
- and sometimes disturbingly vulnerable,
- but who is also
- smarter by half than everyone else in any room,
- competent through-and-through,
- scribbling tales of wonder,
- and going to save to world.

...and one helluva gamer.

Sources/Recommended Reading

2001: A Space Odyssey, Arthur C. Clarke. New American Library, 1968.

The AIs and Androids of Star Trek, Scott Robinson. Paleos Media, 2020).

Andy Buckram's Tin Men, Carol Ririe Brink. Viking Press, 1966.

Back to the Batcave, Adam West (with Jeff Rovin). Berkeley Publishing, 1994.

Beyond Uhura, Nichelle Nichols. G.P. Putnam's Sons, 1994.

Chasing the Enterprise: Achieving Star Trek's Vision of the Human Future, Scott Robinson. Paleos Media, 2019.

Children of Dune, Frank Herbert. Ace Books, 1975.

Dune, Frank Herbert. Ace Books, 1999.

Dune, Messiah, Frank Herbert. Ace Books, 1969.

Foundation, Isaac Asimov. Doubleday, 1951.

HAL 9000: An Unauthorized Biography, Scott Robinson. Paleos Media, 2020.

The Hugo Winners, Vol. I, II, III, ed. Isaac Asimov. Doubleday, 1962, 1977.

In Joy Still Felt: The Autobiography of Isaac Asimov, 1954-1978, Isaac Asimov. Doubleday, 1980.

Logan's Run, William F. Nolan, George Clayton Johnson. Dial Press, 1967.

The Making of Star Trek, Stephen E. Whitfield, Gene Roddenberry. Ballentine Books, 1970.

Origin, Dan Brown. Anchor Books, 2017.

Science Fiction Hall of Fame, Vol. I, Robert Silverberg. Avon Books, 1971.

Science Fiction Hall of Fame, Vol. II, Ben Bova. Avon Books, 1974.

The Smell of the Lord (and Other Charming Heresies), Scott Robinson Paleos Media, 2020.

The Space Trilogy, C.S. Lewis. Simon & Schuster, 2011.

Star Wars, Alan Dean Foster (writing as George Lucas). Del Rey, 1977.

Star Trek: The Motion Picture, Alan Dean Foster (writing as Gene Roddenberry). Pocket Books, 1979.

Star Trek Lives!, Jacqueline Lichtenberg, Sondra Marshak, Joan Winston. Bantam Books, 1975.

Star Trek Memories, William Shatner. HarperCollins, 1993.

Star Trek: The New Voyages, Sondra Marshak and Myrna Culbreath. Bantam Books, 1976.

Star Trek: The New Voyages 2, Sondra Marshak and Myrna Culbreath. Bantam Books, 1977.

Stowaway to the Mushroom Planet, Eleanor Cameron. Little, Brown & Co., 1956.

A Treasury of Great Science Fiction, ed. Anthony Boucher. Doubleday, 1959.

The Trouble with Tribbles, David Gerrold. Ballentine Books, 1973.

The World of Star Trek, David Gerrold. Ballentine Books, 1974.

World's Best Science Fiction 1968, ed. Donald A. Wollheim, Terry Carr. Ace Books, 1968.

About the Author

Scott Robinson is a journalist, social scientist, public speaker and musician, and was for 20 years a music critic with the *Louisville Courier-Journal*. He is also a member of the Scottish Society of Louisville. He has also been published in *Rolling Stone* and *The Wall Street Journal*.

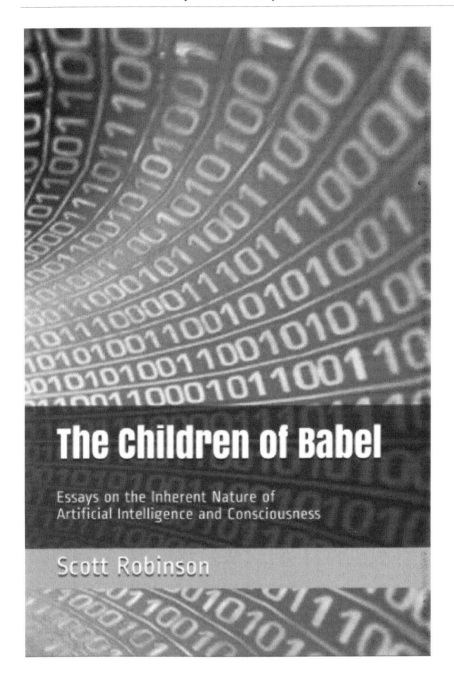

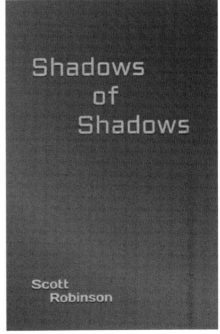

Manufactured by Amazon.ca
Bolton, ON

32079836R00171